DIGITAL MEDIA CONTRACTS

DIGITAL MEDIA CONTRACTS

Alan Williams
Duncan Calow
Andrew Lee

OXFORD
UNIVERSITY PRESS

OXFORD
UNIVERSITY PRESS

Great Clarendon Street, Oxford OX2 6DP

Oxford University Press is a department of the University of Oxford.
It furthers the University's objective of excellence in research, scholarship,
and education by publishing worldwide in

Oxford New York

Auckland Cape Town Dar es Salaam Hong Kong Karachi
Kuala Lumpur Madrid Melbourne Mexico City Nairobi
New Delhi Shanghai Taipei Toronto

With offices in

Argentina Austria Brazil Chile Czech Republic France Greece
Guatemala Hungary Italy Japan Poland Portugal Singapore
South Korea Switzerland Thailand Turkey Ukraine Vietnam

Oxford is a registered trade mark of Oxford University Press
in the UK and in certain other countries

Published in the United States
by Oxford University Press Inc., New York

First published 2011

British Library Cataloguing in Publication Data
Data available

Library of Congress Cataloging in Publication Data
Data available

Typeset by Glyph International, Bangalore, India
Printed in Great Britain
on acid-free paper by
CPI Antony Rowe, Chippenham, Wiltshire

ISBN 978–0–19–956220–6

FOREWORD

I was extremely pleased when the Andrew, Duncan, and Alan approached me to write the foreword to *Digital Media Contracts* . . . until I realized I would actually have to write something insightful about the topic. Given that this is quite unlikely, I thought I would relate some experiences I have had with the aforementioned authors.

I originally met them fifteen years ago when they were the legal team hired to support the commercial and legal launch of the UK-based online service provider I was working for. Our task was to close numerous contractual agreements with multiple partners to populate the online service with e-commerce offerings, advertisements and rich multimedia content; whilst also ensuring that agreements were in place to enable the technical infrastructure, provide end-user customer care and offer a range of payment options.

This was a major undertaking. At one point I think we were managing around 140 agreements at various stages of execution. The greatest challenge, however, was what seemed the almost complete lack of direct commercial and legal precedent for what we were doing.

The major high street brands wishing to engage with us to sell their goods to our subscribers did not actually have websites to which we could link, so we had to also contract to build an online shop window for them; the advertising agencies and brands were still trying to work out the appropriate commercial model, banner adverts and CPM were brand new; the content owners were uncertain whether they had the necessary rights to license the content for Internet distribution; and although the payment providers knew how to manage risk in a 'card not present' environment, they were uncertain how to apply these principles online.

When we added these challenges to the consumer-facing issues around data protection, privacy and child protection, you can imagine that there was a fair amount of head scratching going on. The wonderful thing was we just got on with it and managed to launch the service pretty much on time; it worked, we did not get sued or arrested (well, not yet anyway). And whilst the service did not turn out to be the huge commercial success we hoped for, mainly due to the emergence of the free ISP model and the wealth of 'free' advertiser-funded content, the great personal benefit for us all was that we shoe-horned ten years of direct digital commercial and legal experience into about a year and a half.

A few years later, I had the pleasure this time of sitting across the table from Andrew, whilst working on the negotiation of a major content platform and services outsourcing agreement. He was the head of legal for a major international mobile telecommunications company, I was in sales at a successful medium-sized US digital commerce vendor and Duncan and Alan were at the law firm, DLA Piper, we had selected to represent our company in the EMEA region. By this time, about nine years later, the risks and liabilities arising from the distribution of branded digital content over the Internet, in this case the mobile Internet, were very well understood . . . especially by both Andrew and Duncan. Let us say the negotiation between them got a little heated as times; however, we are all still friends.

Andrew and I are now working together at a fast-growing venture-backed mobile payments company focused on providing online merchants with pay-by-mobile as an alternative payment option—this time combining payments with online goods and services in sixty-four countries around the world, which amounts to a degree of risk. I am glad to have Andrew on our side to help navigate the way.

The key learning for me over this period has been that good quality legal advice counts. Whilst the changes arising from the advent of digital have amounted to more of an evolution rather than a revolution in the law, it is always better to consider and take commercial risks on the basis of knowledge rather than gut feel.

James Patmore
Richmond, UK
October 2010

CONTENTS

B. Licensing and Distribution

Part I

INTRODUCTION

1

INTRODUCTION

A. Digital Media Contracts

This is not a legal textbook. It is designed as a handbook to the law and business of digital media. It has grown out of two books we wrote in the 1990s[1] in which we had aimed to do the same thing. Fifteen years ago the technical and commercial landscape was, of course, very different. PCs still weren't on every office desk—let alone in every home, wireless meant a radio and television was analogue. Multimedia, to use the buzz-word of the day, was promising more than it was delivering. The CD-Rom and CD-I were failing to capture the public's imagination, video games consoles were still for children and the information superhighway was a political idea not reality.

For lawyers too there were more questions than answers. The law has always had to, probably will always have to, play catch-up with technology and the greater the technological changes involved the greater the time lag. There is also a key distinction between the theory, and the practicalities, of the law. Although the former obviously influences the latter, guidance on the latter cannot fully develop until there are sufficient real-world experiences in which the law can be applied. All in all, therefore, there was often talk rather than action and that was reflected in those earlier books. Our focus was 'what if?' rather than 'what is currently the case?'.

This book is different because we have taken the contracts and documentation of digital media as our focus. Following well over a decade of digital media businesses trying to develop appropriate documentation to fit their activities it is now possible to draw upon a set of real world agreements rather than legal theory. We must stress at the outset, however, that these are not precedents in the traditional mould, and in most cases not even industry standards. They are sample agreements, illustrations of how a document dealing with a particular aspect of digital media might look—designed to give a general guide to what the readers can expect to find coming across their desks or screens.

---

[1] *Multimedia: Rights, Contracts and Licensing* (FT Law & Tax, 1996); *Digital Media: Rights, Contracts and Licensing* (with Nicholas Higham) (Sweet & Maxwell, 1998).

As such we aim to go beyond traditional precedents by assisting readers intending to draft their own documents but also those looking for hands-on guidance when reviewing standard form documents received from other parties. Many readers will of course be doing both at different times in different cases with different types of digital media. We therefore hope to reflect that commercial reality with this collection of sample agreements in a realistic 'look and feel' which cover that wide range of circumstances. Some may well help as a template for drafting, whereas some may be an aid for reviewing—and some may just stimulate ideas and debate.

As a result we believe we are showing the reader what to expect rather than what is necessarily ideal. There are usually many ways to approach any given drafting task and specific choices have to be made about style, format and approach: short form or long form? Aggressive and one-sided provisions or a fairer and more mutual stance? By the nature of this book we must leave it to our readers to make some judgments of their own in each case. We do, however, provide our own suggestions where we can in the relevant commentary added in the introduction to each chapter and within the body of each agreement. Whilst, hopefully, always reflecting the real world, the agreements have also been simplified and clarified where necessary to aid this process.

We have also tried very hard to be practical not legalistic. There are no tables of cases, statutes or regulations. This is certainly a specialist publication for those with some specialist interest in the topic: for fellow lawyers, business affairs executives and contract managers whether in private practice or in industry. Yet we hope that it is user-friendly enough for anyone who might need to consider or deal with digital media contracts to find something of use here. We also believe this style will help to limit the degree of built-in obsolescence, given our subject, that any endeavour of this kind must carry.

We also hope that such an approach means that although this book is written by English lawyers with an unavoidable UK bias—with each agreement an English law document—this book will still have value to readers outside the UK. Certainly many of these forms of document are international in style in any case and we have tried to give some pointers to show how other jurisdictions may approach things—whether with similarities or differences—throughout. We must stress again, however, that these cannot be anything other than very limited illustrations only *and are not, nor intended to be, a replacement for proper local law advice.*

B. Format

Part I of this book provides a short introduction: first, to the markets and technology of digital media and, then, to the law. Neither is intended to be comprehensive, but they should help to provide some necessary background to aid understanding of the agreements and the world in which they operate. In our previous books we had attempted an ambitious overview of the law applicable to this sector. What was challenging then is now—given the extensive work of courts and law makers in the interim—in our view almost impossible, even on a strictly national basis. Therefore, instead of presenting an analysis of every potential topic of interest from patents and design rights to tax and competition/anti-trust law readers are directed to other specialist sources (in some cases we have added text into the commentary but this is in no sense comprehensive, eg see reference to anti-corruption legislation, p. 159). We focus solely on some high-level themes that have consistently featured—and not just between ourselves—in legal discussion and debate over digital media.

The main element of the book, Part II, is split into two sections:

A. Acquisition and Development: which will essentially deal with 'rights-in' issues; the process of pulling together content and services to develop a digital media product or service; and
B. Licensing and Distribution: which will focus on 'rights-out' and the external facing exploitation process.

By definition, Part A will seem more generic and potentially multi-purpose than Part B but both should still help provide a genuine 'feel' for real-world documents. On the whole, the documents and the commentary are tailored toward the interests of a digital media producer and publisher rather than the counter-parties covered in these documents. That does not mean, however, that the contracts are always favourable to them, we have tried to reflect likely reality rather than simply present pro-producer/publisher terms, and in some cases there is no clear split between the two.

Each section is made up of ten chapters, each chapter presenting a different agreement or legal document. Each begins with an introduction—using checklists and box-outs to help provide practical input—before setting out the document in full with clause-by-clause comments to explain legal and commercial context.

2

COMMERCIAL THEMES

A. Convergence

1. Digitization and convergence

In the original incarnation of this book (first published in 1996) we began by introducing the technical and commercial background to digital media. That introduction included an overview of how different content sectors: publishing, music, broadcasting, film, video games, sport and advertising, had each been influenced by the process of digitization. To attempt to cover that ground now, fifteen years on, would require a volume in itself. So instead, as a starting point for this book, we have drawn together a short summary of key themes—written, we stress, from our personal perspective as commercial lawyers, not technologists or management consultants.

In that earlier book we described how:

> One of the much discussed consequences of digitization has been the resulting process of convergence both within the traditional media industry and also between the media, the computer and the communications industries and other sectors.

By way of example, at the time that was written, we were the lawyers advising on the launch of one of the first online services in the UK. That service was a joint venture between a major telecoms company and a large media group. The media group had interests in newspapers, books and film but also in other sectors including travel. As such it seemed to represent convergence in action: it was the 'wires' business, joining with the 'content' business, to deliver multi-media information to the user's computer.

As with other digital media projects, then and now, various factors conspired to limit the success of that service. Perhaps it was ahead of its time. Indeed, the CEO brought in to try to turn things around famously remarked that it combined everything a media group knew about telecoms and everything a telecoms company knew about media.[1] Yet, in a way, that was the point of convergence, players in different sectors were crossing boundaries to experiment and explore new opportunities.

---

[1] Ajay Chowdhury. Ajay is now CEO of EnQii the global digital media company.

The high watermark of this initial enthusiasm for, and belief in, convergence was the formation of AOL Time Warner in January 2000. This remarkable merger—that combined the world's then leading online brand with an 'old media' empire that spanned film, television, music and publishing—appeared to embody the potential of a convergent future. It seemed a natural fit. As one commentator was moved to say in the feverish media coverage that followed the announcement, 'it put together the pipes and the poetry'.

In just a few months, however, came the stock market falls that triggered the dotcom crash. The bursting of the economic bubble on which so many of the assumptions regarding digital technology had been based brought a swift re-evaluation on all sides. It was nearly ten years before AOL and Time Warner would go there separate ways, and in that decade came further troubled unions as existing players tried to

Digitization

Digitization is the basic enabling technology behind the forms of media discussed in this book. Much has been written about the fundamental nature and impact of digital technology but in essence, digitization is the breaking down of complex information into a series of simple instructions that a computer processor can understand and to which it can respond. In this context, we use the term 'information' in its widest sense, to include all types of material whether text, graphics, speech, music, film or video—what has come to be known, simply, as 'content'.

'Old' media such as traditional broadcast radio and television, vinyl records or even printed books, are analogue systems. Information stored or transmitted by them is in the form of a continuous signal, which recognizes changes in the information by moderating the amplitude or frequency of the signal. As such those media simply reflect the natural world—it is the way in which we are able to see or hear information.

Digital media rely on a totally different system of recording and reproducing information. Digitization involves taking information, in its natural analogue form, and 'sampling' it to create a series of individual binary notations. By creating a sufficent number of samples the information can be replayed as an apparently continuous signal like the analogue original. The information has however been translated into a common 'language' of simple binary codes which can be recorded, stored and manipulated by computer.

DIGITIZATION

▼

ACCURACY AND STABILITY OF RECORDING

▼

STORAGE CAPACITY, ACCESSIBILITY, AND INTERACTIVITY

▼	▼
EASE OF REPRODUCTION	**EASE OF TRANSMISSION INCLUDING ONLINE**

Using information in digital form has many advantages. It allows information to be recorded and stored with more accuracy and stability. Analogue recordings may be less accurate to begin with and, in addition, the storage medium, such as paper, tape or film stock, deteriorates over time. A digital recording can also be accessed and manipulated more easily, allowing large amounts of data to be stored and searched more effectively. That permits the development of non-linear products that in turn allows increased interactivity between the user and the content. Reproduction and transmission of the information is also quicker and easier. Perfect copies of a digital work can be made indefinitely with limited marginal cost and no loss of quality either in the copy or the original.

Digitization agreement checklist

Much of the content available today, certainly in the professional media sector, will have been created, developed and produced in digital form. Yet there are, of course, still many media archives around the world, both public and private, that remain in analogue form. The process of digitizing that older material can be a significant undertaking, especially for major media organizations or public institutions which have amassed significant libraries over many years.

Where a third party is brought in to assist in that process—particularly in the context of a specific project for further use—there are a number of legal and commercial questions that ought to be dealt with in some form of digitization agreement.

- **Cost**—The digitization of major collections can be a long and expensive process so the basis upon which the work is priced and paid for is important. In return for the digitization partner carrying out and funding (or at least sharing the costs of) that process, some archives have been prepared to grant rights in the resulting digital material to the digitization partner as a cost-effective means of creating a digital archive. Whatever the arrangement, the agreement should set out a clear budgeting process which allocates all ancillary expenses such as delivery and handling costs.

- **Clearance**—The archive owner must be comfortable that the digitization activities that it is authorizing, ie the copying and, potentially, the adaptation and making available of the original works, is something it has the rights to do and is not an infringement of third party intellectual property rights. Older archives should not present a problem, although given the length of copyright protection, care is needed as a safe cut-off date can be as far back as 70 years to 1940, plus the working life of the author, say another 60 years, or 1880. Why so far? An author starting out his writing career in 1880 at, say, 20 years old, could live to 80. Born in 1860, he would have then died in 1940. That is an extreme case but it puts down a marker. More recent material can be a problem if the archive owner holds only limited rights. So, for example, a television broadcaster will not normally own its library of programmes outright but may need to obtain further permission from contributors (for a wider discussion of digital rights see section 3 below). The digitization partner actually carrying out the restricted acts will usually look for contractual protection on this point. That said, Google, which is probably digitizing more material around the world than anyone else, attempted to argue in the US (although not elsewhere) that its digitization of in-copyright books from the collections of its partner libraries, without the permission of the relevant authors and publishers, was not an infringement of copyright. It was sued by a coalition of those authors and publishers and an ambitious settlement arrangement is still being negotiated (see section 3 below).
- **Ownership**—Just as important is determining who will own any rights in the digital material that is created. It can be argued, in some countries, that the process of digitization may in certain circumstances (essentially where there is sufficient effort, even skill, involved—so more likely with photographs and artistic works) produce a new copyright in the digital version. This has significant value where the original analogue version is no longer itself protected by copyright. Even if there are no new intellectual property rights generated, the rights to physical ownership and control of, and access to, the digital material should still be set out with great care. The agreement should establish how the short-term and long-term rights in:
  - the underlying analogue material; and
  - the digitized versions;

  will be cross-licensed and/or assigned between the archive and the digitization partner. There could be a difficult stand-off where only the partner has access to those digitized versions but the archive's rights in the underlying analogue material prevent any further use of them.
- **Service levels**—The process of digitization may be a significant undertaking, especially if it forms part of a wider project then to further develop and

exploit the digital content which is created. As a result both sides will want to be clear about:

- how the material is delivered, prepared, stored and returned and who will do what;
- the timetable for this process;
- quality assurance for the digitized material and any associated activities;
- security arrangements; and
- project management and administrative support.

Other commercial provisions as commonly found in digital media agreements—as discussed in the rest of the book—will obviously also be included as appropriate.

Note that the issues raised above may also be relevant in a project where content is already in digital form but is being transposed into a proprietary digital format, perhaps to be delivered as part of a specific service or otherwise provided from one party to another to be held on a third party platform, for example books being held for print-on-demand or video clips repackaged for wireless delivery.

The time, effort and cost in reformatting between different versions of digital material should not be under-estimated and is a point to remember when agreeing contractual terms on the details of content delivery.

buy into new success stories in Web 2.0,[2] but the focus for that next generation of digital media had changed.

2. Platform divergence

By 2004 one of the major international consulting groups was announcing that 'Convergence is dead: Long live convergence'.[3] Whilst the 'ill-considered value destroying application of convergence at all levels' had perished with the dotcoms, there could be no denying that digital technology was still transforming the creation, production, distribution and consumption of media content. It was becoming clear, however, that this transformation, and its business impact, could be highly variable in scale and scope.

Indeed, there was now consideration of the concept of digital *divergence*. Although digitization allowed multi-media content to be created and distributed in common

[2] For example, News Corp's and AOL's purchases of the social networks MySpace and Bebo respectively.

[3] Deloitte, 'Convergence Revisited' (October 2004).

form that did not mean producers had to provide, or that technology standards would allow—or, indeed, that users actually wanted—uniform products and services. Many of the more successful applications of digital technology had in fact managed to engineer entirely separate platforms and markets. Digital content might be repackaged and resold several times over on different platforms—in addition to the traditional concept of reselling at different times (see discussion of rights 'windows'—section 3).

Whilst that also brought its own legal and commercial challenges it did, in particular, highlight the complexity in demand for digital content devices, as a succession of games and music platforms, handheld players, smart phones, e-book readers and digital tablets of increasing sophistication have appeared over the last twenty years. That path, from the very original version of Nintendo's Game Boy from 1989, through the Diamond Rio PMP300—one of the very earliest portable MP3 music players to appear ten years later, to the Apple iPad and its competitor products, has been instructive.

Whilst certain products and brands may dominate at certain times, and with certain users, there may never be a one-size-fits-all solution for digital content, just as consumers have never defaulted to the same automobile or kitchen appliance. Indeed, the ability to maintain a closed, proprietary format and control the delivery of content within that—to the exclusion of other alternative formats—has been a key element in successful business models for digital media. We return to this in our discussion of monetization and of digital rights management below.

3. Sector specifics

One of the first sectors within the media industry to face the full impact of digitization was the music business. If the world was converging, it therefore seemed to make sense for other media sectors to learn lessons from that experience[4]—especially as conventional wisdom (see box below) held that the record labels had got it so wrong. Yet even if all content was digital, there were still very different cultural and technical factors present in the music business—from its target demographic to the way in which popular recorded music is consumed—that distinguished it from other sectors.

There were also key legal differences. Compare a music track and a sports clip. If an online service wants to carry, say, match footage of top-flight English soccer it has simply to approach the Premier League in London to acquire the relevant rights. 'Simply' is, of course, an understatement—those are extremely valuable rights and

[4] At the one-day e-book conference that prefaced the London Book Fair 2010 several speakers acknowledged that with the rise of latest generation e-readers trade book publishers, ie producers of mainstream fiction and non-fiction works, now faced the same digital issues that other media had done previously but remarked that before publishers looked to the music industry for guidance they might actually consult with publishing colleagues in the educational or professional sector (STM), with their own valuable experience, often in the same publishing company.

may only be available on a semi-exclusive basis to the highest bidder.[5] The Premier League will also have carefully tailored those rights to fit within its existing licensing framework. Even so, the licensing of music is a very different business.

Like any other content, the music track represents a bundle of different legal rights but, more than any other sector, licensing those involves a number of different parties. Music publishers, on behalf of the composer/songwriter, will typically control the rights in the underlying composition, ie the music and lyrics of the song being played, but they will usually be represented by a third party licensing body: a collecting society (whose role has itself been under challenge: see Chapter 3). Separate to that are the rights in the sound recording of the song, which will usually be owned by the relevant record label, which must also grant an appropriate licence. The label may or may not do so through a collecting society.

Other rights could need clearing too. Combining the music with a video will require a synchronization right. For certain new uses, in certain territories, local rules may require specific adaptation rights to be cleared in addition. This was necessary, for example, when clearing the first mobile/cell phone ringtones in certain European territories. Ancillary rights such as promotional support might also need to be acquired from the record label or even the recording artist. Thus, the logistics are not straightforward and developing any new form of music use can take longer as a result. None of this helped to make the launch of digital music services any easier.

The bottom line is that, because different people and procedures are involved, generalizations about different forms of content are often problematic. Custom and practice in individual media sectors has not been harmonized automatically through digitization. Sometimes, of course, these are superficial rather than substantive differences: largely a matter of style rather than form. The licensing jargon of film and television is not that of, say, the newspaper business. Despite this there are also some fundamental similarities between all forms of digital content that are reflected in the commercial and legal themes that we address in the rest of this chapter.

The record labels

By any measure,[6] many elements of the music business, and in particular the record labels, have suffered a decline in fortune over the last ten years.

[5] Note also that sports teams, leagues and governing bodies around the world organize the sale of their media rights in different ways.

[6] The British Phonographic Industry (http://<www.bpi.co.uk>), the Recording Industry Association of America (http://<www.riaa.com>) and the International Federation of the Phonographic Industry (http://<www.ifpi.org>) have all regularly published sales and other industry statistics. There are of course those who challenge the industry's own figures, for whatever reasons, but even on the basis of more independent studies (see for example the reports of the UK's Strategic Advisory Board for Intellectual Property Policy http://<www.sabip.org.uk>) there can be little doubt about the overall impact.

The availability and use of unauthorized copies of sound recordings through the Internet has, despite periodic court victories against supplier platforms and the often controversial action taken against users,[7] continued to rise. In the meantime, sales of CDs have fallen steadily and revenues from authorized online services, though growing, have failed to make up the difference. As the veteran music lawyer, Robert W Allan, memorably once described it, it seemed that by the time the industry had got its digital act together 'the barbarians weren't just at the gate, they were driving up Park Lane in their bling with the stereo on eleven'.[8]

A commonly expressed view is that the record labels must themselves accept much of the blame for this state of affairs. It is perceived that, whatever the rights and wrongs of their action against illegal music use, they were far too slow in offering and supporting authorized online music services and that this allowed the illegal online music sources to flourish which made it harder to win back users when lawful services did launch. Is this fair?

- **New Rights**—The relative complexity of the licensing framework used in the music business, as described above, meant that adapting quickly to the requirements of digital technology was never going to be easy. The record labels were important participants in that framework but they were not alone, working alongside the music publishers, the collecting societies and ultimately the artists, as both composers and performers. If there was a failure to move fast enough we would argue that it was a collective failure.
- **New Business Models**—The challenge of online distribution was not just to put in place the necessary licensing structure but also actually to find a business on which it could be built. Popular music had, since the 1960s, been based around an album model, ie where the key product is a collection of several tracks, released periodically whether as an LP or CD, for which single sales and live touring often acted largely as promotion. It underpinned the economics of the business, as well as the contracts and careers of those in the business, regardless of the preferences of the record-buying public. It was, however, much easier to distribute single tracks online and that's what the unlawful services offered, to the benefit of the user. Record label executives

[7] See for example the key US decisions: *A&M Records v Napster* (2001) and *MGM Studios v Grokster* (2005) in favour of content owners. Since then there have been a range of prosecutions against infringing individuals by recording industry bodies such as the RIAA in the US and the BPI in the UK. In several countries, notably France and the UK, so-called 'graduated response' laws have been introduced, which seek to establish formal procedures for ISPs and content owners to follow in monitoring and acting against illegal file sharing and other infringing uses. These follow support from all sides for action against unlawful use to be introduced alongside increased availability of authorized content, but also frustration at the failure of industry self-regulation to develop.

[8] International Association of Entertainment Lawyers Conference at the Midem (2005) music industry event, Cannes

might be excused for taking pause before embracing that—and any other new approach that online might require—while abandoning the model that had paid the bills for forty years. And again they were not the only ones in the business who had to back that decision. In particular, many artists, and their advisers, were reluctant to abandon the economic certainties on which their recording careers had been based.

- **New Technology**—Popular music was the most vulnerable form of content as unlawful online distribution methods first emerged. The three-minute pop song was easy to share and consume online, even with early limits on memory and bandwidth, and attractive to the early adopters most interested in online media. So the threat came to record labels first but at a time when both the technology, and the business infrastructure, needed to launch a successful online service were far less advanced. Even with the licensing structures and business models agreed, the physical process of building the services and digitizing the content, from the platforms on which the services would operate to the creation of metadata for, and the provision of, the necessary administration of that content, would take time. That's without considerations like DRM and how far the labels, rather than other rights owners should actually be involved (see below). Even if the lawful services could have been built faster could they ever have grown so quickly as the illegal services?

B. Disintermediation

1. The chain of distribution

Alongside convergence, disintermediation was another new concept which we described in the earlier version of this book:

> The new digital forms of media and the new products and services which they offer create new and direct relationships between user and producer which can threaten the commercial logic behind the existing roles of players in traditional industry models. In particular, 'middlemen' in any chain of distribution risk disintermediation from that chain unless they can create a new role or add value to re-intermediate themselves.

However, for a better and more striking description of disintermediation, here's what Timo Hannay, a leading e-publishing expert, wrote on his blog in 2007 when Amazon launched its new CreateSpace self-publishing platform that allowed users to upload, publish and distribute their literary works (as well as music and video):

> Amazon becomes the ultimate clearing house for books of all kinds with none of the traditional middlemen getting a look in. Genius. If you're an agent, publisher,

> wholesaler or retailer of books and you haven't just soiled your undies then you don't understand what's going on.[9]

And to describe *re*-intermediation better, here's Clare Alexander, the then president of the UK Association of Authors Agents, writing at around the same time in the publishing press:

> It seems the booksellers are turning into publishers, publishers into booksellers, and practically everyone thinks they are a writer...if this story is to have a happy ending then we all need to keep doing what we have always done—only better.[10]

Amazon, of course, is a classic example of a new player, originally for physical media but increasingly for online delivery, in the content distribution chain. Yet anyone who recalls the many others who launched similar e-tailing services over the last fifteen years will be aware that even well-funded entrants, with the synergies of long-established media and entertainment interests, had no guarantee of success. Amazon, however, is as much an incredibly successful warehousing and logistics operation as it is an e-commerce and digital media company.

Since then, the process of getting online has become simpler. Hosting and operational technology has improved and so has the ability to sub-contract and outsource. Freed from physical delivery constraints some social network sites and other Web 2.0 services have been able to support huge user growth and develop truly global brands in a very short period. Even so, just how prevalent and disruptive disintermediation has actually been remains the subject of much debate. It has not been as inevitable, nor re-intermediation as impossible, as we once thought.

Certainly, high street retailers in many territories have suffered from the impact of e-commerce and digital distribution (whether authorized or otherwise). Yet, overall, there has been a reluctance on the part of labels, studios, broadcasters and publishers to step too far, too quickly, from standard distribution chains and the commercial and legal relationships that sustain them. The traditional roles of producer, wholesaler/distributor and retailer have often survived in digital media distribution even if the names have changed; for example for mobile/cell phone content read 'developer', 'aggregator' and 'operator deck/portal'.

Perhaps the biggest question has been how far content owners should seek to develop a direct relationship with the user online. The earliest authorized online music and film services[11] were joint ventures by the labels and studios who, for various reasons, eventually stepped away from them. Most book publishers have offered books for sale on their websites but have never promoted this channel of distribution in competition with Amazon or traditional booksellers. This may be changing.

---

9 <http://blogs.nature.com/wp/nascent/2007/08/amazon_a_new_kind_of_publisher_1.html>.

10 *The Bookseller* (September 2007).

11 EMI and BMG launched MusicNet (1999), Universal and Sony launched PressPlay (2002) and MGM, Paramount, Sony, Universal and Warner Bros launched Movielink (2002).

The interactivity at the heart of social networks and user generated content is encouraging a re-evaluation of the value of direct relationships. Broadcasters are looking to operate their own services to deliver online television content and the video games platforms all operate their own online networks.

2. Territorial distribution

One other disruptive force with the potential to disintermediate is, of course, the Internet's global reach. The distribution of content has traditionally been a territorial business. The requirements of local languages, tastes and laws were reflected in rights deals and distribution networks that followed national boundaries. A truly 'world-wide' web, however, was clearly a challenge to that—demonstrated, even before digital delivery arrived, by the increased ability for consumers to obtain content from another territory, for example by someone in the UK to order US editions of books, CDs and DVDs from a US website, well beyond existing opportunities by telephone sale or mail order.

The Internet has certainly been part of a wider globalization effect that has challenged the logic of territorial restrictions. There are a vast range of sites and services online that draw upon and thrive thanks to an international audience. Several years ago, the CEO of a major media group commented to us that the practice of publishers in New York and London dividing up the world for sales of their separate English language editions would probably not survive and we think that recent developments in e-book distribution will likely have supported that view. Yet the demand for the localized still remains and the practicalities of delivering and paying for digital media must often reflect geographical realities.

This is where legal and regulatory considerations intersect with commercial aims and technical limitations. Anyone looking to expand into new markets has always had to factor in the practicalities of doing business in another country. This is no different with digital media. As we described in the earlier version of this book:

> the ability to communicate globally brings not only opportunity but also potential liability. Whilst a site of service might be lawful in one territory in which it is hosted, the situation may be quite different in the many legal jurisdictions in which it can be downloaded.... the law relating to transnational liability and the relevant rules and procedures in any connected litigation can be highly complex [and] the uncertainties raised by new digital media clearly add further complications. It is clearly impossible to provide a detailed analysis of the relevant laws of all countries in which [a site or service] may be downloaded.

Digital media may no longer be so new, but these jurisdictional complexities and the impossibilities of truly global legal and regulatory clearance remain—as does the potential liability. High profile examples of territorial limitations catching up with the possibilities of digital delivery have appeared regularly around the world, in many different contexts, since we wrote that. US portal Yahoo! was prosecuted in France for materials sold lawfully in the US and US publisher Dow Jones has faced defamation claims in Australia. Operators of gambling websites, lawful in the jurisdiction in which they are hosted, have been arrested when travelling to countries in which their service may be unlawful. Other website operators have been caught out when travelling to a country where an extradition request from a third country is honoured even though the alleged offence is not recognized in their home country. Many sites and services are simply unable to acquire rights on a global basis.

A cautious approach of actively limiting access to a site or service on a territory-by-territory basis remains an option. So-called 'geo-blocking' techniques, of varying degrees of sophistication, can be used to identify user location and limit access. These range from technical measures such as analysing the IP address of a user, ie using the Internet's own computer numbering system to trace where the access request has come from, to more administrative measures such as checks on a user's home address, bank and credit card. Such steps may never be 100 per cent accurate (see wider discussion of Verification of Identity in next section) but are now commonly relied upon commercially and are often included as contractual commitments.

Territorial limits

With portable devices the ability to access services from outside a 'home' territory may need to be recognized with an explicit carve-out from a territorial grant of rights using wording such as the following:

Territory clause content—Owner acknowledges that to the extent it is technically impossible to prevent End Users ordinarily resident in the Territory but situated temporarily outside the Territory from accessing some or all of the Mobile Content by 'roaming'. Licensee shall not be liable in respect of any such access *provided* that (i) Licensee accepts that no exclusivity commitment given by Content Owner shall apply to Content accessed in this manner; and (ii) Licensee shall ensure that all customary checks are made to verify that each End User is ordinarily resident in the Territory and the fact that the Content may be so available outside the Territory is not actively marketed or promoted.

Many operators will not always choose to adopt such a black-and-white approach to territory online. A risk assessment process will usually be undertaken based on a range of factors. First, of course, certain content will be more sensitive or controversial and require more care than others. Secondly, on the basis of the old '80/20 rule of thumb' (ie a high percentage of revenue or other important elements of a business may often derive from a proportionately low number of sources) only certain territories may be of importance. Finally, although even the largest digital media companies cannot clear sites and services on a global basis, experience may suggest that the position in certain countries can prove more problematic than others and so may require the investment of further time and effort.

Notwithstanding the examples above, and the health warning that comes with them, the trend already identified in our earlier books of courts and regulators in many territories moving away from the notion that simply because a site can be accessed in their territory does not mean they should or will have jurisdiction over it has continued in recent years. Courts and regulators have generally looked for connections over and above that. So a key part of any risk assessment is to look at what additional connections with a territory exist and whether they will be commercially and legally significant—see the checklist below. As with all such generalizations care is needed in applying this approach. In some cases this is based only on an assessment of the likelihood of local legal or regulatory action actually being taken rather than the strict letter of the law.

CHECKLIST

Connections that may trigger local legal or regulatory activity include:[12]

- localized elements of a site or service, eg language, content, domain names
- local registration and data collection
- collected data held/processed locally
- content, software, cookies or other deliverables supplied to local users
- physical delivery to local users
- technical delivery: hosting or additional content delivery networks used in the local jurisdiction
- payment using local currency or other devices sold locally
- advertising and promotion in other media in the local jurisdiction
- own or third-party local support, eg helpdesk, customer support
- local affiliates operating in the territory

C. Monetization

1. Competing with free

Ultimately, all commercial digital media services need to make money to survive. Finding a successful way to do this has been—and remains today—a significant challenge for many businesses. In particular, the process of moving from the comfort of traditional analogue formats to new a digital framework has often proved to be a painful transition.

[12] For specific EU rules for 'targeting' of consumer websites see the 2010 ECJ decision of Hammer/ Hotel Alpenhof.

That said, the earliest digital content plays were at least supported by clearly defined business models. Content on CD-Rom, CD-I or other physical products could obviously be sold in the same way as more traditional media had been, even if pricing was a challenge—is an encyclopaedia on disc worth the same as a set of bound volumes? (a dilemma which those pricing e-books today still face)—retail shelf space was hard to find and consumer demand ultimately proved to be weak. The first mainstream online content, whether for consumer or business use, was delivered through proprietary services that were usually subscription-based or in some cases even metered: charging by the time spent online. These were closed environments often seen as scarce valuable resources with limited competition.

Then came the web. Getting online became easier and there was now a world of website content to discover. Proprietary networks became so-called 'walled gardens' with content and access services still often bundled together. However, the ubiquity of the Internet encouraged interconnectivity and challenged the value of separate networks—especially when alternative website content was available for free. Competition also drove down the cost of dial-up access itself. These and a combination of other factors—including difficulties with early payment systems; not least an initial resistance to providing credit card and other personal details online, and the discovery that the void left by a lack of authorized content could and would be filled with unlawful copies—led in one direction. There was a growing expectation that accessing and downloading content from the web should be free—or very close to it.

The focus for digital media businesses therefore shifted to other ways to 'monetize' digital content. With the growth in online ads and sponsorship, business models based around advertising revenues became dominant for many services—the most famous example, perhaps, being Google engineering itself from a popular search engine into a billion-dollar advertising system.[13] Advertising was, of course, the way in which parts of the broadcasting industry had been successfully funded for many years, but it was only ever a partial funding element for some sectors, eg magazines and newspapers, and was entirely new to many other forms of content, such as music services. Questions over the ability for advertising to support the full range of digital content services have grown following the recession of 2008–9. Accordingly the pressure to maintain, or in some cases re-introduce, paid-for content models have increased.[14]

Of course some online content has prospered on a paid-for basis. In general, closed or semi-restricted environments such as those created by Apple for its iPod, iPhone and iPad devices—or by many of the mobile/cell phone networks around the world—as well as those providing content in particularly unique or compelling online experiences such as virtual worlds, multi-player games and remote gambling

[13] For an enthusiastic analysis of 'free'conomics, see Chris Anderson *Free* (Random House, 2009), following *The Long Tail* (Random House, 2007)

[14] For example the high profile steps taken by Rupert Murdoch's News Corp to place content behind so called 'pay walls'.

services have found it easier to 'monetize' (it has, though, still proved difficult to transfer such services, when once made available for free, into a paid format). Further, certain branded material, for example targeted at specialist business markets or to parents looking for reliable educational or entertainment material for their children, has also faired better online.

Clearly a range of factors will be relevant in determining which specific content will succeed with any given business model. It remains to be seen whether current attempts to extend paid-for content succeed, set as they are against continuing demographic and technical changes (see Chapter 3).

2. Revenue and value

It is perhaps not the role of lawyers to lead the debate over business models, but it is important that those models are accurately and effectively documented. With that in mind we set out below a chart which includes some of the possible elements that should be taken account of, or at least considered and discounted, when preparing contract documentation for digital media projects. It is intended to be a generic and content-neutral summary—but it could easily be adapted and developed for certain sectors—and should hopefully provide a useful checklist for readers, as it has for us.

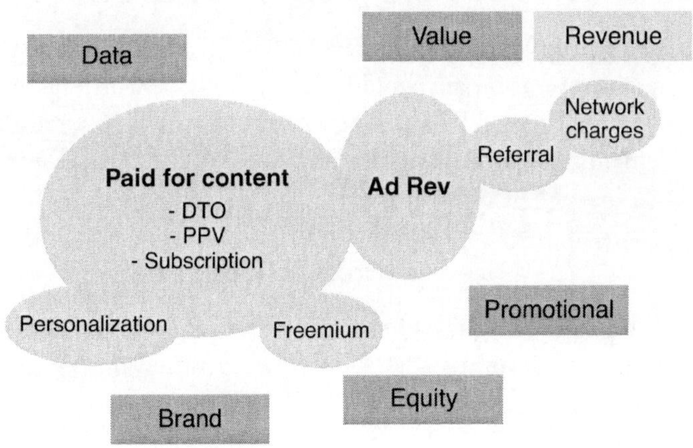

Figure 2.1 Monetization

As you can see, we have divided the elements into two: in lighter shade—actual cash-generating sources of revenue, and in darker shade—possible sources of more indirect value. The former obviously includes paid-for content including permanent downloads, sometimes called download-to-own (DTO) or electronic sell-though (EST),[15]

[15] Though the terms are open to debate given the licensing issues—see next chapter.

plus alternative access models of pay-per-view/use and subscription. It also includes hybrid models where payment for bespoke or additional content may follow an initial free offer, eg personalization and so called 'freemium' content.

Alongside these are advertising revenues—in all their forms. It is usually worth taking care to think through whether, alongside more straightforward paid-for space, any other possible promotional, marketing and sponsorship opportunities might be relevant and ensuring that these are adequately captured. We have also flagged the possibility of there being other pots of revenue such as referral fees (for more discussion see Chapter B4), or network charges (while mobile/cell phone networks have traditionally resisted sharing their access revenues, models which bundle the sale of content with access continues to resurface[16]).

The sources of value should clearly include personal information and other valuable data derived from the operation of a site or service. The economic value of such data can obviously be huge although the legal responsibilities that flow with it, particularly for personal data (see Chapter B9), are also significant. Indeed, there is often a key distinction between a contractual agreement over owning data and the statutory or regulatory requirements governing its use, both of which must be addressed. More intangible elements include promotional benefits, so often discussed as a basis for online business model—but of course reliant on that promotion leading to a revenue source, and brand value—which reinforces the need to ensure that contracts include appropriate provisions for the use and ownership of trade marks and domain names.

We also mention equity value. The days when the offer of a share in the ownership of another digital media company would automatically be worth taking, over any immediate payment of revenue, have gone with the dotcoms. It is, however, always an option to remember in any financial discussion.

E-commerce checklist

The focus of this book is digital content not electronic commerce but while we are looking at monetization issues the following issues are certainly worth flagging:

- **Online contracting**—Many of these transactions are international in nature with buyers and sellers from different countries transacting business on a platform potentially operated in a third territory. The security, validity and enforcement of these transactions can therefore be subject to various laws and regulatory requirements. As we discussed below, several countries have

[16] The ultimate model perhaps being licensing at point of access. For a detailed analysis of that concept and relevant legal and commercial considerations, see *Collective Licensing at the ISP Level: The 2010 Yearbook of the International Association of Entertainment Lawyers* <http://www.iael.org>.

established rules and regulations relating to the use of electronic signatures, contracts and invoices. In addition, where records and documents need to be maintained, it is important that the electronic archiving methods used guarantee legal certainty.

- **E-commerce regulation**—Establishing a business online, or simply engaging in an online transaction, may subject a business to varying regulations in one or more countries including the jurisdiction of local taxing authorities and courts. It is important to understand the framework of regulation in which any e-commerce site is operating. As an example, the EU E-Commerce Directive is considered the cornerstone of European legal regulation of e-commerce. It contains rules on applicable law, information duties, electronic contracting, liability and publicity online. A wide range of other EU legislation is also relevant including many provisions focused on protecting consumers, such as the distance selling regime.
- **E-money** (including payment systems, invoicing and tax)—E-commerce requires secure and efficient transactions. These require appropriate arrangements with banks, credit card companies, payment processors and other partners. Mobile operators are promoting their own purchase solutions. The contractual requirements of the card schemes in particular are often restrictive and compliance can be a challenge where innovative payment arrangements are being developed. Legal and regulatory controls can also restrict the use of such arrangements, eg in operating electronic gift cards and loyalty schemes. Non-compliance with the legal requirements of electronic money and related financial legislation can raise serious liability issues. Special online rules covering VAT and sales tax, as well as place of establishment, have been developed by the authorities in many territories.
- **Operations**—Operating a sales platform of any type requires establishing and hosting a potentially complex infrastructure involving software and hardware issues as well as systems integration and development services. Some choose to outsource these operations to third party providers. The success or failure of business is completely dependent on its infrastructure and the third party tools and services that support it. Contracting for these tools and services may require a different approach than when purchasing for the backroom operation of an offline business. Obviously failure to obtain the right solutions or the right service level commitments from third party providers can negatively affect a company's brand, and ultimately its bottom line.
- **E-marketplaces**—Online auctions and other forms of e-marketplace provide alternative electronic trading platforms that bring together entities with the purpose of buying and selling. Such platforms are now well established in both B2B and B2C sectors. B2C platforms have succeeded in a wide range of

markets supported by distance selling and other online sales related legislation aimed at protecting the consumer from unfair trade practices. Operators can, however, face legal challenge for the actions of their participants.

- **Data privacy**—The management and protection of information, including personal data, is now high on the policy agendas of many countries, as well as of many self-regulatory organizations. Data protection issues arise in the context of virtually all consumer-facing e-commerce activities, and raise particularly complex issues for operations that have a presence both inside and outside the EU (for more details see Ba below).
- **Advertising and marketing**—Any marketing or promotional aspect of a site, service or other online activity—from banner ads, viral campaigns and other direct/indirect advertising to the use of targeted search and navigation tools and site sponsorship—will usually trigger a number of legal and regulatory issues.

3

LEGAL THEMES

A. Copyrights and Wrongs

1. The challenge to copyright

From the beginning of the digital age, reports of the death of copyright have been greatly, and consistently, exaggerated. Fifteen to twenty years on, in all practical senses, copyright remains the lifeblood of digital media. Of course, digital technology has presented, and continues to present, undeniable challenges. But copyright has faced technological challenges before. In fact copyright's natural habitat is one of changing technology. A legal concept that was developed in response to the printing press has since evolved from the invention of the photograph, through sound recording and film, to terrestrial and satellite broadcasting and computing. Copyright has continually proved itself to be an adaptable and resilient legal animal. So why has the digital debate so often seemed to question copyright's very fitness for purpose? Indeed, why is that debate virtually unchanged from the one we reported on in the our earlier books?

Copyright has always needed updating over time. Copyright is based around the concepts of 'protected works', 'restricted acts' and specific 'exceptions', ie descriptions of the types of content that are protected and the things that can or cannot be done with that content. As media and technology change so those definitions can become outdated. There has, though, been extensive work in the last ten years on both the updating and harmonization of copyright law at a national level, at a regional level through bodies such as the European Commission and at an international level through the World Intellectual Property Organization (WIPO). Indeed, we have already passed the 10th anniversary of WIPO's 'digital agenda' for such reform. As a result of the international treaty arrangements that WIPO administers,[1] there is

[1] The WIPO Copyright Treaty of 1996, along with the WIPO Performances and Phonograms Treaty of the same year, updated existing international copyright agreements such as the Berne Convention and the Rome Convention.

currently an obligation in 88 nations from Albania to Venezuela—and certainly in the US and all the EU—to have some 'digital copyright basics' in place.

First, they must provide for a technology-neutral 'communication to the public' right to make it possible for content owners to license new digital content services just as they can traditional media. Secondly, they must give explicit legal protection for DRM systems (see Content and Control below) by making it unlawful to circumvent effective technical protection measures applied to content or to remove rights management information from content or to distribute content from which such rights information has been removed or altered without permission. As always with the law, the devil is in the detail. There has been significant variance in the timing and scope of national implementation—even within Europe. But while those national differences remain crucial, the law should in theory make it possible for content owners to license distribution by web or wireless device just as they can by hard copy or traditional broadcast.

2. Reframing the debate

Of course, for copyright to have a value it still needs to be enforced—and that has always, and will always, mean time, effort and money.[2] We discuss just how far technology itself has been able to assist that in the next section. We should also stress that law makers can only go so far in trying to keep up with technology. Statutes now attempt technology-neutral provisions, but technology-specific answers are still needed. Many questions over the scope of copyright protection are left for the courts to settle and the high-profile Google Books dispute is a good example of that (see box). Yet the continuing copyright debate has been rarely about legal detail. It continues to generate a more fundamental tension, almost a paradox. Through digital media, it is true to say that copyright works have never before played such an important and exciting role in the lives of users. Yet, as users interact with that content on an array of platforms and devices, it is probably also true to say that never before has there been such apparent disrespect for the copyright in those works.

Google Books

The Google Books project involved the scanning of books from the shelves of major libraries into a searchable database allowing Google to display bibliographic data and snippets of text in response to search requests. In the UK and elsewhere this project only ever extended to out-of-copyright works or with

[2] See Chesterman and Lipman, *The Electronic Pirates* (Routledge, 1988) for a reminder of the significant problems even in a pre-digital age. For an even earlier discussion of piracy and the 'challenge' to copyright law, see the 1878 Report of the Royal Commission on Copyright, in which even then some were questioning copyright's fitness for purpose.

rights holder permission. In the US it has included copyright works. Google argued that the fair use exceptions in US copyright law can be extended to include this type of digitization, although Google did agree not to scan the works of rights holders who opted-out. This effective reversal of the copyright permission process led to high profile US lawsuits from publishers and authors who disputed this interpretation of fair dealing and saw an opt-out approach as unacceptable.

Some saw this as essentially a commercial battle to see how far either side could go in establishing legal principles before striking a hard bargain to deliver that material. There was, however, a more fundamental legal concern. If copyright law prevented hard copy digitization, it might also be used to control online activities. In Belgium, Google had lost a claim that its Google News Service went too far in not only linking to other sites but also carrying excerpts and making available entire cache copies from them.[3] That decision was limited in its scope and court decisions elsewhere, notably in the US, have declined to outlaw the activities of search engines generally, but any judgment on Google's hard copy digitization would almost certainly have had an impact on the way in which search engines and others captured and catalogued online data.

As a result, the very basis of Google's core business could have been affected. The commercial impact on authors and publishers could also have been significant. Perhaps the stakes, and the costs, were too high, so it is unsurprising that both sides agreed to a settlement. The scope and scale of that settlement did surprise many however. In a hugely complex and ambitious document, over 300 pages long, the parties attempted to establish a framework, through a central registry,[4] for Google to continue to expand its database, allow certain library use and compensate publishers and authors on an international basis. It attempted to use US class action rules to put in place arrangements that would normally be achieved through legislation and public consensus rather than contractual agreement (as highlighted by comparisons with European digital library initiatives).

[3] As will be discussed in Chapter B4, the underlying legal rules for linking and related online activities are confused and confusing. Indeed in the UK, a 2005 Government response to a consultation on 'the liability of hyperlinkers, location tool services and content aggregators' effectively admitted as much but put off any reform until an EU-wide policy had been developed, something that the European Commission's Digital Agenda, launched in 2010, may finally address. In the meantime commercial disputes, such as that in the UK between the Newspaper Licensing Agency and media monitoring business Meltwater News, may result in further guidance from the courts.

[4] Other plans for international registers of content have also emerged in recent years such as ARROW: Accessible Registries of Rights Information and Orphan Works <http://www.arrow-net.eu> (discussed later in this chapter) and the Global Repertoire Database <http://www.globalrepertoiredatabase.com> which aims to develop a common framework for rights ownership information for musical works.

Unsurprisingly, the impact those arrangements would have on others, in particular the perceived competitive disadvantage for anyone else seeking to obtain similar licences, and the effective unilateral reform of the overall regime for orphan works,[5] as well as those outside the US, brought a range of challenges from different parties in the subsequent court hearings necessary to ratify the settlement. Despite some concessions and amendments the settlement has still not received court approval and such approval will still likely trigger appeals from those who object.[6]

This can be particularly observed in the behaviour of the so-called 'digital natives', ie minors and young adults who have grown up with new technologies and who perceive digital content as a given. For them, instant access, unlimited copying and seamless remixing are self-evident. Many do not realize that copyright law prohibits these acts without permission, and are often sincerely surprised when copyright rules are explained to them. Many 'digital immigrants'—ie the rest of us—have also grown accustomed to the availability of digital content. In contrast to digital natives, however, digital immigrants grew up in an analogue media world. Most digital immigrants therefore (still) realize that free digital content is not automatic, and why unauthorized use is unlawful, even if some may succumb to it. We discuss the practical impact of a 'copy and paste culture' further below.

It is also intriguing to speculate whether there will be a further shift, as current decision makers, digital immigrants accustomed to traditional copyright rules, are replaced by tomorrow's digital natives. Certainly media coverage in the last eighteen months has focused on that possibility. We would compare the reception to a fifty-something UK trade minister introducing pro-copyright legislation and predictably, and unfairly, being attacked for 'not getting it', with his much younger opposite number in Belgium known for brandishing his iPhone to make points about hacking and DRM.[7] It is, perhaps, still too early to claim that an irreversible generational influence is at work but it must be recognized that this has been a factor within the public arguments.

A further factor to consider is that too often challenges to business models have been mistaken for challenges to the legal framework on which they are based.

[5] How best to tackle the issue of clearing rights in copyright works, especially online material, where the owner is not easily identifiable, has proved difficult with legislative proposals in the US, UK, Australia and elsewhere proving controversial. See also the EU's Accessible Registries of Rights Information and Orphan Works (ARROW) project—<http://www.arrow-net.eu/>.

[6] The official site summarising progress: <http://www.googlebooksettlement.com/>.

[7] See Patrick van Eeche and Duncan Calow 'We need bold solutions for paradoxical times' FT.com, 2 November 2009.

What has been labelled a copyright debate has often been more about economics and power than the law: a commentary on the major corporations whose businesses are based on copyrights and their role, responsibilities and relationship with the consumer. That of course is an entirely legitimate debate to hold, and the law can never be separated completely from a wider political and social background, but it is often a frustrating complication for anyone wishing to focus on the more practical aspects of copyright law.

It is also worth noting that developments that are often framed as alternatives to copyright, such as the Copy-left or Creative Commons initiatives[8] (which essentially promote the distribution of material with standardized usage and re-usage information) or wider ideas based around so-called 'open source' or shared development concepts (which have extended from software to wider content through the growth of user-generated content whether in the form of public sources such as Wikipedia or media organizations like the BBC making material available for such use) are not necessarily incompatible with copyright law. In most cases they represent a different way of licensing and/or an alternative distribution model for content rather than a challenge to the overall legal framework. Indeed, the commercial exploitation of those licensing ideas may yet develop within the mainstream just as the use of open source software has become a million-dollar business.

A copy-and-paste culture?

That the copying of others' work has always played a part in literary, artistic and scientific endeavour is not open to challenge. The words of Shakespeare and Newton are quoted on the topic. Christopher Hitchen's essay *In Defence of Plagiarism*[9] provides a rich history of such re-use, describing the benefits enjoyed as a result. One example is Dr Martin Luther King, presented with an original but third-rate speech, throwing away notes and extemporizing, calling upon all he'd ever read, to 'synthesize borrowings into something higher'.

Now, however, virtually everyone—from classroom to boardroom—is able to access, use and manipulate 'content' to an unparalleled degree. Indeed, for a younger generation happily downloading from peer-to-peer networks and mixing and sharing multimedia 'mash-ups', reportedly with neither payment nor contrition, adding plagiarism to their list of infringing behaviour might not seem such a big deal. Take Georgetown University's online guidance notes on this topic. They begin not with a review of copyright rules but actually a

[8] See, for example, <www.gnu.org/copyleft> and <http://www.creativecommas.org>.
[9] See Hitchens, *Unacknowledged Legislation* (Verso, 2000).

justification of why, just because someone has already said it better, a student should still actually bother trying to write something original rather than copy it off the Internet—after all, 'Michael Jordan can hit a fade-away jump shot better than you can, and Miles Davis could play a better blues than you'.

Of course, if those students were actually to review applicable copyright law they might be surprised. In many territories, and contrary to popular wisdom, the law does not set down neat limits based on the number of words or percentage of content taken to determine whether or not a work has been infringed. In the UK the law says that copyright will be breached when a 'substantial part' has been taken and the courts stress that this can be assessed on the basis of quality as much as quantity. Clearly, some words do have greater value than others and flexibility is needed to deal with a diverse range of works, but that does mean differences of interpretation do develop, and theoretical differences can lead to inconsistencies in practice.

That's not to say that copyright cannot spot open and shut cases of plagiarism. The court will not need evidence of the defendant 'caught in the act', which by definition will rarely be available. It will often be enough to show that two works are similar, that one pre-dates the other, that the defendant would have had access to the former and that the similarity is too close for it to be coincidence. Where whole passages of text have been taken from one work into another, where there is identifiable word-for-word copying, courts will usually have no difficulty in deciding when the law has been broken. One of the reasons that author James Herbert fared less well than Dan Brown, on superficially similar facts, in two famous infringement cases (over twenty years apart) was that with Herbert's novel, *The Spear*, the claimants could identify examples of near identical wording, something that claimants simply could not find in Brown's *The Da Vinci Code*.

More difficulties are likely to arise when the copying is non-literal. Certainly, despite what many believe, paraphrasing another's work can still amount to copyright infringement. Permission is needed to re-word a website in English just as it is to translate it from English to Italian. But as you move away from the use of identical, or at least very similar, wording to merely similar themes and configurations, establishing infringement becomes more difficult. Stealing the structure of a story is harder to deal with than theft of the actual words used to tell it; and in digital media taking from computer programs and databases will often involve acts of non-literal copying of architecture and function. Similar difficulties have been encountered in the many disputes that have arisen in the television industry over competing quiz game and reality show formats where courts have been reluctant to give protection.

There are then difficulties, but copyright still grapples relatively successfully with these issues, proving once again its surprising adaptability. The courts have had many cases over many years to develop their thinking. Technology has, of course, made a difference and will continue to do so. It is intriguing to consider whether the wealth of content that digital media immerses us in today increases our potential for subliminal copying. The more blatant examples of infringement will usually require an active hand, however, and if the computer processor makes plagiarism easier it also makes it easier to analyse and detect—from simple word counts to the use of sophisticated tracking devices across networks.

B. Content and Control

1. The answer to the machine

It is ironic that at a time of significant online piracy, many of copyright's detractors have been reacting to the fact that in a digital environment copyright can actually be seen as too effective. Again let us stress that we are not discounting the cost of online infringement and piracy, but the experience of digital rights management is instructive.

The late Charles Clark famously said that 'the answer to the machine is in the machine'[10] in an article which examined how the challenge of unauthorized digital reproduction and distribution of copyright works might be met by the use of technical controls, so-called digital rights management or DRM. Since then of course DRM—in theory and in practice—has proved to be an often controversial solution. Content owners have enthusiastically adopted, and in some cases then retreated from, its use. Confusingly, DRM has come to mean different things to different people. To some it is a purely technical issue of developing and operating potentially competing systems. In other contexts it is a shorthand for the payment models and other business terms with which it can be used. Very often it is simply seen as a more basic symbol of economic power and control.

That reflects the fact that such technical protection measures can police the letter of copyright law more effectively than was ever possible with analogue distribution means. The home copying and analogue format-shifting debates of the 1980s have been transformed now that the copyright legend on the back of an LP or VHS tape can actually be enforced through a technical wrapper around digital content.[11] In very simple terms, DRM systems identify content, in a similar way to existing systems

[10] *The Answer to the Machine* was first published in 1995, but appears in Jon Bing and Thomas Dreier (eds), *The Answer to the Machine is in the Machine: And Other Collected Writings* (NCCL, 2005).

[11] Courts and regulators are still reviewing how far the digital equivalents of that wording: end-user licence agreements and standard terms of use, with or without DRM, should be permitted to restrict the use of content.

for physical products, but also describe the work and its uses, trying to break down what things can be done with that content, so usage rules can be set.[12] They must then provide the content in such a way that those rules can be enforced. This is often achieved through encryption, which effectively wraps and unwraps the content. Content owners may, however, be just as interested in watermarking and fingerprinting systems, ie markers to help identify and track the content and its use.

2. Legal and commercial challenges

There are a number of core legal and commercial themes that flow from this. As mentioned above, copyright law includes exceptions, permitting protected works to be used without permission. Some are obvious, others are more technical and they can cover a broad range of circumstances from scientific research to use in religious celebrations. The big question for a DRM system is how far these exceptions can and/or should be respected. Indeed, are these *exceptions* or effectively *rights*? For example, with a printed newspaper it is easy to take advantage of those exceptions. The reader can copy it, share it, amend it, and do many things that do not fall within an exception. When the reader downloads that same text in a DRM-protected format they may only be able to do those things that the system actively permits. Law makers have wrestled with whether and how they should step in and regulate.

Unlocking DRM

- In the UK provision is made for the government to designate circumstances when DRM restrictions may be circumvented—currently no such list of activities has been issued.
- In the US, every three years under powers granted under the Digital Millennium Copyright Act there is a 'Rulemaking on Exemptions from Prohibition on Circumvention of Technological Measures that Control Access to Copyrighted Works'.
- In Australia there has been a recent Parliamentary 'Review of technological protection measures exceptions'.

The latter two have both produced a more detailed set of circumstances where they think that DRM technology could be circumvented. These included for obsolete and unsupported software or other so-called 'abandonware', software installed without permission, disabled access and material handled by libraries.[13]

[12] Two interesting developments have been ACAP (Automated Content Access Protocol), a labelling system for publishers to inform search engines of the rights status of online content <http://www.the-acap.org> and hNews a descriptive microformat <http://www.microformats.org/wiki/news> being developed as part of Associated Press' initiative for a news content registry.

[13] See the most recent US Rulemaking at <http://www.copyright.gov/1201> and details of Australian measures at <http://www.aph.gov.au/home/committee/aca/protection>.

Then there is the linked issue of private copying—especially in Europe. Many EU states responded to the cassette tape and the VCR by permitting private copying in return for a levy or tax payment on those analogue systems, which was used to compensate rights-holders. Those countries have had to decide whether digital devices should now also be included. The European Commission was originally very keen to phase out levies in favour of DRM but the countries themselves have generally preferred to retain the certainty of their existing structures. Indeed now the focus of the Commission is on harmonizing those levies not necessarily replacing them.[14] Interestingly some platform providers for both handheld devices and online services have begun to investigate almost voluntary levies—collective licensing deals on behalf of their users. Even in countries without a levy, such as the UK and the US, consumers have been accustomed to making copies.[15] So a successful DRM system, and the licensing structure below it, may need to reflect what users did in the pre-digital era and have come to expect, regardless of their precise legal basis as exceptions, rights or even whether they were allowed by law at all.[16]

There is a related privacy issue. If a consumer buys a video in a store with cash there is no (identifiable) record of that purchase. If they download it to a handheld device the relevant DRM system could begin to compile a detailed record of when, how and even where they consumed that content, including with whom they shared it. EU law specifically makes clear that support for DRM technology does not override the need to comply with data protection law. The European Commission has also looked at the issue of interoperability. Their ideal was to develop open standards: like VHS or DVD,[17] but failing that they have looked for an ability for dominant proprietary standards to allow content downloaded to one device to be transferable to another. In such a young and aggressive market, however, neither industry agreements nor the use of competition law have succeeded. An attempt in France to enshrine specific mandatory interoperability requirements into copyright law also proved to be a non-starter given the technical and commercial sensitivities involved.

DRM also highlights accessibility issues, which also have a far wider importance for digital media and should be considered in any arrangements to develop new services (see Chapter B5). 'Accessibility' primarily addresses the ability of all people, regardless

[14] See <http://www.ec.europa.eu/information_society/digital-agenda/index_en.htm>.

[15] Partly of course because the courts did not ban the analogue technologies—photocopiers, video cassette recorders or tape-to-tape machines—that permitted those copies to be made. This was largely on the basis that the supplier had no control over whether or not the user decided to use that technology to infringe copyright—see key decisions such as *Sony v Universal* (1984) in the US, *CBS v Amstrad* (1988) in the UK, and *RCA v Fairfax* (1981) in Australia. The same approach has not always been applied when particular digital services have subsequently been reviewed by the courts in each of those territories.

[16] It may be that there is room for collective as well as individual licensing solutions for the industry. If the answer to photocopying of copyright works in most countries was a collective licensing solution, might that have a role in digital use?

[17] In the wireless sector that has been partially delivered through something called the Open Mobile Alliance Initiative <http://www.openmobilealliance.org>.

of any physical disabilities, to use and access services without discrimination. Many countries including the UK now have laws making it unlawful not to take account of accessibility in the delivery of services to the public. As online services play an increasingly important role in all aspects of life so the obligation (legal as well as moral) on the providers of websites and digital services to ensure that their technology does not discriminate against certain users increases. Bodies such as the RNIB in the UK have consistently argued that this should include online content and any technical controls, such as DRM, that may limit access to it.[18] Consumer groups, libraries, archives and other public bodies have also led a vociferous campaign over wider access issues. In particular they have been concerned that technical protection measures should not 'lock-up' content from society, for example effectively extending the copyright term by making it difficult to remove DRM from public domain material where the same system is being used for copyright protected content (see Unlocking DRM above).

3. Future developments

Of course some business models are DRM-free—in the sense of not applying access controls to digital content. Most notably, the music industry has retreated from wholesale DRM controls for many digital services, in particular permanent downloads. This move came in the face of customer opposition and a perception that services already competing with free illegal alternatives could not afford to impose additional usage restrictions that the illegal alternatives did not have.[19] Crucially, however, not all online music is currently DRM-free with a different approach taken between some of the services including those based on subscription or for mobile/cell phones. Other sectors also remain committed to DRM so the notion that DRM has been killed off by the music industry is certainly premature. That said, for less well-known content providers obscurity may often seem more of a danger than uncontrolled distribution and digital piracy. Others in the media industry are choosing to focus on time-sensitive or 'disposable' content precisely because it is less susceptible to longer-term misuse and can be provided DRM-free.

It is perhaps worth remembering at this point that Charles Clark's original article, mentioned above, led with the following quote: 'the question is not so much how we shall prevent access and use, as how we shall monitor access and use'. So from the beginning, DRM—in its widest sense—was about more than just locks and keys for content. Digital fingerprints, watermarks and tracking may be as valuable as access controls. Numbering systems and metadata have always been a vital part

[18] See <http://www.rnib.org.uk/professionals/webaccessibility/pages/web_accessibility.aspx> for information on the RNIB's approach to digital accessibility.

[19] Commercial pressure also came in the form of an open letter to the industry in 2007 from Steve Jobs the Apple CEO entitled 'Thoughts on Music' <http://www.apple/com/hotnews/thoughtsonmusic> which proposed the 'abolishing' of DRM—in part a reaction to pressure on Apple to license others access to its FairPlay platform.

of the equation too. Some of the key technical developments currently involve management of the wider ecosystems that digital content inhabits. They form part of various steps towards potential collective, or at least centralized, digital licensing possibilities (including development of key registries of digital content as discussed above). So even if content providers decide—whether for technical or commercial reasons—not to apply encryption technology that controls access to content, they will still likely want an ability to identify and trace the use of that content. YouTube was reportedly only able to sign a deal with one of the major music groups because it promised to launch a form of 'advanced content identification and royalty reporting system' for its platform.

Whilst the implementation of DRM in practice has probably not developed as its original promoters might have expected or wanted, and a range of legal questions (as listed above) still remain, the use of technology to protect, police and support the distribution of digital content will continue.[20] There is, however, a more fundamental point to capture here. Returning to the above discussion of traditional analogue content and users' expectations—whether legitimate or not—an obvious but important factor to note was that content and the rights in that content were effectively always bound together. Possession of a printed book gave with it the ability to read it. The act of giving or selling that book to someone else passed that ability with the book.

This need not necessarily apply online. The content and then the right and ability to use that content can be thought of separately. So whatever the *physical* solutions for digital distribution the *rights* questions need to be dealt with in addition. In simple content delivery systems the two might still be combined, and it may be that consumer demand requires that link to be maintained, but in more sophisticated alternatives they can be separated.[21] Even if technical DRM controls are not applied to content this consideration is still relevant to the licensing and commercial terms that the user is offered and will likely trigger developments in copyright, contract and consumer law.[22]

C. Copyright and Contract

1. Who has the rights?

Even if the potential business models and monetization of digital content have been in doubt—and the effectiveness of relevant legal and technical protection

[20] See the latest initiatives such as DECE's 'Ultraviolet' <http://www.uvvu.com> and Disney's 'KeyChest' discussed further in Chapter A6.

[21] See the OMA website (<http://www.openmobilealliance.org>) for details of how the OMA DRM options separate the content item itself from the rights permissions allowing access and use of that item.

[22] A recent US case (*Verner v Autodesk* (2010)) has grappled with the issue of whether the EULA (an end user licence agreement) for digital content determined whether that content had been sold or licensed on the basis of its legal, rather than technical, restrictions on use.

measures open to question—this has not stopped stakeholders arguing over who gets what. This is nothing new of course. Just as copyright has always adapted with and to developments in media and technology, so arguments have always arisen whether the rights and revenues derived from an existing medium extend to each new alternative and/or replacement. As a result courts have regularly had to scrutinize older contracts to determine whether or not they cover newer rights, eg did owners of theatre rights also hold film rights, did film rights include television, did television rights include video, did VHS cover DVD etc?

Such disputes, and the application of the legal principles used to rule on them, have been revisited over developments in digital media in many different contexts in many countries.[23] Those principles vary from territory to territory, and such cases always turn on their specific facts, so it is dangerous to make generalizations. It is probably fair to say, however, that courts around the world have often been willing to protect the position of content creators who argue that they should be entitled to restrict—or at least be entitled to additional benefits from—any exploitation of the work in new digital media by other parties. Of course, it is possible to draft documentation that sets out more clearly that any such further uses are included—the *'any and all media now known or hereafter invented'* type of provision—but commercial reality often means such contractual clarity is not provided for.

As a result, most digital media producers have had to carry out a degree of due diligence in checking that their older rights contracts permit exploitation of content in new digital formats. This can be a slow and, ultimately, frustrating process where the grant language is particularly unclear or the relevant financial provisions vague or equivocal. Going forward, of course, new contracts need to make allowance for future technical developments too. A further complication arises with industry-wide agreements. As discussed above, the music industry relies on collective licensing arrangements that were slow to adapt to new online delivery requirements.[24] Many other media sectors have some form of collective, or industry, agreements that can be relevant to rights and revenue.

In particular, the film and television industries largely rely on terms of trade agreements between talent unions, producer representatives and broadcasters that establish standard deal terms for rights acquisition. These have had to been re-negotiated to take

[23] Key digital decisions include the well-known *Tasini* (2001) and *Rosetta Books* (2002) cases in the US as well as the more recent *Greenberg v National Graphics* (2008). In the UK there has been less case law but see *Excelsior v YTV Ltd* (2009).

[24] Moreover, all the networks have run into difficulties with the music collecting societies within Europe in arguments over who is the appropriate licensee in the mobile distribution chain; the relevant income to which royalties apply; and why cross-border deals cannot be struck with just one or two societies. Under pressure from the Commission the last of these has begun to change with pan-European one-stop shop licensing becoming a reality—EMI struck a high profile deal with MCPS/PRS and GEMA in 2007 (see <http://ec.europa.eu/competition/sectors/media/online_commerce.html>.en>. The other questions are currently being argued over in court but the outcome is as likely to make off-portal licensing easier as it is for network deals.

account of digital exploitation—for instance the development of online availability of television programming required specific additions to broadcasting agreements. In the US a long-running dispute over the terms of these new arrangements led to high-profile strike action by the unions. The nature of those industry deals are outside the scope of this book, and neither is this the forum for a clause-by-clause analysis of how all rights agreements need to change, but let us provide some thoughts on some generic issues which will be relevant to some of the sample agreements in Part II.

2. A non-disruptive rights template

Whatever the commercial arrangements, lawyers still have to ensure that the underlying rights and licensing structures are able to support them. As discussed above, all the media sectors are having to deal with digital technology transforming the roles and relationships throughout the chain of development and distribution. Many of the same pressure points are emerging: from the definition of digital rights to the extent of any exclusivity and the nature of promotional activities in interactive media. The music industry has grappled with these issues longer the most. Recording contracts traditionally only took rights to an artist's recordings leaving the artist to exploit other opportunities, in particular concerts and merchandize. In a digital world, where recordings may generate less income, some labels now think their business ought to be in those other areas. So they are looking for a wider grant of rights and a completely different relationship in return for a different upfront deal with the artist.

So-called 360 degree contracting may have a value elsewhere. Hamish McCrae, principal economic commentator in *The Independent* newspaper in London, picked up on this when he wrote:

> Whereas half a century ago pop stars made most of their money from records, now they make it from live performances. That is why the Stones and Madonna keep slogging round the world. I suspect authors will find themselves pushed in the same direction. We won't quite get to the stage where books are given away free, leaving all the money to be made from the authors making personal appearances, but that is the way it seems to be heading.[25]

As warned earlier, there is a limit to how far lessons learnt in the music industry can be applicable in other media. Book authors and other content creators are not rock bands, and the commercial and legal structures within the music business are often very different from other media sectors. So, for example, self-published authors may never top the bestsellers in the way that 'unsigned' artists can now have a number one single on the back of successful touring on the gig circuit and through self-promotion. Yet given the power of blogging, social networks and reduced distribution costs (and, in the case of books, technologies like print-on-demand) the parallels are clear. Indeed, educational publishers have commented to us that many

[25] 'Why intellectual property is a vital trade for the English-speaking world', *The Independent,* 12 October 2006.

academic authors, though otherwise distinctly dissimilar to rock stars, are engaging with their audience in a similar way.

At the very least it shows how contract parties will increasingly need to think outside the analogue box. At the same time, and switching from the acquisition of rights to their exploitation, many content providers have been trying very hard to stay within that box; seeking to fit new digital distribution methods into their existing licence structures. They aim to develop a so-called 'non-disruptive rights template' that allows the introduction of new markets without harming existing ones. Clearly, if a business is still enjoying very considerable revenues from traditional formats it makes no commercial sense to damage those by licensing new rights which produce far less reward. Balancing the two is not always so straightforward, of course, and the licensees may seek to acquire both rights in any case as a defensive measure.

So, for example, this impacts upon the traditional distribution 'windows' used in certain media to maximize revenue with different forms of media licensed at different times (and often different territories). An example of this is where a film is given a cinema release before video and television showings, or sports rights are split between live, recorded and highlight television packages or a hardback book appears before a paperback version. In some cases digital media platforms have been slotted into the existing structure, that is simply *adding* new rights to the old ones for minimal disruption. Others, however, have found that factors such as piracy mean it makes more sense to squeeze these release windows so that different media are licensed together, *re-arranging* the rights to accommodate digital. Others have kept the time windows but tried to license rights on a media-neutral basis, effectively *transforming* the way in which rights are sliced and diced (see the table below).

Film	Sport
Theatrical	**Live TV**
(+ 6–12 months) Video	(+ hours) Delayed TV
(+ 18 months) Pay TV	(+ day) Highlights TV
(+ 33 months) Free TV	(+ week) TV Archive
re-arranging the rights:	*transforming the rights:*
Theatrical and DVD	**Live**
(+ 6 months) Pay TV/VOD	(+ hours) Delayed
(+ 12 months) Free TV/web	(+ day) Highlights
	(+ week) Archive
Shrinking windows	*Technology neutral*

That last development is partly because technology is making it increasingly difficult to distinguish between, say, wireless rights and existing television and radio markets. Mobile TV, particularly when DAB, DVB-H or other mobile broadcast standards are used, makes it much harder to draft robust rights definitions that avoid market disruption—see for example below the alphabet soup of mobile technologies that might form a definition of wireless technology:

'Wireless technology' includes any of the following technologies with radio frequency spectrum in any band: the Global System for Mobile Communications (GSM) but including GPRS, EDGE, HSCD, MBMS and TDtv; Code Division Multiple Access (CDMA); Universal Mobile Telecommunications System (UMTS); Wideband Code Division Multiple Access (W-CDMA); DCS-1,800; HSDPA; HSUPA and their derivative systems and services or any combination of them; but *excluding* (a) any wireless standard or technology that is used during the term of the agreement for the point to multi-point broadcast of content to portable devices including DVB-H, DAB, DMB-T, DMB-S, ISDB-T and MediaFLO; and (b) any fixed-wireless systems including Wi-Fi (802.11), W-MAX (502.16), Bluetooth, MMDS, LMDS and IrDA.

Moreover, the competition/anti-trust law regulators in the EU have taken a very close interest in sports markets generally and new media rights in particular. They are keen to ensure that rights are 'unbundled', in other words that television broadcasters will not necessarily grab newer rights alongside their traditional media packages. Further, SMS alerts, wallpapers and even simple apps and other short-form content are far easier to distinguish as 'wireless content' than increasingly sophisticated services that will look and feel the same on a mobile/cell phone or portable device as a PC or a TV. So at this point some rights might need to be established more often by function as well as, or instead of, format.

3. Future-proofing contracts

Rather than argue whether, say, print on paper rights are different from e-book rights, or trying to distinguish between audio CD, audio download and radio, contracts might—in some contexts—be better off focusing on the consumer's acts of 'reading' or 'listening' regardless of the medium. Clearly much will depend on from which end of the grant of rights the contract is being reviewed as well as the other specific factors of the deal: exclusivity, term, other deals being entered into etc (see Chapter A4). Sticking closely to the technology, however hard that may be to specify, may still feel more comfortable for some.

There may still be a wider benefit, however, regardless of the issues discussed above, in re-evaluating the nature of the deal and the way it is documented. In fact what we are getting down to is a debate about what it is to be a 'producer' or 'publisher' of digital content and how that needs to be reflected in commercial agreements. For example, is it just about deciding how and when access is granted to something, or more about branding and quality—about what should be selected and how it should be promoted? Or is the primary concern a continued need for project finance, ie funding talent through advances, allowing works to be created in the first place?

Actually this has not been such a defined process in the media business. In music, film, broadcasting and publishing the producer/publisher is usually left to get on with what it does best and industry contracts usually reflect that. This is less about bargaining power (although clearly the relative position of contracting parties is a factor) than certainty over what it is that is being produced: an album, a series, a film or a book. Contrast that with technology contracts where the development and production process is constantly reduced to a collection of specifications and procedures that can quantify and measure performance. Perhaps unsurprisingly, digital media products have often followed something of a middle ground. We try to address this in some of the agreements in Part II.

Even without such fundamental considerations contracts need to take account of digital rights properly. It is no longer possible to hide them or the issues they raise in the boilerplate or secondary clauses in the hope no will notice or argue. Many traditional media documents also need updating more generally since digital issues will usually run right throughout a contract, not just the definition of rights. In some cases these raise very specific commercial questions. In book publishing, a common example is the author's reversion clause where the possibilities of digital media might mean a work never went 'out of print' under older clauses. More generally, however, many operative clauses may simply assume that material is delivered and exploited in physical form. Again, in book publishing, everything in an author agreement from 'proofs and production', 'cover artwork', and 'credit provisions' through to 'reserves' and 'remainders' may still be based entirely around print on paper.

The practical answer is to step back and work out what any provision is actually trying to achieve. Contract wording is not magic—even though industry standards and expectations can sometimes seem to invest it with that power. Contracts can always be re-worded to do a different or better job. The updating does not have to be dramatic or extensive, it can be evolutionary not revolutionary, but it does have to be done. As we suggested in the previous section, copyright and the structures upon which it is based are likely to be around for some time to come. Obviously it will pay to keep an eye on tweaks and changes to that legal framework—as it always has done—but the basic rules of the game will likely remain the same. It is the contracts that will have to change; though not necessarily dramatically. It is often less about how many changes we make and more about how much thought we put into those changes.

D. Content and Consumer

1. Regulation 1.0

As our former colleague and co-contributor Nick Higham used to say, the business of regulating content in new media is a shotgun marriage between law and technology.

Like most such unions it involves some misunderstandings, a fair degree of reluctance but an overwhelming desire to protect the children. The rise of more sophisticated digital media content is, however, putting a strain on the relationship.

When we wrote our earlier books, the UK, like many others,[26] was struggling to get to grips with the concept of the Internet and online content. Suddenly the type of material that the relevant authorities had previously been so successful at restricting and regulating was finding its way onto people's hard drives. It is easy to forget the sense of moral panic of the time: tabloid newspapers were running banner headlines, difficult questions were being asked of politicians, and raids and arrests at Internet service providers were a serious possibility.[27] Happily, however, the situation was diffused through a combination of industry control, international co-ordination and a good deal of common sense on all sides.

What emerged was a light-touch regulatory regime that has served as a model for many other countries and allowed online media to develop. It was acknowledged that what was illegal offline should be illegal online—so the same general rules that content providers followed in physical format should be upheld in digitally delivered versions of their content—that cross-border co-operation was vital but that attempting to establish a special super-regulator for the information super-highway was simply unrealistic. Service providers could not be expected to police the networks (from a content regulation rather than a content rights perspective) but they should be expected to take steps to help control the most extreme content. So, for example, the industry-funded Internet Watch Foundation hotline service was set up in the UK, alongside sister organizations overseas, to work with law enforcement bodies to identify and remove child pornography.

Content regulation

In many countries there are often three levels at which content is regulated:

1. **General law**—Provisions relating to any activities in any media and society generally, eg defamation, obscenity, privacy, racial hatred etc. Specific services and content might fall within this level of control, eg gambling. These laws vary from territory to territory according to local political and social factors—so the First Amendment protection of freedom of speech in the US has resulted in very different rules in this area than in Europe (and even within the EU there is little effective harmonization). The law itself will

[26] Obviously in certain territories—in line with local political realities—the control of the Internet like any part of the media is far more restrictive than described here.

[27] Headlines and moral panics over Internet content have continued from time to time but they have now become part of the media landscape.

likely have developed before digital media so its practical application online may sometimes be difficult (see Chapter B10 and the review of defamation law).

2. **Formal media regulation**—Some forms of media will operate under specific rules designed purely for that form of content distribution. The obvious example is broadcasting where the original need to manage the allocation of the analogue broadcasting spectrum led to state controls on many aspects of the way in which radio and television operates. This often includes controls on both editorial content and advertising—in addition to the general law. The extent to which these controls should extend to new forms of audiovisual distribution remains an area of debate (see below). Similar debates will likely apply to other forms of media regulation.
3. **Self-regulation**—In some cases the media will establish its own set of rules to control certain aspects of its operation including content regulation. Often this will be a step taken to avoid more formal regulation being introduced by government. In some cases the regulation will become as entrenched within industry practice as more formal controls. Obviously in addition to industry-wide agreement individual companies may choose to apply their own standards and procedures—over and above those that might apply in compliance with 1 or 2 above. In the digital media sphere this may be particularly important when new forms of content and services first appear.

It was also recognized, however, that the public should take some responsibility too. Through new media literacy programmes and technology solutions such as rating and filtering software, users—in particular parents—could control the content that electronic networks brought into their home. Children should not just be allowed to surf unsupervised to stumble across unsuitable, even if legal, material. Unlike television the Internet was a pull not a push media that required the user to seek out content rather than receive it, as the old British Broadcasting Corporation maxim used to have it, like an uninvited guest.

When richer media content began to appear in both fixed and mobile Internet, along with the first emergence of video on demand and interactive TV, a similar approach was taken. Even as new forms of content emerged as part of so-called Web 2.0 industry was expected to take protective steps, alongside best practice suggestions from government—and special self-regulatory codes emerged in each of those content areas, largely based on existing regulatory controls in traditional media. Social networks and mobile/cell phone operators employed teams to keep their services free from unlawful uses just as ISPs and portals has done before them. No-one, though, had suggested that the kind of wide-ranging and highly prescriptive regime that controls the broadcast world—certainly within the EU—should be constructed for or extended to these new media.

2. Next generation regulation

That initial consensus is now being challenged. In the EU, the relevant legislation establishing the regulatory framework for television broadcasting regulation, the Television Without Frontiers Directive, which first appeared in 1989 and was revised in 1997, has now been reformed as a technology-neutral Audiovisual Media Services Directive (AMSD). This has introduced the concept of regulating 'television-like' programming whether it is traditional 'linear' content or provided on demand. As such it attempts to establish a level playing field for similar forms of content being supplied using different technology. In particular it attempts to avoid different rules applying to what appears on the TV screen in one corner of the home and the PC screen in another corner.

The European Commission has stressed that it is not trying to go back and regulate the Internet on a wholesale basis—just that the existing regime of controls needed to be updated as technology improves and the process of convergence continues. Clearly, services that have not previously had to work within the confines of TV regulation would not welcome the imposition of such controls on their online activities. Limits on the number of advertising minutes per hour, impartiality and right-of-reply requirements, detailed broadcast-style editorial and advertising restrictions that analogue television has worked within could severely limit the creative and commercial attraction of new media. Concerns that user-generated content sites might be caught by the AMSD have been specifically allayed, however, and a two-tier approach to regulation of linear and on-demand programming, as well a relaxation of some areas of regulation for all television, has recognized the need not to over-regulate online and for broadcast television to compete with new media alternatives.

Other regulatory initiatives within the EU are less advanced but could still have a significant impact. Many of these have a focus towards protecting children but could be relevant to wider content and services.[28] These include support for a standardized approach to content rating that would harmonize the classification of video games[29] but could also extend to other forms of content,[30] guidance for the regulation of social networks in particular those targeting children and agreed solutions for verifying age online (see the Verification of Identity box below).

Crucially of course many younger users access phones and mobile devices that are not used like home TVs and PCs that parents can monitor and supervise. For their part the mobile networks have always been very active in seeking to self-regulate the

---

[28] See the Bryon Review (2008) and the Bryon Progress Review (2010) for action proposed and implemented in the UK <http://www.dcsf.gov.uk/bryonreview>.

[29] See the Pan European Game Information (PEGI) rating system <http://www.pegi.info>.

[30] A range of initiatives in the UK have developed on varying legal and regulatory terms including the Association for Television on Demand (ATVOD) <http://www.atvod.co.uk>, BBFC online <http://www.bbfc.co.uk/bbfc-online> and the Internet Mobile Classification Body (IMCB) <http://www.imcb.org.uk> .

content that can be downloaded via their handsets (in some cases their opt-in rating system has actually been extended off-portal from their own material to third party content). Even fixed ISPs have been coming under renewed pressure to adopt measures, such as the BT clean-feed software, to filter out certain web content. Many of the initiatives are probably best described as 'soft-law', by their nature some way short of strict mandatory requirements, but they are a clear sign-post as to the expected shape of future content regulation.

Verification of identity

The 5 July 1993 edition of *The New Yorker* carried a now famous cartoon by Peter Steiner. It depicted two canines at a desk: one looking down from his keyboard to the other with the words 'on the Internet, nobody knows you're a dog'. The phrase had been much quoted and mis-quoted since. Yet doubts over the expression and verification of identity in all aspects of online life, whether private or commercial, do, however, remain.

Concerns regarding online communication with individuals posing as something they are not, in particular by those seeking inappropriate contact with children through chat rooms and similar services, have always, rightly, received much attention. It must be recognized at the outset, however, that the anonymity, or at least perceived anonymity, of the online world provides many of its benefits as well as its disadvantages. Some online activities can be disturbing but at least the technology allows monitoring and tracing by operators and the authorities.

In a different sphere, libellous or offensive emails whether anonymously posted to websites and bulletin boards or targeted at the individuals themselves, are also a clear menace (see Chapter B10) but, in the hands of someone sharing valuable personal life experiences in a chat room or social network to others or even a 'whistleblower', such communications offer users—and society—a real benefit. Anyone seeking to develop successful online services, and anyone advising or regulating them, will do well to remember and respect this.

In many cases, though, the need to confirm online identities remains of great importance and, like so many other aspects of the Internet, a decent starting point is to look first at the offline world. There, manuscripts signatures obviously play a central role. In the UK a quick review of case law shows a robust approach by the courts with judges unfazed by the assortment of proxies, copies, faxes and rubber stamps which have been used to 'sign' documents over the years. It is function, rather than form, that is paramount and this reasoning has complimented the development of 'electronic' or 'digital' signatures, notwithstanding the implementation of enabling legislation such as the EU Electronic Signatures Directive and the Electronic Communications Act (see Chapter B9).

E-signatures have not become widely adopted by consumers or the norm for most business users. Consequently few e-commerce operators, be they B2C or B2B, can rely on such means to confirm identity. Even in the offline world, however, other means are often used to check aspects of identity especially with sales of age-restricted products. A good example in the UK is the sale and rental of video recordings, both because the certification scheme operated by the British Board of Film Classification (BBFC) adopts several age limits, eg 12/15/18, and because the e-tailing of tapes and discs has been a relatively successful area.

Under the Video Recordings Act it is an offence to distribute a video recording in breach of its BBFC certificate. As a result, industry body the Video Standards Council suggests that rental stores use their membership application procedure, usually requiring production of a range of identification, to put in place pre-agreed restrictions on under-age family members using the store's membership card. Retail transactions are, however, less easy to police and in both cases the shop assistant is usually left relying on their own assessment of the customer's age. In an automated e-shop that physical assessment of the customer is not an option and privacy concerns on the part of the customer, as well as the need to keep conversion rates high through swift purchase procedures, make the provision of additional evidence impractical.

As a result, e-tailers usually rely on the fact that most sales are made by way of credit/debit card which are only issued to over-18s (though in some cases over-16s) and then a self-certification by the purchaser that they or the person for whom they are buying the product is old enough to view it. Back in the offline world, however, other retailers have developed their own specific forms of identification. In the UK age verification cards are operated for use in pubs and clubs. In other territories more formal identity cards and schemes, whether publicly or privately operated, have obvious potential for online use. Electronic age verification systems have long been supported by adult-themed sites; many US schemes for such sites already exist, whether as an alternative or in support of credit card information.

The UK government has issued Good Practice Models for social networks and interactive services such child-focused chat and instant messaging. The Good Practice Models stress the importance of compliance with data protection legislation and although, unlike the US (see Chapter B9), specific provisions relating to children's data do not exist, even though the US age limit of 13 is commonly followed by default, anyone who operates data collection through online promotions in the UK is advised to follow the industry standards proposed by Trust UK. These state that data from the under-12s should not be collected without verifiable consent from a parent or guardian.

The 'verifiable' nature of that consent brings us back to a fundamental question of online identity. Whether sites try to use third party registration schemes or more simple mechanisms using IP-based cookies or PIN numbers and passwords (and the latter includes many banks or financial institutions despite being under significant identification obligations), one problem remains. As a UK court said in an anonymous email libel case; 'analysis of computer contents cannot conclusively identify whose fingers were on the keyboard at the relevant time'.

In that case serious defamatory allegations were made against a company director. The source of the emails was eventually tracked to an account owned by a third party which, in turn, traced use of the account to a specific laptop computer used by certain of its employees and, finally, the defendant. The court appointed a single joint expert who provided both a preliminary and final report finding that the use of the defendant's email account with the laptop computer in question closely matched the dates and times of the malicious emails. Even though the laptop in question had been 'contaminated' by continued (possibly malicious) use after its supposed isolation, the expert was able to satisfy himself, and the court, that the emails had indeed come from the defendant. It remains to be seen how far other courts, criminal as well as civil, are able to be satisfied of such technical matters.[31]

3. Looking after the consumer

When we wrote our previous book there was great concern over the 'Millennium Bug', ie that the advent of the year 2000 would reek havoc upon anything with a processing chip. We all spent millions upgrading our computers and it is unclear whether it was this that averted meltdown—or whether computer salesmen had simply dreamt the whole thing up. However, we have always argued that the real Y2K problem was something more enduring. In the late 1990s, law-makers (particularly in the European Commission) felt the need 'to do something' in response to the dramatic growth of the Internet and the dotcom boom. They produced a raft of proposals for regulating the 'information superhighway': in 1999 we counted nearly 100 items of online or e-commerce law grinding their way through Brussels.

The result—ten years later—is an extensive framework of regulation (in part overlapping and in some cases now outdated or in the process of review) that, if not a bug, can certainly be a headache. As stated above, this is a book on digital media not e-commerce or the regulation of the Internet generally but since the focus of many of these provisions was the protection of the consumer they will have some relevance

[31] Which household member is behind the activities traced to a shared family computer and inbox can be an issue in data protection law as well as steps taken against unlawful P2P use.

to the supply and promotion of content and digital media services to end users. These include:

- Misleading Advertising Directive
- Unfair Terms in Consumer Contracts Directive
- Distance Selling Directive
- Misleading Price Indications Directive
- Consumer Goods and Guarantees Directive
- E-Commerce Directive
- Unfair Commercial Practices Directive
- Data Protection/Electronic Privacy Directives

Clearly where digital media producers and publishers seek to 'own the relationship' with the user they must accept that, in regulatory terms, consumers are high maintenance. The days when a business could get away with dealing with consumers in a similar way to other businesses are long gone. Unfair contract terms, advertising and sales promotions, data protection law, distance selling and e-commerce requirements all apply to consumers in a different way to businesses. Obviously retailers and many other consumer-facing businesses have always managed these requirements so none of this should be seen as show-stoppers or legal rocket science. It can, however, involve a different way of looking at things (see below).

Consumer law drafting

The spirit of UK and other consumer law requires a fundamental re-assessment of standard business contract drafting. We discuss this further in Chapter B9 but set out below is an example of how a standard provision from a business contract might need to be amended to comply:

EXCLUSION OF LIABILITY
Big bad digital media company ('bbmc') does not accept any liability whatsoever for any loss or damage (direct, indirect, punitive, actual, consequential, incidental, special, exemplary or otherwise) resulting from any use of, or inability to use, the bbmc service or the material, information, software, facilities, services or other content on the bbmc service, regardless of the basis upon which liability is claimed and even if bbmc has been advised of the possibility of such loss or damage. Without limitation, the consumer (and not bbmc) assumes the entire cost of all necessary servicing, repair or correction in the event of any such loss or damage arising.

would be replaced with

OUR LIABILITY

We'll compensate you for any loss you may suffer if we fail to carry out our obligations under this contract to a reasonable standard or breach any duties imposed on us by law unless that's due to:

- your own fault; or

- a third party unconnected with our performance of this contract; or

- any other events which neither we nor our suppliers could have foreseen or prevented even if we or they had taken reasonable care.

Part II

THE AGREEMENTS

A1

NON-DISCLOSURE AGREEMENT

Introduction

It is sensible to start at the beginning. The question of whether to have a Confidentiality or Non-disclosure Agreement (NDA) in place is often a vital first stage for anyone considering entering into a relationship for any digital media project, whether they might be providing—or receiving—technical data, business intelligence or other proprietary or sensitive information. Care is needed. Trade secrets are often protected by the general law; indeed in some European countries and the US there are criminal sanctions against the misuse of such information.

In the UK, confidential information is protected, to an extent, by the law of confidence which implies, in many relationships, a duty to keep information confidential provided the information has the necessary 'quality of confidence' and is disclosed in circumstances from which it is reasonably apparent to the recipient that the information has been imparted in confidence. A duty of confidence will be implied in many commercial relationships; it is a feature, for instance, in employment contracts and in many professional relationships such as with a lawyer or a doctor.

It is often unwise, however, to rely on an *implied* duty as to confidence whenever valuable information might be disclosed. It is much better to have a clear description, in a binding agreement, of the confidential information that is to be disclosed, the duties of confidentiality relating to it and how it may be used. The process of negotiating and signing that contract also encourages the internal discipline that is necessary to prevent an unauthorized leak in the first place. It reinforces in the minds of the recipient—and critically the individual personnel involved—the need to maintain confidentiality.

Where information is intended to be protected by an NDA, the disclosing party should give careful thought to the extent of the information to be disclosed, depending on its sensitivity and value. Consideration should first be given to whether it is safe to disclose the information to this particular party:

- Is the proposed recipient a sound viable business?
- What is its track record and reputation?

- Which circle of individuals need to be party to the information within the recipient organization?

Clearly these considerations will not only have a resonance beyond the NDA but also to whether the recipient is a suitable partner for the digital media project itself. As such the process of entering into an NDA can have a value beyond the confidentiality protections that it seeks to put in place (and see the final paragraph below). They are also of practical concern since any breach of confidentiality may often be discovered too late to allow the disclosing party to obtain an injunction effectively to prevent misuse, and damages may not provide a satisfactory remedy to compensate for a missed commercial opportunity.

A particular difficulty faced by anyone entering into an NDA, whether as a discloser or recipient, is being able to identify clearly and accurately the nature of information to be disclosed and the purpose or project for which it is to be used. Rather than simply reaching for the last agreement and re-using generic descriptions, the person creating the NDA should discuss this with relevant team members and try to ensure that it is defined as appositely and as tightly as possible. A closely drafted confidentiality agreement makes it easier to apply to the courts to obtain an injunction preventing an unauthorized disclosure, ideally before the damage is done.

Equally important in practice is rigorous internal adherence to procedures for signing NDAs. They should be cleared through the appropriate internal business affairs or legal function and only certain personnel, eg Directors or other sufficiently senior staff, should be authorized to sign such agreements. This is particularly important for the recipient, who may find that an ill-considered NDA had unexpected repercussions in restricting its freedom of activity. The larger the organization (and the more subsidiary and affiliated companies it has that may be subject to the NDA) the greater the problem and the greater the need for control.

It is also important, whether as a discloser or recipient, to have a structured approach to keeping a record of which information has been disclosed and/or received and to ensure that the confidentiality obligations are adhered to. Traditionally, confidential documents could be kept separately in a safe and secure place which, apart from anything else, made their return, if requested, pursuant to an NDA easier to achieve. Such documents are now often held and provided digitally. As ever, we discuss throughout this book, this has benefits as well as risks. Technical security measures to limit and track their use and disclosure are avoidable—see for instance DRM, which we refer to in Chapter 3. Yet any breach or failure of those measures can of course lead to rapid and uncontrollable further distribution.

The signing of an NDA is often, and wrongly, seen as a simple formality that can quickly be got out of the way to enable work on the project to begin. The pressure to conclude the agreement, however, should not prevent the NDA being properly considered with appropriate protection built in to defend the interests of both the discloser and recipient. This sample agreement is a typical 'one way' and has been drafted from the perspective of the discloser. A 'two way' agreement, where both parties are disclosing information, will be similar, but the mutual obligations might, but perhaps should not, result in a lessening of the duties of confidentiality.

Of course, commercial reality may mean that in negotiations between parties of unequal bargaining power the weaker side may face resistance from the stronger in signing up to an NDA—even if a 'two-way' NDA is proposed. Some organizations apply a standard policy of refusal, or at least take such a stance initially in negotiations. Even if an NDA is agreed, the weaker side may not feel it has the financial ability, or commercial will, to enforce its terms in court. Despite such concerns, however, the very act of tabling an NDA can help demonstrate that a party is a serious, business-like operation.

Indeed, as the NDA is often one of the earliest forms of contact between parties at the beginning of a relationship, the style and tone of the document is important. We provide here a typical document, in the form of a letter agreement, which is relatively simple and straightforward and which might easily be made mutual—without too much prejudice to the presenting party. Far more detailed NDAs are also common but should still conform to the basic style and structure presented here.

CHECKLIST

1. What is the information that needs to be disclosed?
2. Can it be, and has it been, properly identified and listed?
3. Has the information been marked appropriately, whether in physical or digital form?
4. Which personnel need to receive the information?
5. Where are they and how will they use it?
6. What are the recipient's internal control procedures?
7. What are the physical and technical security measures that will be applied to the information?

Non-Disclosure Agreement

XYZ Ltd
1 Confidential Avenue
London NW

Date:

To: ABC Limited
27 Open Road
London SW

Project

This letter, when counter-signed by You, shall constitute an agreement between us with respect to the following, which shall remain in full force and effect unless and until varied or terminated by written agreement between us both.

1. For the purposes of this letter agreement, the following words shall have the following meanings:

   '**Company**': shall mean ourselves, XYZ Limited.

   '**Confidential Information**': shall mean all ideas, concepts, codes, proposals, data, documents, notes, analyses, materials, research and information of whatever nature relating to the Project and/or to the Company obtained by you, disclosed to you by the Company or to which you have access at any time whether in written, pictorial, oral, magnetic, film or audio, electronic, digitized or machine-readable form and shall include the name of the Project and the specific documentation listed [in the attached Schedule 1]. (1)

   '**Project**': shall mean the digital media project [described in the attached Schedule 2]. (2)

   '**Permitted Recipients**': shall mean [the personnel listed in Schedule 3][those of your employees, directors, officers, representatives, agents and advisers who are or shall be permitted by us to be admitted to the group of persons who know about the Project] (and who shall have signed a letter in similar form as this one). (3)

   '**You**' or '**Your**': shall mean ABC Limited. (4)

2. In consideration of Confidential Information being made available to You, You undertake:

   (a) not to use the Confidential Information otherwise than in connection with the Project; (5)

   (b) to keep and continue to keep as private and confidential the Confidential Information and not to disclose or allow the Confidential Information to be

1 This definition is typically wide, trying to catch all types of information. In the context of the Project that may be defendable, though maybe less so in the context of the Company generally. The limitations in Clause 3 should make the width of this acceptable but the additional qualification of 'confidential' might need to be added to this list. Another typical issue is to decide whether or not to limit confidential information to information imparted in writing or other tangible form, or whether it should also include information imparted verbally. Sometimes it is thought commercially desirable to include all information, whether written or verbal, but this can lead to uncertainty as to what has been disclosed and whether or not it is confidential. A solution often proposed by the recipient is to insist that any information that is imparted orally must be confirmed in writing within a certain period of time as having being imparted in confidence if it is to enjoy the protection of the agreement. A wide-ranging definition should not be a substitute for careful thought as to particular information that may be sensitive in an organization and that needs to be identified. Indeed it is surprising how often a pre-contractual review is limited to certain specific documents eg a proposal, a business plan or a technical presentation. One other key concern is whether the NDA needs to cover information already disclosed. If the NDA is being signed after some information has already been provided (again not uncommon!) then this should be made clear.

2 It is obviously important, for the same reasons, to define carefully what is meant by the 'Project'. This might be focussed further to a 'Permitted Purpose' or other specific activity.

3 An alternative approach is to identify, either by name or job function, a limited circle of individuals within a recipient organization who may be party to the confidential information. The same applies to outside advisors and consultants who may be named in this way and indeed individuals within such outside consultants and advisors. The recipient may often try to resist requiring each of these individuals to sign separate NDAs themselves.

4 It is vital to consider whether one is dealing with a parent or subsidiary company and whether or not the implications are intended to apply to the entire group of companies of which the recipient forms part. If the recipient is a subsidiary it might be appropriate to include the parent company or obtain some other written assurance that the subsidiary has authority to bind the group. Bear in mind that the legal structures within companies rarely reflect the precise operating structures and that project teams and functions now operate across a series of the legally incorporated companies. It is unlikely that in a large group of companies all the employees who need to have access to the information will be employed by the same legal entity within the group.

5 This obligation is as important as the duty of confidentiality; for the recipient this could prove to be of greater commercial significance as it could impact on activities in the future. Hence the need to understand and define clearly the extent of the Confidential Information and the Project and to agree on a sensible period for the NDA to last.

disclosed to any third party (other than Permitted Recipients) at any time without the Company's specific prior written approval;

(c) to keep all physical documents and electronic versions of the foregoing safely and securely stored [in accordance with the minimum control procedures set out in Schedule 3] and in any event no less securely than You hold Your own confidential information; [6]

(d) not to disclose or allow to be disclosed the Confidential Information to anyone (other than Permitted Recipients) unless (i) the Company has approved such disclosure [in writing] and (ii) such other approved persons (whether a company or individual) agrees to be bound by the terms of this letter and signs a copy of it; [7]

(e) inform all Permitted Recipients (and those other approved persons to whom Confidential Information is disclosed) of the restrictions contained in this letter and ensure that such Permitted Recipients and permitted person shall observe such restrictions;

(f) not to copy, transmit, summarize, quote, adapt or otherwise reproduce the Confidential Information; [8] and

(g) not to use or allow the use of the Confidential Information to the detriment of the Company or the Project.

3. The restrictions contained in this letter agreement shall not apply to any information which:

   (a) at the time of disclosure was already known to You as evidenced by Your written records pre-dating such disclosure;
   (b) at the time of disclosure was generally available to the public or subsequently became available to the public other than by an act or omission on Your part or on the part of any Permitted Recipient;
   (c) is made available to you on a non-confidential basis by a third party having the lawful right to do so; or
   (d) is required to be disclosed by law or order of a court of competent jurisdiction provided that You:
      (i) shall inform the company as soon as You become aware that such disclosure may be ordered; and
      (ii) shall authorize the company to make representations to the Court on the proposed order for disclosure and/or any terms applying to such disclosure.

4. You agree that nothing contained in this letter agreement shall be construed as obliging the Company to disclose any particular information to You or to enter into any further agreement with You or to continue discussions relating to the Project with You if the Company does not wish to do so. All intellectual property rights in the Confidential Information are reserved to the Company and nothing in this letter agreement grants any such rights in or with respect to the Confidential Information to You. [9]

6 It may be appropriate for the relevant project leaders to maintain a register of all Confidential Information disclosed or received. The security limitations may be nothing more than requiring material not to be taken from a named site or location or they could be a detailed list of specific steps that must be followed to maintain physical and technical security.

7 This can be extended as desired to include other public bodies having some regulatory control over the recipient.

8 With physical copies this restriction should not raise any issues—unless the recipient needs to make specific copies as part of the pre-contractual process which, if agreed, can be addressed with a suitable reference. With electronic versions, local acts of copying, transmission and storage may have to take place. Often NDAs fudge this issue but again a specific reference could be included.

9 It is common for the disclosing party to want to reserve its position on these points. Again, the recipient might dispute whether some form of 'licence to use' has actually been granted for digital material (see note 8).

5. Without prejudice to any other rights or remedies that the Company may have, You acknowledge and agree that damages would not be an adequate remedy for breach of this letter. In the event of a breach or threatened breach by You, the Company shall be entitled to seek the remedies of injunctions, specific performance and any other equitable relief and no proof of special damages shall be necessary for the enforcement of this letter. No delay in exercising any right, power or privilege under this letter shall operate as a waiver thereof, nor shall any single or partial exercise thereof preclude any further exercise of such right power or privilege. [10]

6. You agree that you will immediately on demand deliver or procure the delivery of the Confidential Information to the Company and permanently delete all copies of the Confidential Information held on any computer, word processor or other similar device under Your possession and control and provide to the Company a certificate of such destruction signed by one of Your directors. [11]

7. The obligations in this letter agreement shall continue in force for a period of [5] years and shall survive any subsequent agreement between us relating to the project, unless expressly stated otherwise. [12]

8. The parties do not intend that any term of this letter agreement shall be enforceable solely by virtue of the Contracts (Rights of Third Parties) Act 1999 by any person who is not a party to this letter.

9. No failure or delay by any party in exercising its rights under this letter agreement will operate as a waiver of that right nor will any single or partial exercise by either party of any right preclude any further exercise of any other right.

10. Each party confirms that this letter agreement sets out the entire and only agreement and understanding between the parties regarding its subject matter. Neither party has relied upon any statement, representation or warranty of any person other than as expressly set out in this Agreement but nothing in this Agreement shall limit or exclude liability either parties' liability for fraud.

11. Nothing in this Agreement will be deemed to create a partnership or joint venture between the parties.

12. This letter agreement shall be governed by and construed in all respects in accordance with English law and both parties agree to submit to the [non-] exclusive jurisdiction of the English courts. [13]

10 This wording originated from US NDAs. Although under UK law it probably achieves little technically (since the remedy of an interim injunction is an equitable one at the discretion of the court), it is now quite common in UK NDAs and should probably be left in. It does provide evidence of the intention of the parties that this remedy would be appropriate, which may help.

11 Consider whether or not one copy may be retained for record purposes in the event of later legal proceedings. It could be stipulated that such copying might be held by recipient's external lawyers or even by an in-house department. The clause does not go so far as to require the director to certify compliance with the agreement as a whole. We have also not included an indemnity from the recipient to the disclosing party for breach. That is a common provision but it is also one which, in our experience, is often argued over unduly in these circumstances.

12 In theory Confidential Information should be kept confidential by the recipient for as long as the information remains confidential. In practice it is better to agree on a period for the obligation to apply, not least because of the difficulty otherwise of determining when something has ceased to be 'confidential' and when the obligations have ended. The recipient will want to know when it can draw a line under the NDA and become free to engage in any venture that might arguably include or rely on the Confidential Information. Disclosing parties often ask for lengthy periods (ten or twenty years) that are almost certainly more than their commercial needs; three or five years should suffice and that period is often agreed. Confidentiality provisions in other documents may of course become relevant in due course anyway whether in an initial heads of agreement (see Chapter A2) or the actual agreement entered into for the digital media project.

13 Where both parties are UK companies, the standard choice of law clause should not be contentious. If one party is located overseas, it might be appropriate to consider agreeing to a non-exclusive jurisdiction of the English court to that the matter could be tried in the country of the recipient (perhaps albeit subject to English law). If there is concern that an unauthorized disclosure may occur in an overseas country, obtaining a court order in England may be of little practical use and it may be preferable to take one's chances with the overseas law.

Please indicate Your acceptance of the terms of this letter by signing the enclosed duplicate of this letter.

Yours sincerely

....

For and on behalf of
XYZ Limited

Agreed and accepted:

....

For and on behalf of
ABC Limited

SCHEDULE 1—Confidential Information
SCHEDULE 2—Project
SCHEDULE 3—Security Procedures

A2

HEADS OF AGREEMENT

Introduction

Many digital media projects will involve initial discussions as the parties explore the creative, technical and commercial elements of the intended arrangements. In addition to a Non-Disclosure Agreement (see Chapter A1) there may also be the need to put in place some form of wider legal document to record progress and/or intent. We asked Martin Delaney, Legal Advisor, Copyright Licensing Agency Ltd, to describe some of the background to such a document.

Often parties in commercial negotiations may sign a Letter of Intent or Heads of Agreement document before moving to formal binding contracts. This document is typically not meant to create legally binding relations, although it sometimes can have that effect (whether deliberately or otherwise) and this is discussed below. Non-binding Heads of Agreement may provide one or both parties with a measure of comfort that the deal will proceed to a conclusion, or that they are the only party with whom the other party is negotiating. It might be a useful summary of the negotiating position that has been reached and can provide a platform for the contract drafting to be taken forward. Typically the stage is reached when there is a 'business agreement' following which detailed work on preparing the legal agreements can begin. It can be a guide as to what should be included in the legal contracts and it can also serve to highlight important points of principle that have been agreed and that should inform the negotiations and drafting of detailed points.

There is, however, a danger that the Heads of Agreement can become a negotiating exercise in itself. This can prove counterproductive if it is allowed to get out of hand and not achieve the desired effect of shortening or clarifying the process to an exchange of legally binding contracts. Sometimes time and effort spent on negotiating Heads of Agreement might be better spent on settling the formal contract itself. Heads of Agreements can attempt to cover too much ground that might be more efficiently tackled at a later stage of detailed drafting. Relatively minor points can present themselves as a greater stumbling block than they ought to be and become elevated to the status of 'deal breaker'. The Heads of Agreement, therefore, as their name applies, should be limited to key terms only. What the 'key terms' are will vary depending on the type of contract being negotiated, but a checklist with suggestions is set out below.

Sometimes the parties do intend that the Heads of Agreement are meant to commit both parties and not just in terms of individual items such as confidentiality or exclusivity that often do involve (or are intended to involve) legally enforceable obligations. The lead negotiators may have struck a deal in principle to which both do wish to be committed, even though many details may remain to be addressed. So it is vital that the status of the Heads of Agreement is clear. Care is needed here as the different countries' laws can vary as to when binding legal commitments are made—the English position is summarized below. If (as is most often the case) they are not intended to be legally binding this should be clearly stated in the document to avoid any risk of them being interpreted as binding by a court should the parties fall out and litigate.

Some items that are often meant to be legally binding are:

- Confidentiality obligations (which are perhaps better covered in a separate Non-Disclosure Agreement) and ought always to be stated to be legally binding.
- Any exclusive dealing arrangements such as a 'shut-out' period (during which one or both parties is precluded from engaging in discussions with any other party) should be identified as legally binding if they are to be of any use.
- An undertaking to negotiate in 'good faith' whether with or without some exclusivity period.
- If the continuing negotiation process would require one party to take certain steps before any deal could be concluded, this might be stated as a legally binding obligation, eg that they should use reasonable endeavours (or best endeavours) to seek and obtain such consent as may be necessary to take such steps as are identified.

A timetable for moving forward to a conclusion of the contract should be realistic and not assume that a subsequent process of detailed negotiation and preparation of the contracts is a formality and merely writing up the terms. Often this process throws up new points, reveals new problems or presents existing ones in a different light. It may be helpful to identify any steps that have to be taken that could impact on the timetable, any internal or external consents that have to be obtained and any 'due diligence' or disclosure exercise that needs to be undertaken before contracts can be signed. If the Heads of Agreement are to be binding then any 'conditions precedent' to signing of contracts (eg to obtain written copyright permissions to use some illustrations in a work) should be clearly stated.

Heads of Agreement, even if not legally binding, should be reviewed and discussed with legal advisers to ensure that they:

- do not create any unintended legal obligations; but
- do provide legal protection in areas where agreed;
- do cover all the key points of principle; but
- do not include points which may become a hostage to fortune and render the subsequent detailed negotiation and drafting process more difficult.

Is it binding?

As a matter of contract law in England, this type of agreement will only be binding if:

- the parties intend to be bound by it;
- there is clear agreement on all the key terms of the intended contract; and
- there is 'valuable consideration'.

Intention can often be evinced from the conduct of the parties, but it is better to state clearly whether the Heads of Agreement or Letter of Intent is intended to be legally binding or not. The document can be labelled 'subject to contract' but preferably there should be a separate paragraph clearly stating that the document is not to be legally enforceable unless and to the extent that certain specific items are agreed as being intended to create legal relations.

The risk is that a 'contract' is not formed, or is void for uncertainty, either where it is not clear that the parties have agreed on a particular point or where they have not addressed a point. The court cannot easily imply (where the parties themselves have failed to be specific) what that term is because of a different understanding between the parties as to what is a major point. This is a complicated area of law. One measure that can be adopted to overcome this risk is to provide for some form of alternative dispute resolution (either mediation or arbitration) to resolve individual points that may not have been thought sufficiently important to include in the Heads of Agreements; that is certainly one way to try not to jeopardize the validity of the contract.

One of the elements of a binding contract under English law is the presence of 'valuable consideration', that is to say the parties have to give some value or benefit to one another, or undertake some obligations. This might be by paying money, providing other assets, or providing some service, such as agreeing to perform/undertake an obligation or to refrain from doing something. Consideration will normally be easily identified in most commercial relationships where, typically, both parties agree to do something, eg an author to write a book, and the publisher to publish it. If, however, there is any doubt, it is safest to express that the consideration provided by one party is the payment of a small sum—such as £1. 'Valuable' simply means that some value can be identified, there is no subjective analysis of how valuable that is. For instance, a clause providing exclusivity (where it is intended to be legally binding in an otherwise non-binding Heads of Agreement) can be expressed as being in consideration of party A entering into negotiations/disclosing information and so on to provide the necessary consideration to make the obligation enforceable.

CHECKLIST

1. Are the Heads of Agreement (or the Letter of Intent) intended to be legally binding? If not, include 'Subject to Contract' wording such as:

   It is not the parties' intention in signing these Heads of Agreement/this Letter of Intent to create any legally binding obligations except [unless otherwise expressly stated] [cross refer specifically to particular obligations that are intended to be legally binding, eg confidentiality, exclusivity].

   It is prudent to ensue that all subsequence correspondence is also labelled 'subject to contract', but sometimes for safety an expanded clause is added to the Heads of Agreement to cover the ensuing correspondence as follows:

   It is not the parties' intention for any legally binding agreement to be established in correspondence, or in any other pre-contract documentation. These Heads of agreement, and all other correspondence or documentation, will remain on a 'Subject to Contract' basis whether or not so headed or stated until either the correspondence specifically removes the 'subject to contract' qualifications, or binding contracts are formally exchanged.
2. Identify any obligations that are intended to create legal relations—see the list above.
3. Is there an obligation to pay any costs in the event of one party pulling out of negotiations whether at any time or before a certain date? Are the costs to be capped and how are they to be calculated? Is there to be a 'liquidated damages' clause for breach of exclusivity obligations?
4. If the Heads of Agreement are intended to commit the parties legally, provide a mechanism for resolving disagreements on matters of detail not included in the Heads of Agreement. This could be by naming a more senior individual from each organization (previously unconnected with the negotiations) who should meet to attempt to resolve the problem and/or by reference to standard mediation or arbitration clauses.
5. A timetable—this should be realistic and state when the parties envisage that contracts will be exchanged, as well as possibly setting out a sequence of steps and key dates for the necessary steps to be taken to arrive at that point.

Heads of Agreement

HEADS OF AGREEMENT [1]

BETWEEN

1. XYZ LIMITED of 1 Confidential Avenue, London NW ('XYZ') and
2. ABC LIMITED of 27 Open Road, London SW ('ABC')

XYZ and ABC (the 'Parties') wish to negotiate detailed written terms for an agreement between them relating to the digital media project [described in the attached specification] (the 'Project') which terms will be contained in a full long form agreement (the 'Formal Agreement').

The Parties now wish to confirm the following terms in respect of the Project on a legally binding basis which where relevant are intended to form the basis of the Formal Agreement in due course.

For good and valuable consideration, the receipt and sufficiency of which is hereby acknowledged the Parties agree as follows:

1. The Parties agree to negotiate in good faith and use all reasonable endeavours to agree and execute the Formal Agreement within [ ] weeks of signature of these Heads of Agreement. The Parties are entering into these Heads of Agreement on a non-exclusive basis and neither Party shall be prevented from entering into similar arrangements with any other persons. [2]

2. In order to meet the intended Project launch date of [ ] (the 'Launch Date') the Parties have agreed to commence preliminary work and incur initial expenditure on the Project [in accordance with the attached statement of work, expenditure schedule and timetable]. [3]

3. Except where otherwise identified in [the statement of work or the expenditure schedule] each Party shall perform the preliminary work using its own existing personnel, equipment and facilities and at its own cost and expense and in accordance with all applicable laws and regulations. If either Party needs to undertake additional work or incur additional expenditure beyond that agreed above it shall obtain the prior written agreement of the other Party. [4]

4. Each of the Parties has appointed a Project manager set out in [the statement of work] who shall meet to discuss and minute progress in accordance with [the timetable] or as otherwise necessary to ensure the work is completed by the Launch Date. If there are any problems or delays the Project managers shall escalate the matter where necessary and the Parties may agree to amend the [timetable] and if necessary the Launch Date.

1 This document is intended to be legally binding. As such, and mindful of the comments made in the Introduction, it does not attempt to provide a short-form version of the final version of the contract. Such a document always risks becoming either as heavily negotiated as the long-form agreement and/or simply the only contract ever signed by default! Instead this Heads of Agreement aims to set out the specific and limited initial actions that the parties wish to carry out while the long-form contract is negotiated. This is normally triggered by an impending launch date or other commercial imperative and although this document describes a largely mutual arrangement might well be more of a one-sided deal where one party is essentially committing to some initial deliverables from a supplier.

2 In a more one-sided arrangement the party effectively buying initial services from the other might want to go further and state that it was not committed to entering into the Formal Agreement, which remained subject to contract.

3 Even in a mutual arrangement it is probably in both sides' interest to be clear as to what initial work is being undertaken and at what cost. Here that is set out in a separate statement of work and costs schedule alongside an agreed timetable and the overall project specification. There may not always be the time and opportunity to create detailed additional documentation but since the Formal Agreement will likely have similar schedules based on these initial materials it is usually worthwhile doing so.

4 Clearly the position becomes more complicated where additional overhead, special employees or other specific commitments are required or indeed if some form of joint venture or corporate vehicle is needed. Equally in a more one-sided arrangement service commitments and associated warranties might need to be included.

5. Each Party shall co-operate with the other to provide such reasonable information and assistance as the other Party may request including in relation to any regulatory or other due diligence investigation deemed necessary by the Parties. [5]

6. Any revenue generated from the Project shall be allocated in accordance with the cost and profit share breakdowns set out in the [expenditure schedule]. [6]

7. No intellectual property rights, except those identified in [the statement of work], shall be licensed or transferred either from one Party to the other or to any other person by reason of these Heads of Agreement unless otherwise agreed in writing between the Parties. Any intellectual property rights created by either Party in performing [the statement of work] or otherwise in connection with the Project or these Heads of Agreement shall, unless otherwise agreed, be owned by that Party. [7]

8. The term of the Project is intended to be no less than [ ]. The minimum notice period required to terminate the Project after the Launch Date shall be [ ]. The Project territory shall be [ ]. [8]

9. Each party shall bear its own legal costs relating to these Heads of Agreement and the Formal Agreement. [These Heads may be terminated on [ ] written notice and if so terminated neither Party shall have any liability to the other.] [9]

10. Neither Party may assign, sub-contract or transfer any of its rights or obligations under these Heads of Agreement without the prior written consent of the other Party. Nothing in these Heads of Agreement will be deemed to create a partnership or joint venture between the Parties. The Parties do not intend that any term of these Heads of Agreement shall be enforceable solely by virtue of the Contracts (Rights of Third Parties) Act 1999 by any person who is not a party to this Agreement. Any variation to these Heads of Agreement must be in writing and agreed by the Parties. [10]

11. The Parties agree and acknowledge that the Non-Disclosure Agreement entered into between them dated [ ] shall apply to the provisions of and the activities undertaken under this Heads of Agreement.

12. These Heads of Agreement are legally binding on the Parties and shall be governed by and construed in accordance with the laws of England and the Parties submit to the exclusive jurisdiction of the English courts.

Schedule

- Project specification
- Statement of work
- Expenditure schedule
- Timetable

5 As mentioned in the Introduction in particular cases either Party may wish to use this period to carry out further checks on the legal or regulatory requirements for the project or specific content uses within it.

6 This may well be something that the negotiations for the Formal Agreement will establish but on the basis that initial costs have been agreed in an attached schedule then potentially profit shares could be too.

7 A default position reflecting the general law: each side retaining ownership of its IPR and also owning anything that it creates. The statement of work may set out specific exceptions—perhaps where test content is being licensed from one side to the other or some form of technology shared. In those cases the Party licensing or supplying might be better using a specific short form licence or supply agreement (see other chapters).

8 This is the closest to a summary of some of the provisions that will be the basis of the Formal Agreement. Obviously more detail could be included where the negotiations have progressed. It is common to see references to the long-form agreement including 'standard clauses' or 'reasonable boilerplate' (which can often involve further debate rather than clarity) or even the listing of specific clauses and a short summary of their content.

9 The question of whether and how the Parties can terminate the Heads of Agreement—and whether that should be on a different basis to the eventual long-form agreement—should be addressed. Here either side can walk away reflecting the overall sense that there is specific period leading up to the Launch Date when initial investment costs are limited, no rights are being transferred and regulatory checks are continuing. But in other circumstances where wider commitments are involved it may be more appropriate to include full termination provisions that the Formal Agreement will likely include.

10 As with any short-form document judging the amount of boilerplate needed is an art not a science, but it will usually be sensible to include some of the usual provisions.

For and on behalf of XYZ

....

Name:

Date:

For and on behalf of ABC

....

Name:

Date:

A3

ASSIGNMENT OF RIGHTS

Introduction

Assignments need to be distinguished from licences. If full ownership of any particular element of a digital media project is required to pass from one party to another—usually some form of creative content and, in particular, the intellectual property rights to that content—then an assignment will be needed. If a more limited usage right is intended then a licence will be used. Something similar applies in other industries and situations: for example, a building or piece of land might be sold outright or it might be leased (indeed in the UK and some other common law countries copyright and intellectual property share many legal attributes to real property).

Of course an exclusive, worldwide and unlimited licence of rights for the full period of protection may in practice be very similar to an assignment of those rights (just as a very long lease of property may seem very close to ownership) but care is sometimes needed. Special provisions apply to the ownership and enforcement of intellectual property rights, which vary from territory to territory, so there may be technical reasons why a licence does not give the benefits of an assignment. There may also be technical requirements to perfect and record the assignment (or licence). This is especially important where the rights are registered, eg as is the case for formal trade mark protection in most territories and copyright in the US.

There is no copyright registration in the UK but an assignment of copyright must be in writing, although there is no specific format required and it is not strictly necessary to include the words 'grant' or 'assign' if the intention is otherwise clear from the document. UK copyright law also provides specific benefits to exclusive licences that are made in writing, but otherwise licences of copyright can be made orally and indeed implied into situations where necessary (a court may step in to uphold a so-called equitable assignment in a similar way where the writing requirement has not been complied with, but clearly a written agreement will always be preferable, as Samuel Goldwyn would agree).[1]

[1] The legendary film producer Samuel Goldwyn is attributed with the statement that 'a verbal contract isn't worth the paper it is written on'.

There are also legal health warnings for older copyright content, where special rules may apply under earlier copyright legislation (in particular pre-1956), and for particular types of content; copyright in music and photographs can be particularly complicated. In essence, however, the same principles that apply to any other sale from one party to another also apply to rights assignments. The primary concern for the buyer is establishing that the seller is the owner of those rights—in the absence of or even in addition to a register of ownership the buyer may need to review a long set of ownership documents (a 'chain of title'). The seller's primary concern is to ensure that the agreed price is safely received before ownership passes.

Both sides will also be keen to make clear what is actually being sold. Although assignments are often associated with the entire ownership of the relevant content, ownership can be divided up, with only limited parts assigned. A key distinction is between the physical form of content and the copyright in that content. For example, an original manuscript or letter may be owned by the person to whom it was sent by the author, but the right to publish that manuscript or letter will remain with its author unless otherwise licensed or assigned. It is also possible to assign only part of that copyright, so that while the right to publish the manuscript in a printed book is transferred the right to publish it online is retained (see Chapter A4 for more on dividing rights).

CHECKLIST

1. Who owns or controls the rights (are there documents or registers to inspect)?
2. Are there any existing competing or non-competing grants?
3. Are they exclusive or non-exclusive?
4. Are they territory specific or worldwide?
5. What languages are available?
6. Which platforms are available?
7. What term of rights is available?
8. Is the price negotiable?
9. Can moral rights be waived?
10. Are rights of publicity or privacy or other content liability issues a concern?

Assignment of Rights

THIS ASSIGNMENT is dated [ ]

BETWEEN

(1) [OWNER] (**Owner**). [1]
(2) [ASSIGNEE] (**Buyer**).

INTRODUCTION

(A) The Owner owns the Intellectual Property Rights in the Content (as defined below).
(B) The Owner has agreed to assign to the Buyer all the Intellectual Property Rights in the Content on the terms set out in this Assignment. [2]

IT IS AGREED AS FOLLOWS:

1. DEFINITIONS

In this Assignment the following terms shall have the meanings set opposite them:

Content: the [content] more specifically described in the attached Schedule. [3]

Intellectual Property Rights: all copyright, know-how, trade secrets and other confidential information, registered designs, design rights, database rights, semi-conductor topography rights, trade marks, service marks, logos, domain names, rights in the nature of unfair competition rights and rights to sue for passing off, patents, inventions and all registrations or applications to register any of the aforesaid items and rights in the nature of any of the aforesaid rights or affording equivalent protection to the foregoing in any country or jurisdiction, and all other rights of whatever nature, whether now known or created in the future.

Clause and schedule headings shall not affect the interpretation of this assignment.

Unless the context otherwise requires, words in the singular include the plural and in the plural include the singular and a reference to one gender shall include a reference to the other genders. The words include and including will be deemed to be followed by the phrase 'without limitation' or 'but not limited to'.

A reference to a statute or statutory provision shall include any subordinate legislation made from time to time under that statute or statutory provision.

Writing or written includes faxes but not e-mail. [4]

1 Whether an incorporated entity or an individual (in the UK rights in a work created by an employee in the course of their employment would pass automatically to their employer but with freelance workers a separate assignment would be needed. In both cases formal assignment wording should probably appear in their engagement terms).

2 As mentioned in the Introduction above, the ownership of copyright in a work is distinct from the ownership of the physical material in which the copyright work is embodied. The transfer of title to the physical material does not necessarily transfer the title to the copyright, any more than the assignment of the copyright necessarily transfers the title to the physical material. This should be remembered if physical access is actually needed to material to exploit the copyright!

3 If only part of the copyright is being assigned, take particular care to describe that part.

4 Notices can, of course, be served by email, but both parties have to be geared up to cope with this.

2. ASSIGNMENT [5]

In consideration of the sum of £[AMOUNT] [6] (receipt of which the Owner acknowledges), the Owner hereby with full title guarantee [7] and where relevant by present assignment of future rights assigns [8] to the Assignee irrevocably and absolutely the Intellectual Property Rights in the Content throughout the world for the full period or protection including any renewals, reversions, revivals and extensions together with all rights of action arising or accrued in relation to the Intellectual Property Rights including without the right to take proceedings and recover damages and obtain all other remedies in respect of any past infringements. [9]

3. WARRANTIES AND INDEMNITY

3.1 The Owner warrants and represents that: [10]

(a) the Owner is the sole legal and beneficial owner of the Intellectual Property Rights in the Content and free to assign the Intellectual Property Rights to the Buyer;

(b) the Owner has not assigned, licensed or otherwise transferred any of the Intellectual Property Rights in the Content and the Intellectual Property Rights in the Content are free from any option, mortgage, charge, lien or security interest;

(c) the Content is original and has not been copied in whole or in part from any other work or material and does not infringe the rights of any third party;

(d) the Owner has procured absolute waivers from all authors of the Content in relation to any so-called moral rights or similar rights in any territory so far as is legally possible;

(e) exploitation of the Intellectual Property Rights in the Content will not create any liability for the Buyer or be otherwise unlawful; and

(f) the Owner is unaware of any present or prospective claim, proceeding or litigation regarding the Intellectual Property Rights.

3.2 The Assignor indemnifies the Assignee from any claims or actions against the Assignee and against any expenses or costs (including legal costs and expenses on a solicitor and client basis) incurred in respect of any claim arising from any inconsistency with the warranties set out in this Assignment.

3.3 The Owner shall at all times at its [11] cost perform, or procure the performance of, all such further acts and execute, or procure the execution of, all such further documents as are required by law or which the Buyer may reasonably requests to give effect to this Assignment and maintain the Intellectual Property Rights in the Content. The Owner hereby appoints the Buyer as agent to perform such acts and execute such documents on its behalf if the Owner fails to do so within a reasonable period following written request by the Buyer.

5 There are formalities with transfers of copyright—see Chapter B8.

6 The consideration does not have to be money. But it does need to be 'valuable'. The law will generally not enquire into adequacy: £1 will do, or services rendered etc—see Chapter A2.

7 This phrase has a particular meaning under UK law—effectively including implied warranties as to ownership—notwithstanding the express warranties below.

8 The CDPA does not require that an assignment of copyright should be in any special form, beyond that it should be in writing, signed by or on behalf of the assignor.

9 Where legal action against a third party over a title is contemplated by the assignee, he should take care to include an assignment of the cause of action.

10 Drafted from the Buyer's perspective the Seller may well resist some of these—(c), (d) and (e) may be harder to agree to where the Seller is not also the author or at least aware of the circumstances of production. If the Seller is the author then the warranties could be made more personal, eg the waiver of moral rights given directly. The Buyer might extend the warranties to expressly refer to content liability issues such as defamation or obscenity.

11 Who bears the cost of 'further assurance' is a matter for negotiation. The owner's argument is usually that the purchaser had the opportunity when drawing up the assignment and during due diligence, to insert appropriate requirements, and should not have the opportunity to have a second bite at the cherry later on down the line. The purchaser will ar gue that he is entitled to good title and, if problems occur, it is for the owner to resolve them!

4. GENERAL

4.1 Each Party undertakes to the other that it will treat as confidential the terms of this Assignment together with all information whatever nature relating to the business or affairs of the other Party as may be communicated to it under or in connection with this Assignment and will not disclose such information to any person (other than to its affiliates, auditors and other professional advisers subject always to equivalent undertakings of confidentially) or to the media and will not use such information other than for the purposes of this Assignment subject always to any prior and specific authorization in writing by the disclosing party to such disclosure or use. Notwithstanding the above, such restrictions shall not apply to any information which: is in the public domain other than by default of the recipient party, is obtained by the recipient party from a bona fide third party having no apparent restraint on its free right of disposal of such information or is required to be disclosed by law, applicable regulation, the valid order of a court of competent jurisdiction or the request or direction of any governmental or other regulatory authority or agency.

4.2 Any notice or other communication required to be given by either party to the other shall be given in writing and served at the other's address stated above (or such other address as each party may notify to the other in writing) by first-class post, facsimile or by personal delivery and shall be deemed to have been given in the case of first-class post forty eight (48) hours after posting, in the case of facsimile upon transmission and in the case of personal delivery immediately upon such delivery to that address.

4.3 Each party confirms that this Assignment sets out the entire agreement and understanding between the parties regarding its subject matter and that it supersedes all previous agreements, arrangements and understandings (whether written or oral) between them relating thereto. Neither party has relied upon any statement, representation or warranty of any person other than as expressly set out in this Assignment but nothing in this Assignment shall limit or exclude either parties' liability for fraud.

4.4 This Assignment shall be governed by and construed in accordance with English law and the parties hereby submit to the [non-]exclusive jurisdiction of the English Courts as regards any claim or matter arising in relation to this Assignment.

SIGNED by [ ]	)
authorized signatory	)
for and on behalf of	)
[OWNER]	)

SIGNED by [ ]	)
authorized signatory	)
for and on behalf of	)
[BUYER]	)

A4

CONTENT SUPPLY AGREEMENT

Introduction

Content is king. Or at least, in the world of digital media talk is often not of text, graphics, speech, music, film or video, but 'content': a catch-all for any type of digital information that is provided for viewing, access and use.

Today that content will increasingly be delivered online via streaming, download or other intangible means. There are no physical copies, just digital ones. So the business of procuring and supplying such content is primarily the business of licensing the intellectual property in that content: first and foremost, in most territories, the copyright. Thus the main objective of any form of content supply agreement is to secure a licence that is crafted sufficiently widely (from the point of view of the licensee) to enable the use of the content in the intended ways, and narrowly enough (from the point of view of the licensor) to prohibit use of the content outside of the agreed scope.

CHECKLIST

A licence may be framed in terms of:

- Content—what is being supplied (and when and how).
- Time—it will usually be limited to a set period, perhaps with provision for that period to be renewed or extended.
- Technology—the scope of the licence must be specified with sufficient detail to the satisfaction of both the parties, often around some or all of:
  - the digital media product or service which is to be supplied
  - its delivery platform or set of platforms
  - its delivery means or format
  - its method of reception, consumption and/or use.
- Territory—even in an online world rights are still limited to permitted geographical territories.
- Exclusivity—the licence may be exclusive or non-exclusive or even switch between the two in different circumstances.

The traditional principles of licensing material will often still hold true:

- When acquiring content one should seek as wide rights as possible and when supplying it one should seek to limit rights more closely, eg 'license-in wide and license-out narrow'.
- As a distribution media matures from the cutting edge to the established the degree of technology detail needed to define the scope of the licence may fall, ie short generic industry-accepted terms replacing long specific definitions.
- As licences for new forms of products and services emerge care should be taken not to harm existing arrangements, eg the development of a non-disruptive rights template.

See Chapter 3 of this book for more background on the development of digital rights and licensing.

These factors will be at the heart of both the commercial bargain and the legal agreement between the parties. The degree of detail and format of that legal agreement will vary widely in different circumstances, but what else do parties usually seek to cover in a content supply agreement?

1. **Payment**—Clearly, there will be consideration for the grant of the licence, so the agreement will need to capture the agreed commercial terms, whether these are a licence fee or a share of the revenues generated by the licensee's exploitation of the content, or some other form of benefit—as well as any other costs involved in the arrangement.

2. **Regulation**—The distribution of content can carry legal risk, whether in terms of the potential for claims that the content infringes the intellectual property rights of a third party, or that it breaches the law or regulation in some other way. The degree of risk will vary dependent on the nature of the content in question: clearly sexual content will carry a relatively higher risk than, say, cooking recipes. The agreement should, then, allocate those risks between the parties, typically by means of the giving of warranties, ie specific contractual commitments as to the legality of content, and/or indemnities, ie specific contractual obligations to refund costs incurred if problems arise.

3. **Obligations**—In addition to the main licence parameters there will usually be other commitments that either side must fulfil, for example:

   - When and how must the licensor supply the content?
   - Can the licensee decide whether to use the content or not—or must it 'use it or lose it'?
   - Can the licensee make changes/additions to the content—and who approves and owns those?
   - Are there restrictions on which other content can appear with it?

- Are there specific copyright notices or other markings that must appear with the content?

4. **Risk**—Typically, commercial parties will want to ensure they do not have a potentially open-ended financial exposure, so a cap on liability may be agreed, and the interplay between this cap and the risk allocation provisions will often need to be given careful consideration.

Obviously there may be other specific commercial, creative, technical or operational requirements that will need to be recorded in each case along with the usual 'boilerplate' terms that any legal document will contain. Accordingly content supply agreements vary enormously in style and approach.

So, rather than attempt to provide a typical form of content supply agreement we present here a stripped-down form of structure that will highlight the issues mentioned above and from which a more project-specific document could be developed.

Content Supply Agreement

CONTENT SUPPLY AGREEMENT [1]

Special Deal Terms

1) [ ] of [address] (the 'Supplier')
2) [ ] of [address] (the 'Distributor')

Commencement Date:	[*date of agreement*]

Content:	[*description of content*]
Fee:	[*licence fee/revenue share/other*]
Site/Service:	[*intended use of content*]
Term:	[*term*]
Territory:	[*territory*]

Additional Terms

Delivery Requirements:	[*how is content supplied*]
Timetable:	[*timing for supply and updates*]
[Device Requirements]:	[*limit of the licence to certain platforms*]
[Usage Restrictions]:	[*further limit on use of content*]

[*Any additional provisions*]

Contact Details

The Distributor wishes to obtain a licence of the Content for use on the Site/Service, and the Supplier wishes to grant the Distributor such a licence, on and subject to the terms of the Agreement.

1 The agreement is structured as two documents. The 'Special Deal Terms' set out the key commercial terms of the deal—the names of the parties, a description of the content, the territory, the licence fee—all the key aspects of the licence. The 'General Provisions' set out everything else.

This kind of structure, which is very common, is often intended to minimize negotiation. The General Provisions are presented by the party who has drafted them as an effective 'fait accompli' with the express or implied suggestion that only the Special Terms need to be discussed which should be a relatively simple exercise in reflecting the commercial agreement between the two parties. Of course, this position of the inviolability of the General Provisions is merely a matter of optics (often the General Provisions will be presented in smaller font, in columns, or with some amendment, as an online agreement with a tick box), and relative bargaining position.

Since the licensor will usually look for more control and therefore more detail, this simplified sample agreement effectively favours the licensee or 'Distributor'.

The Agreement consists of these Special Deal Terms and the attached General Provisions.

....

Signed by

Duly authorized for and on behalf of the Supplier

....

Signed by

Duly authorized for and on behalf the Distributor

General Provisions

1. BASIC PRINCIPLES [2]

(1) The following provisions set forth the terms and conditions (the '**General Provisions**') governing the supply and use of all text, data, images, graphics, audio and/or audiovisual material, games, software programs, marks, logos, brands and/or other material as relevant and more particularly specified in the Special Deal Terms (together, the '**Content**') by the Supplier to the Distributor.

(2) Capitalized expressions used in these General Provisions shall have the meanings set out in the Special Deal Terms or as otherwise specified in this document. The General Provisions, Special Deal Terms and any documents referred to in them together constitute an agreement for granting of a licence in and to the Content by the Supplier to the Distributor (the '**Agreement**').

(3) In the event of inconsistency between parts of this Agreement, the Special Deal Terms shall take precedence over these General Provisions.

2. PROVISION OF CONTENT [3]

The Supplier shall provide the Content to the Distributor in accordance with the Delivery Requirements and the Timetable and otherwise in accordance with this Agreement and the reasonable instructions of the Distributor as provided from time to time.

3. LICENSING [4]

(1) The Supplier grants to the Distributor by way of [non-]exclusive licence the right to make available and distribute the Content by means of the Site/Service to users in one or more Territories [including without limitation by browsing, streaming, downloading, playback, storage and purchase] [subject always to the Usage Restrictions and the Device Requirements].

(2) In addition, the Supplier grants to the Distributor the right to use the brands, logos, names and trade marks relating to the Supplier and the Content, together with screenshots, demos and/or excerpts of the Content, on the Site/Service (and on all other media subject to the prior approval of the Supplier) for the purpose of marketing or advertising the availability of the Content. All use of the Supplier's brands, logos, names and trade marks under this Agreement shall be subject to the Distributor's compliance with the Supplier's practicable usage guidelines (if any), as supplied to

2 This confirms the structure of the agreement as mentioned above and the basic nature of the deal—supply of content of whatever nature (the list is non-exhaustive) by one party (the 'Supplier') to the other (the 'Distributor').

Whenever an agreement consists of more than one document there is the potential for inconsistency between those documents. We make it clear that in the event of any such inconsistency, the Special Terms take precedence over the General Provisions. This allows the commercial document to override the General Provisions, so that deal specific variations to those General Provisions can be recorded in the Special Terms and have binding effect. Sometimes this may not be considered appropriate and the order of precedence might be reversed.

3 This clause specifies the technical provision of the content from the Supplier to the Distributor. These specifics may, depending on the requirements of the Supplier, be complex or simple, and accordingly be set out in the Special Terms, a separate technical document annexed to the agreement, or left to the reasonable instructions of the Distributor.

4 As explained in the Introduction this is the legal meat of the agreement.

Sub-clause 1 links the deal specific licence terms—as defined in the Special Deal Terms—into the basic grant of rights. This may be exclusive or non-exclusive—if this is likely to be a variable, the exclusivity can be moved to the Special Terms.

We also deal with the method(s) of consumption here, in the list in square brackets—'browsing, streaming, downloading, playback, storage and purchase'. Again, this list will vary dependent upon the nature of the Distributor and its purposes for the licensing of the Content. As discussed above, in theory, the Distributor will seek the widest list of permitted exploitation, and the Supplier will be seeking to limit that list to its essentials. In practice, the scope of exploitation is likely to be fairly standardized, and will of course go to the price paid for the licence. Having said that, given the nature of the technologies within scope, and the speed of change in the business models spun out from those technologies, this part of the licence is potentially complex, and will require careful consideration. Concepts such as the 'Device Requirements' and 'Agreed Restrictions' are suggested as further definitions helping to set the overall scope.

It is usually necessary to stress that the supplier is not just licensing the content itself but also the associated trade marks and other brand elements that may be included within that content, and this is dealt with in sub-clause 2. The Distributor will need to use these within the Site/Service to enable users to know that the Content is available and to be able to find it. The Distributor may also want to use the marks for a number of other purposes, including the advertising and marketing of the availability of the Content on the Site/Service in external media, though this is usually by prior agreement with the Supplier.

the Distributor from time to time. All goodwill from such use shall accrue to the Supplier.

(3) Solely except to the extent technically necessary to facilitate the distribution of the Content in accordance with this Agreement the Distributor may not make any changes to the Content unless requested to do so by the Supplier. If requested to do so by the Supplier the Distributor shall make such changes as soon as reasonably possible. Unless otherwise agreed or where technically unfeasible in the circumstances, the Distributor shall refrain from removing or concealing the copyright notices contained in the Content.

(4) Each party acknowledges that save as expressly set out in this Agreement nothing shall operate to transfer the title of any intellectual property rights owned and/or controlled by one party to the other party.

4. FEE PAYMENT [5]

(1) Within 10 working days from the end of each month, the Supplier shall issue the Distributor with an invoice for the agreed Fee. Within 30 days of receipt of the Supplier's invoice, the Distributor shall transfer the Fee to the Supplier.

(2) Unless otherwise specified, all amounts are shown excluding VAT, which must be levied, if necessary, on the charges and reported on the bill, in addition to any withholding tax which may be imposed by any relevant taxing authority or government.

5. WARRANTIES [6]

The Supplier represents and warrants that: (a) it holds the unlimited right and title to grant the licence set out under this Agreement, and no additional licences, permissions, waivers, consents or payments with regard to copyrights, trade mark rights, patents, rights to names/personality/likeness/image, privacy rights, performers rights, database rights, moral rights, design rights, rights to images or other industrial or intellectual property rights of any kind ('IPR') are necessary in order for the Distributor to use the Content in accordance with this Agreement, and that such use will not infringe any third party rights whatsoever; (b) it shall always use its best efforts to prevent the Content from being infected by viruses or other harmful programs; and (c) the Content will not be, or contain anything which is defamatory, obscene or otherwise unlawful in any part of the Territory.

6. LIABILITY

(1) Neither party limits its liability to the other for (a) fraudulent misrepresentation or (b) death or personal injury caused by the negligence of, in either case, that party or the employees, agents or sub-contractors of that party.

(2) Subject to sub-clause (1), neither party shall be liable under contract, tort or any other head of law, to the other party for any indirect loss, consequential loss or loss of anticipated savings. In respect of all other loss, [each party's] aggregate liability to the other Party under this Agreement is limited to [the higher of £[ ] and the fees paid or payable to the Supplier].

(3) The Supplier hereby indemnifies and holds the Distributor harmless

5 Extremely straightforward payment provisions and as such favouring the Distributor. Depending upon the actual fee arrangements, the Supplier may require further detail on tax, late payment and audit rights.

6 These warranties address the key risks to the Distributor in the carrying of the Supplier's content: infringement of third party rights, virus or other harmful code, and illegality. The first two are usually considered to be within the control of the Supplier and fairly standard—although the Supplier might argue that while it will offer an indemnity to protect the Distributor if a problem did arise it will not commit to a warranty that such a problem won't ever arise. In respect of the latter, the Supplier may only be willing to provide more limited comfort even arguing that this should be the risk of the Distributor, or limit such a warranty to specific jurisdictions. In some cases the Supplier will seek to carve out elements of the Content from the scope of its commitments: for instance where there is user generated material or open-source software, or specific content or a usage involved that requires a third party to grant permission directly to the Distributor eg sound recordings cleared with a collecting society.

against all loss, damage, costs, expenses and liabilities that the Distributor may suffer as a result of (a) any claim or threatened claim (a '**Claim**') by any third party relating to the Content (including without limitation a Claim for infringement of IPR in the Content); and (b) breach by the Supplier of its warranties under Clause 5 above. The limitation of liability at Clause 6 above shall not apply to this indemnity.

(4) The Distributor shall promptly notify the Supplier in writing of any Claim of which it has notice. Unless otherwise instructed by the Distributor, the Supplier shall diligently conduct the defence of the Claim. The Supplier may not settle the Claim in any manner that binds the Distributor in any way without obtaining the Distributor's prior written consent to the terms of such settlement (which consent shall not be unreasonably withheld or delayed).

(5) The Supplier shall ensure that it carries at all times commercially adequate insurance to meet any claims by the Distributor under this Agreement. On written request by the Distributor the Supplier shall provide the Distributor with reasonable documentary evidence of compliance with this sub-clause.

7. CONFIDENTIALITY [7]

Each party undertakes and shall ensure that its employees, agents and sub-contractors undertake to treat as confidential all technical and non-technical information as well as business and operating matters that come to their attention in connection with its cooperation with the other party in verbal, written, graphical or other form and to refrain from making such information and matters accessible to third parties either directly or indirectly.

8. TERM OF THE AGREEMENT

(1) This Agreement shall come into force on the Commencement Date and remain in effect for the Term unless terminated earlier as set out below.

(2) Unless otherwise provided in the Special Deal Terms, either party shall have the right to terminate this Agreement forthwith, without prejudice to its other contractual rights:

(a) if the other party is in material breach of this Agreement and either such breach is not capable of remedy or such breach remains not remedied within 30 days from the date of being notified of such breach by the non-defaulting party;
(b) upon the expiry of [30] days written notice to the other party; or
(c) if the other party becomes insolvent, a petition to initiate insolvency proceedings has been filed, or if the other Party enters into an assignment agreement for the benefit of his creditors.

9. MISCELLANEOUS PROVISIONS

(1) No amendment to this Agreement shall be valid or enforceable unless in writing and signed by duly authorized representatives of both parties.

(2) No assignment or sub-licensing of rights or obligations under this Agreement is permitted without the prior written consent of the other party (which shall not be unreasonably withheld or delayed).

7 It is fairly standard for parties to a commercial contract to wish to limit their liability up front to an acceptable level, which is often expressed as the greater of a specific figure and/or the value of the contract—that is the fees paid.

With content agreements caution is needed, however, since the risks associated with the specific content may not fall within this limit. An assessment of damages in a breach of copyright claim or, in some territories, breach of privacy or defamation, may not have any relationship to the commercial value of the contract. For this reason, the Distributor will want the Supplier to indemnify it against such risks, and for liability arising under the indemnity not to be subject to the agreed cap on liability.

The Supplier also indemnifies against breach of warranty, covering risks of the content breaching law or regulation. Of course, the Distributor has at least in theory some measure of control over such risk in terms of its own compliance due diligence activities, so the Supplier may argue that an indemnity is not appropriate.

(3) If any provisions of this Agreement are or become invalid, this shall not affect the validity of the other provisions. In such an event, the parties shall replace the invalid or ineffective provision with one that most closely approximates the economic interest of the parties.

(4) All notices made under this Agreement shall be made in writing and directed to the contact details specified on the Special Deal Terms, to the attention of the named recipient.

(5) This Agreement constitutes the entire agreement between the parties relating to the subject matter hereof and supersedes all prior agreements. Neither party has relied upon any statement, representation or warranty of any person other than as expressly set out in this Agreement but nothing in this Agreement shall limit or exclude either parties' liability for fraud.

(6) Except as expressly provided in this Agreement, nothing in this Agreement is intended or shall be construed to give any person, other than the Parties hereto, any legal or equitable right, remedy or claim under or in respect of this Agreement pursuant to the Contracts (Rights of Third Parties) Act 1999, or any provision contained herein.

10. JURISDICTION AND APPLICABLE LAW

This Agreement shall be governed by and construed in accordance with the laws of England and Wales and the parties submit unconditionally to the [non-] exclusive jurisdiction of the courts of England and Wales.

A5

DEVELOPMENT AGREEMENT

Introduction

One of the sample agreements we included in the original version of this book was a short-form development agreement. It was intended to serve as a very simple but flexible contract to cover one party (the Client) commissioning another (the Developer) to develop software, content or indeed any other element of a digital media product. As such it was appropriate for a broad range of relatively straightforward procurement requirements.

In the years since the original book was published this form of agreement has been one which has proved particularly useful to us time and again—with appropriate tweaks—from building microsites and widgets to co-developing iPhone apps. We have therefore included it again in an updated form. It remains short and simple, picking out the key aspects of the project. Complex and/or higher value development projects would benefit from an expanded form of document (see eg Chapter A7).

What are the key aspects of a development project? First, there must be agreement as to what is to be developed—which is why the first deliverable under such a contract is often the development specification. The Developer will usually have the expertise and know-how here, especially with cutting-edge products or technology, and is likely to draft the specification; but should do so in response to a requirements document drafted or agreed by the Client that will set out in as much detail as possible exactly what the client intends to commission.

Then there must be agreement as to the price of the development, and the timetable for payment. As with any project, but especially where budgets are limited, it cannot be overstated that from the Client perspective keeping on the right side of the money is the key practical method of controlling a development project. Upfront payments are to be avoided; the better strategy is to use fee payments to incentivize performance, by tying payment to achievement of identified milestones.

Again, for the Client, delivery of the software or other items should not be enough; the software needs to work as the parties intended. Hence the need also for some form of defined acceptance concept. Ideally software should be properly tested for compliance with the agreed specification and only if it passes that test will the Developer have met its obligations. The Client should therefore tie payment to acceptance, not delivery.

CHECKLIST

If a development project is outsourced the essential terms will include:

1. *The specification* for design, performance and functionality—there may also be provision for how changes to the design will be incorporated.
2. *Preparation* of the work in an agreed format.
3. *Project timetable and delivery note.*
4. *Product testing* and approvals before acceptance; and *quality control.*
5. *The fee and payment schedule*: normally this would be a one-off relationship, with the developer agreeing to undertake and complete the development for a fixed fee and without any continuing financial or other interest in it.
6. *Confidentiality* (and maybe exclusivity) especially in relation to any proprietary user interface or where the product is part of a series.
7. *Responsibility for clearance of rights.*
8. *Copyright assignment* (or licence if acceptable).
9. *Delivery* (and/or if needed placing into escrow of any source materials).
10. *Warranties.*
11. *Project management.*
12. *Termination* (and possibly cancellations: this may allow termination and/ or withdrawal by the producer if development does not proceed as planned or if it is impossible or not feasible to change the design specifications; or if the feasibility study suggests there is no future for the product).
13. *Engage the developer to produce further work: support or even production versions etc*: this is perhaps an option (but not a commitment) in favour of the commissioning party.

The essence of a development contract is that the developer is commissioned to develop the product and, on completion or delivery, has nothing further to do with it except perhaps to provide support. Hence, the contract should provide that all rights pass from developer to producer and there is no need to specify a division of rights. Some contracts may, however, give the developer a right to participate in exploitation in some way; it will then be necessary to agree who shares what from which market and the percentages and per-unit royalties from sales.

Development Agreement

Short-Form Development Agreement

Dated: [ ]

Parties

(1) [ ] of [ ] (the 'Client')

(2) [ ] of [ ] (the 'Developer')

1. Introduction

The Client wishes certain software and/or other digital material (the 'Software') to be developed and the Developer wishes to develop such Software for the Client, subject to the following terms and conditions (the 'Agreement').

2. Specification

(a) The Developer shall write and deliver to the Client a technical specification (the 'Specification') within [x] weeks of the date of this Agreement, such Specification to conform to the Client's requirement specification (attached hereto as Annex 1) and also include a detailed timetable and the fixed fee for the development of the Software and any associated documents or material.

(b) The Client may approve or reject the Specification. If the Client wishes to vary or extend the Specification the Developer shall amend the Specification at no charge provided that the work is necessary to cure defects or omissions in the Specification and/or does not exceed [x] man days.

(c) Upon agreement by the parties the Specification shall be signed by both parties and added to this Agreement as Annex 2. The [Developer] shall at this time propose acceptance tests to be performed on the Software to reasonably establish the compliance of the Software with the Specification (the 'Acceptance Tests'), which when agreed by the parties shall be signed and added to this Agreement as Annex 3. 1

3. Development and delivery

(a) The Developer shall develop the Software and deliver the Software and documentation to the Client in accordance with the Specification. The Software shall be delivered in annotated source and object code form together with appropriate user documentation.

(b) The Developer shall assist in the installation of the Software upon the Client's equipment and the parties shall then carry out the Acceptance Tests as soon as is reasonably practical.

1 The Developer generates a lot of important material under this clause: a technical specification, the timetable for the development, and the pricing. All of this is subject to the agreement of the client; only upon agreement are these documents added to the agreement.

The client will need to consider these documents very carefully to ensure they meet its requirements, and that the timetable is suitable. As payment is linked in this agreement to the timetable, the client will need to check what triggers payment; as mentioned in the introduction, wherever it is possible the client is advised to 'backload' its payment obligations so that the development is completed or substantially completed, and accepted, before payment is made. If something must be paid it should be a limited good faith gesture not project finance.

The client may conceivably choose not to go further with the developer, but wish to use the technical specification it had developed—this option would need to be set out here. That will usually involve some form of payment.

Who comes up with the acceptance tests can be a subject of discussion, but this agreement assumes it will the developer—again subject to the agreement of the client. The client will probably carry out the tests but perhaps with the developer personnel in attendance. Again, this is highly important—passing acceptance will mean that the developer has performed its obligations under the agreement and will in all likelihood trigger payment by the client; so the tests need to be adequate to assess the performance of the software.

4. Acceptance testing

(a) The Client shall accept the Software upon it achieving the results set out in the Acceptance Tests. Acceptance shall be notified in writing by the Client to the Developer. If the Software fails the Acceptance Tests the Developer shall cure any defects, redeliver the Software and re-perform the Acceptance Tests, and these steps shall be repeated until the Software passes the Acceptance Tests.

(b) In the event that the Software has not passed the Acceptance Tests within [ ] weeks of the first agreed delivery date, then the Client shall have the option to terminate this Agreement on written notice to the Developer and in such notice specify whether it accepts any part of the Software in which event the parties shall acting reasonably agree a pro rated fee for that accepted part of the Software. [2]

5. Assignment

In consideration of the fee payable by the Client under this Agreement the Developer hereby assigns to the Client with full title guarantee the present and future copyright and all other rights of intellectual property in the Software, the Specification and all other documents or material created by the Developer as requested by the Client (the 'Deliverables') pursuant to this Agreement. [3]

6. Payment of fee

Subject to and in consideration of the Developer developing the Software in accordance with this Agreement the Client shall pay to the Developer the fee in accordance with the payment schedule set out in the Specification.

7. Warranty and indemnity

(a) The Developer warrants that:

- (i) it shall develop the Deliverables and perform its obligations under this Agreement in accordance with the highest industry standards;
- (ii) for a period of 1 year from the date of Acceptance the Software shall perform in accordance with the Specification when properly used on the specified equipment and in accordance with the agreed user documents;
- (iii) the Developer is the sole author of the Deliverables and that the possession and use of the Deliverables shall not infringe the intellectual property and/or other rights of any third party nor be defamatory, indecent, capable of causing religious or racial hatred or be otherwise unlawful; and
- (iv) the Software shall be supplied free of any virus or malware.

(b) The Developer shall indemnify the Client against any loss, damage or other costs incurred by the Client in respect of any breach or alleged breach of the Developer's warranties set out above.

2 The acceptance tests are performed, the software is accepted. But what if it fails? There are a number of options here, but usually the developer must take the software back and work on it until it passes. This cycle repeats until the software passes acceptance, or the client decides that enough is enough, and the agreement includes a 'drop dead' date after which the client can decide to terminate if the software is still not in an acceptable form.

The client can decide it wants to accept part of the software at this stage in which case there will need to be a pro-rating of the fee.

3 Intellectual Property in developed software can be treated in numbers of different ways. From the client perspective, outright ownership is the best position (assuming this is commercially realistic), and this is how it is dealt with in the sample agreement.

It is possible that the developer may use some pre-existing software in developing the deliverable, for example a game engine that is adapted to the specifics of the game that is developed for the client. In this scenario, the developer is likely to resist outright assignment of the pre-existing element as this is part of its 'stock in trade', and offer a simple licence of this element. This is likely to be acceptable, but care needs to be given to the definition of what is subject to the licence, and what is assigned to the client.

Another scenario here is the use of certain third party, or open source software as component parts of the deliverables. In all these cases, the client should be aware of these elements from the specification, and it will be a factor in whether that specification is acceptable to the client. Clear delineation of the component elements and their differing treatment under the agreement is key here.

The developer may be incorporating materials provided by the client—or developing look and feel based on the client branding and additional licensing provisions would need to be added.

(c) Without prejudice to the foregoing the Developer shall modify or replace any part of the Deliverables which has given rise to a breach or alleged breach of warranty provided that such modification or replacement does not materially diminish the performance or functions of the Software, or alternatively procure the right for the Client to continue to use the Deliverables (at no further cost to the Client). [4]

8. Confidentiality

The Developer shall keep confidential all information concerning the business and affairs of the Client received or obtained during the performance of its obligations under this Agreement and shall not use the same without the prior written permission of the Client other than as permitted under this Agreement. This obligation shall not apply to any information which is already in the public domain or which was already in the Developer's possession at the time of its disclosure by the Client.

9. Termination [5]

(a) In addition to Clause 4(b), either party may terminate this Agreement immediately by written notice to the other if the other fails to cure a breach of any provision of this Agreement within 30 days of service of written notice on the party in breach specifying the breach and requiring it to be remedied.

(b) On termination of this Agreement [by the Client], the Developer shall deliver to the Client all the Deliverables in existence at the time of termination.

(c) Termination [other than due to the breach of the Client] shall be without prejudice to the assignment of rights set out above.

10. Notices and consents

(a) No acceptance, approvals or consents given to the Developer shall be valid unless they are provided in writing by an authorized representative of the Client.

(b) Any notice given under this Agreement will be in writing and may be delivered to the other party or sent by pre-paid post or fax transmission to the address or transmission number of that party specified above or such other address or number as may be notified under this Agreement by that party from time to time for this purpose.

11. General

(a) This Agreement sets out the sole and entire understanding between the parties regarding its subject matter. Neither party has relied upon any statement, representation or warranty of any person other than as expressly set out in this Agreement but nothing in this Agreement shall limit or exclude either parties' liability for fraud.

4 We suggest that the essential warranties that are obtained from a developer are a performance warranty in terms of function in accordance with the specification, and a warranty that the software is original and will not infringe any third party rights. Where media content is involved wider content warranties will be needed. Ideally other protection will be included too—see 7(a)(i) and (iv) of this Agreement.

In respect of the former, given the inherent nature of software, the developer will want to time limit the warranty, as well as restrict it to proper performance within the specified environment. This is another reason for the client to be careful in approving the Specification.

As to the latter, this is a key requirement, and it is appropriate for the developer to give an indemnity in respect of this aspect, as it is outside the scope of control of the client. Typically the agreement will allow the developer to modify or replace the offending part of the software, or to procure a full licence in respect of the client at no cost.

5 Standard termination and confidentiality provisions, followed by protection on client consents and general clauses. In reality email may be used far more readily than post or fax so consider amending the notices requirement, eg permitting 'an email message that a read receipt or other positive report or reply from the recipient's computer can be produced in respect showing the recipient's correct email address and the sender has certified that it has not received an undeliverable or other technical error message (for the avoidance of doubt an "out of office" reply shall be deemed such an error message)'.

(b) The rights and remedies of the parties under this Agreement are cumulative and in addition to any rights and remedies provided by law.

(c) The parties do not intend that any term of this Agreement shall be enforceable solely by virtue of the Contracts (Rights of Third Parties) Act 1999 by any person who is not a party to this Agreement.

(d) No failure or delay by the Client in exercising its rights under this Agreement will operate as a waiver of those rights nor will any single or partial exercise by the Client either preclude any further exercise of any other right.

(e) Nothing in this Agreement will be deemed to create a partnership or joint venture between the Developer and the Client.

12. Governing law

This Agreement shall be governed by and construed in all respects in accordance with the laws of England and Wales and the parties agree to submit to the jurisdiction of the English court.

Signed by ——————

For and on behalf of Client

Date

Signed by ——————

For and on behalf of Developer

Date

Annex 1

Client's requirement specification

Annex 2

Specification

Annex 3

Acceptance tests

A6

CLOUD VIDEO SERVICES AGREEMENT

Introduction

The current buzz-words in digital media are content 'in the cloud' or virtual 'content lockers'. As usual with such terms they can mean different things to different people; with some enthusiasts they will be truly transformative developments and others sceptical, at best. In essence, these draw upon a wider concept in the technology and telecoms sector called cloud computing. This refers to the move of computing power and functionality away from the user or 'client side' and into the technology framework of the service provider or 'server side'. Instead of hosting and operating computing activities itself the user accesses these on-demand from the service provider. This 'virtualization' can bring improved flexibility and quality of service, usage efficiencies and cost savings.

Cloud computing has already triggered discussion of a range of legal factors. Security and data protection law issues are regularly raised by users; given the resulting loss of physical control over the computing infrastructure. Service level guarantees and liability risks are also often cited. These are certainly genuine concerns but are, to some degree, merely an extension of the issues businesses and their advisers have been used to handling in the procurement of outsourced technology. In particular, the trade-offs between cost and service commitment, and the technical ring-fencing of data and networks, are commonly dealt with in contracts with providers of telecoms and hosting services (see Chapter A8). Indeed those providers are currently very active in developing cloud-based service offerings for their customers.

The cloud takes on a more specific focus, however, in the context of digital media and content. The sample agreement below is a business-to-business arrangement where the client is pulling video content 'from the cloud' provided by the service provider. To the extent that the client then features the video content in its own digital media service, the client may have to back-to-back these arrangements with its own customers. Indeed, the structure of the document could be reworked relatively easily into a consumer cloud content service—although such an agreement would need to reflect the usual issues discussed in terms and conditions between the consumer and service provider (see Chapter B8).

In some ways the cloud concept represents a logical continuation of the process of digitization (as trailed in Part I): from the standard physical product (eg book, film, tape or disc), through the digitally delivered e-version (ie permanently held e-content—what the film business calls 'download to own' or 'electronic sell-through': though the latter has fallen out of favour as it implies a transfer rather than a licensing of rights—see box below), to a world where content is no longer physically held by the user. This idea of a central repository of content is not new. The 'celestial juke-box' was something mentioned in the earlier incarnations of this book and since then there have been a range of services, enjoying varying degrees of success, with both time-limited downloads and subscription models—which, it must be said, may not be so far away from what the traditional broadcasting industry has delivered for more than ninety years.

Yet the content-in-the-cloud concept is firmly based around current digital media issues, which in turn influence the different ways in which it could develop:

- **Content Storage**—at its simplest it offers users the ability to back-up and store their digital content in an easy-to-access form. That is a function already provided by a range of popular commercial services in particular for photographs and home video, which may or may not include added-value offerings to print or publish content.
- **Content Library**—moving from user-generated content to commercial material it could also allow the creation of a similar secure library of purchased content, as physical products had themselves formerly provided for the user. This clearly raises intellectual property rights issues. The ability to make repeated downloads of content once purchased (perhaps only when a copy is lost or defective) is already common in some online services, and that is now being extended to wider access-model services, but the ability to upload content purchased from third parties is more controversial. Indeed ten years ago a service that purported to allow users to access online versions of music recordings, provided they had already purchased them on CD, was found in a high-profile US judgment to infringe copyright. There were also legal complaints in certain jurisdictions over CD-ripping services offered when iPods first appeared. It remains to be seen how a fully digital content library would function and how far it would need to be licensed by the content owners. As described in Part I, both the law relating to private copying and the liability position of intermediaries varies in different countries. Much would depend on the nature of the service and who was offering it. A service that hosted a hundred copies of a music track uploaded by a hundred users might be treated differently to one that allows a hundred users to access one centralized copy of that track.

- **Digital Rights Management**—As also described in Part I, DRM systems have been criticized for locking away content and not allowing users sufficient flexibility. That has led to proposals for more ambitious systems where the purchase of an item of content in one format would bring with it the right to use that content in other ways and on other compatible devices authorized through a central repository or 'rights-locker'. Ultraviolet (formerly DECE) and KeyChest are two systems currently being developed with significant backing both from major media companies, especially the US film studios, and major device manufacturers.
- **Streaming**—In general terms, and no technology has proved to be completely resistant to circumvention, streaming content to the user rather than making it available for download has assisted in preventing unauthorized re-distribution and misuse. Until now users have, however, remained wedded to holding permanent copies of content even if provided in digital not physical form. If cloud-based content services prove successful the ready availability of content might encourage users to migrate from downloads.

Rights and content

Since 1966 a Beatles fan may well have purchased *Revolver* on LP, cassette and CD. That fan would have talked of owning a permanent copy of the album. In legal terms, at least under UK law, what the fan actually owned was a record, tape and disc but with that they were granted a limited licence of copyright in the recordings held on those physical media (the scope of that licence is discussed in Part I). In practical terms, however, that licence has been limited further by the effective obsolescence (for the mainstream user) of turntables and cassette decks. So talk of permanent copies of content is often misleading. Now that *Revolver* is finally available online it remains to be seem whether the generation of users first listening to it in that form will have the same feelings toward content ownership.

Cloud Video Services Agreement

CLOUD TV Virtual House, New Business Park, Media City 911

Video Services Agreement

Start Date:	
Initial Term:	
Bespoke Services:	

Client Name: Address:	
Client Team: Service Manager: Deputy: Authorized Person: Deputy: **CloudTV Team:** Account Manager: Service Manager: Deputy:	

Cloud TV Limited (**CloudTV**) agrees to provide, and the client detailed above (**you**/the **Client**) agree to accept, cloud video services on the terms of this Front Sheet and the attached Terms & Conditions and Schedules:

A—Service Description

B—Client Digital Media

C—SLA

D—Timetable

E—Bespoke Services

F—AUP

G—Charges

H—Data Controller Agreement

(together, the **Agreement**). [1]

Please read this Agreement carefully; it constitutes a binding contract effective as of the above Start Date between you and CloudTV. If you have any questions please contact your CloudTV Account Manager who is named above.

Signed

For and on behalf of CloudTV

Name

Date

Signed

For and on behalf of Client

Name

Date

CLOUD VIDEO SERVICES—TERMS & CONDITIONS

1. SERVICE MANAGEMENT

1.1 CloudTV and you have each appointed a Service Manager (as detailed on the Front Sheet with a named Deputy for periods of absence) to be responsible for managing technical issues relating to the performance of this Agreement.

1.2 You have also appointed an Authorized Person (as detailed on the Front Sheet with a named Deputy for periods of absence) to be responsible for providing approvals for and on behalf of the Client where this is required under the Agreement. CloudTV shall be able to rely on any approval provided by the Authorized Person (or their Deputy) as given by and on behalf of the Client unless or until CloudTV receives prior written notice from you of any change to your Authorized Person.

1.3 Where Bespoke Services (as defined in Clause 2.4 below) have been ordered by the Client (as indicated on the Front Sheet) the Service Managers shall arrange regular telephone meetings to discuss and minute progress and shall respond promptly to any issues or requirements relating to the provision of Bespoke Services referred to them.

1.4 The Service Managers shall seek to resolve any problems arising in relation to this Agreement as quickly and effectively as possible. Any issue which cannot

1 As with other agreements in this book the structure is based around a front sheet, terms and then specific technical and commercial detail included as separate Schedules. Also like other standard agreements featured it might well be a document that the service provider would turn into a set of online terms agreed as part of a click-wrap contract.

be resolved between the Service Managers shall be referred to the Authorized Person and your Account Manager. If it remains unresolved it shall be dealt with in accordance with paragraph 10 below.

2. PERFORMANCE OF THE CLIENT SERVICES

2.1 The broadband video services to be supplied to you under this Agreement incorporate: [2]

(a) access to CloudTV's proprietary modular video application, end user interface and connectivity solution within the CloudTV distributed hosting network (the **Platform**); [3] and

(b) access to CloudTV's client interface allowing customization and management of the Platform by the Client including customization of presentational templates, video management, publishing and syndication services and control of the content delivery system (the **Dashboard**); [4]

(together, the **Core Services**) all as further detailed in the core services description set out in Schedule A (the **Service Description**) which will allow you to present video functionality as a constituent module of the service operated by you as set out in Schedule B (the **Client Digital Media**).

2.2 Following the Start Date and subject to and in consideration of the Charges, and any other fees due, all as set out in paragraph 5 below, CloudTV shall: [5]

(a) activate the Client's account to allow access to the Platform via the Dashboard to enable the Client Digital Media to be customized and presented to users by you; and

(b) otherwise deliver the Core Services in accordance with the Service Description, the service level agreement set out in Schedule C (the **SLA**) and any relevant milestones detailed in the Timetable set out in Schedule D (the **Timetable**) for the Initial Term (as detailed on the Front Sheet) and thereafter unless or until terminated in accordance with paragraph 10 below.

2.3 Unless agreed otherwise with CloudTV as part of any Bespoke Services, the Platform shall be made available to you for the Client Digital Media with defaults/base settings identified in the Service Description. [6]

2.4 You may also have ordered (as indicated on the Front Sheet) additional bespoke services from CloudTV in relation to the customization, support and ongoing management of the Platform, which where applicable are set out in Schedule E (the **Bespoke Services**) and shall be delivered by CloudTV subject to and in accordance with the other provisions of Schedule [E] and any relevant milestones in the Timetable. [7]

2.5 The Core Services and the Bespoke Services (if any) shall together be known in this Agreement as the **Client Services**.

2.6 Unless expressly indicated to the contrary, all dates set out in the Timetable are estimates only and although CloudTV shall use its reasonable efforts to comply with them it shall have no liability to you for failing to do so.

2 The Client is being offered a standard set of 'Core Services'—which will be further described in the Service Description probably standard documents—with any specific client deliverables covered as 'Bespoke Services' in Clause 2.4.

3 Using a common form of approach there is a 'Platform' concept to cover the base level, non-customizable elements of the 'cloud': hosting, connectivity, storage and use of any proprietary applications.

4 A 'Dashboard' concept to cover the software 'front end' that gives the Client the ability to manage and customize the service.

5 As stated above the use of standard documents for technical and commercial detail would aid use of this type of agreement in online form. As also mentioned in the Introduction where the Client was effectively presenting the same service to its consumer users, and note Clause 3.7 which seeks to regulate and authorize that process, some care would be needed to be taken over how far the terms here could be mirrored in user terms—including service levels and timetable.

6 Again the focus in on a 'default' standard position. The service provider will usually look to maintain a standard level of commitments for its service and avoid offering different terms to different clients. With many cloud-based services the commercial rationale for the service provider is to standardize as far as possible.

7 See Chapters A5 and A7 for suggestions of how the delivery of bespoke services might be defined, tested and accepted.

3. YOUR RESPONSIBILITIES [8]

3.1 To ensure successful integration and operation of the Client Services within the Client Digital Media it is necessary for you to understand and accept your responsibility for some aspects of the work and resources involved. CloudTV shall have no liability for any delays, errors or omissions in delivering the Client Services which arise out of any error, failure or delay by you in providing any assistance or information required from you in accordance with this Agreement and that any Timetable or any timescales for delivery of Bespoke Services may be adjusted accordingly. [9]

3.2 You shall be responsible at your cost for the provision of your own hardware, software and communications infrastructure to deliver the Client Digital Media and sufficient to meet the minimum technical requirements of the Client Services. CloudTV shall not have any liability for any inability to deliver or use the Client Services due to any error, failure, inadequacy or delay of such facilities. [10]

3.3 You acknowledge and agree that the specification of the Core Services shall be subject to upgrade, adjustment and amendment from time to time which may result in interruptions to the Core Service (as governed by the SLA). Although CloudTV shall wherever possible provide reasonable notice of and supporting information for any material changes via the Dashboard, it is your responsibility to remain aware of any such upgrades, adjustments and amendments and ensure your own hardware, software and communications infrastructure remain compatible with the Core Services. [11]

3.4 Access to certain elements of the Core Services, including the Dashboard, shall be provided by CloudTV under such password control and other security restrictions as CloudTV shall set from time to time. You agree to comply with those restrictions and shall keep any passwords or other security mechanism confidential. Only your employees and authorized personnel may be granted access to them. You must report any suspected security breaches to CloudTV immediately. You agree that you shall be solely responsible for any activities undertaken by any persons who access the Client Services using your password (or other security mechanism).

3.5 You acknowledge and agree that the provision of the Platform and other Client Services shall be on the basis of shared resources with other CloudTV clients. Excessive use or access to those resources may impair overall performance for you and others. Accordingly: [12]

(a) you must give minimum prior written notice to Cloud TV as set out in the SLA as soon as you are aware of any circumstances which shall or may be likely to give rise to a need for increased resources to be allocated for any period to the provision of the Core Services to you (for instance, an anticipated increase in user demand for the Client Digital Media); and

(b) you acknowledge and agree that CloudTV may increase the Charges if CloudTV reasonably believes that the resources allocated to you are

8 As discussed in the Introduction to Chapter A7 the Client should take care over the commitments that it is being asked to give—even in the spirit of 'partnership' in any commercial relationship and especially where the supplier will have more technical expertise and understanding of a particular technology platform.

9 Clearly there could be room for debate over the 'adjustments' needed.

10 A common technical challenge in legal documents of this kind is defining where one service, and responsibility for it, ends and another begins. In some cases it would be necessary to ensure that appropriate descriptive detail was added to the specification.

11 The Client might want some protection against this—while the service provider will try to ensure that it can deliver the same basic service to all its customers. Ultimately the Client might look to be given a right to terminate if an upgrade results in incompatibility.

12 A relatively standard concern for service providers that one customer's demands do not impact on others. The Client needs to be comfortable that this can be managed in practice.

insufficient and this is having or may have a detrimental effect on CloudTV's ability to provide services to other clients.

3.6 You acknowledge and agree that maintaining the integrity of CloudTV's technical infrastructure is of prime importance and accordingly in addition to your specific obligations set out in this Agreement you must not act nor permit activity at any time in a manner that might interfere with the use and operation of the Platform (including the introduction of any worm, virus or other malicious code or hacking, denial of service or similar attacks) and you shall report any activity which you suspect may so interfere to CloudTV immediately. [13] CloudTV may suspend your access to the Core Services immediately and without notice if it believes there is such a risk to the integrity of the technical infrastructure.

3.7 You agree not to resell, lease or rent all or any of the Client Services delivered by CloudTV to a third party unless and until you become a member of the **CloudTV reseller programme**—please contact your Account Manager for details.

4. CLIENT DIGITAL MEDIA

4.1 You acknowledge and agree that you shall be solely responsible for the content of the Client Digital Media.

4.2 The Dashboard will allow you to control the content that you, your users or any other permitted person may upload to and make available via the Client Digital Media (the **Service Content**).

4.3 By uploading and distributing or permitting the upload and distribution of any Service Content and by providing any material you use to customize the Client Digital Media (the **Material**) you agree that you shall thereby grant or have procured the grant to CloudTV of a licence of all necessary intellectual property and related rights (at no cost to CloudTV) in such Service Content and Material to the extent and for so long as is necessary for CloudTV to provide the Client Services and to perform its obligations under this Agreement. [14]

4.4 Notwithstanding the above, CloudTV reserves the right to determine what types of Material and Service Content are made available using the Client Services. Accordingly CloudTV has established the acceptable usage policy set out in Schedule F, as may be amended on reasonable notice from time to time, (the **AUP**) which among other things requires you to respect the intellectual property and related rights of others by not permitting the distribution of infringing material and prohibits the distribution of content which is defamatory, obscene, in breach of any right of privacy or data protection law or otherwise unlawful.

4.5 You agree that Material, the Service Content and the Client Digital Media shall at all times comply with the AUP. CloudTV may, but is not under any obligation to, require you to remove any Material or Service Content from the Client Digital Media immediately if CloudTV has reasonable grounds to believe that this Material or Service Content violates the AUP. If you do not

13 Clauses 3.4 and 3.6 might be amplified with further technical detail on security concerns and requirements, eg for encryption and account protection.

14 The document might go further and include a list of required technical activities for the avoidance of doubt, eg reformatting, redistributing etc.

comply with such a request and do not provide sufficient evidence to CloudTV as to why the Material or Service Content does not breach the AUP then CloudTV reserves the right to remove the Material or Service Content itself and/or in serious cases to suspend the Client Services and the Client Digital Media.

4.6 CloudTV may, but is not under any obligation to, review the Client Digital Media and your Material and Service Content from time to time to monitor compliance with the AUP and this Agreement.

4.7 You agree to fully indemnify CloudTV and keep CloudTV fully indemnified from and against all losses, damages, claims and costs of whatever nature (including but not limited to legal costs) incurred by CloudTV as a result of any Service Content or Material provided in connection with the Client Digital Media.

4.8 CloudTV reserves the right to review the form and content of the terms and conditions of service by which you make the Client Digital Media available to your users and to require amendments to those terms and conditions of service where they conflict with the AUP, this paragraph 4 or any other provision of this Agreement.

4.9 Each Party shall comply with its obligations under all applicable data protection law in relation to any personal data processed in the performance of this Agreement and accordingly the Parties have executed a Data Controller Agreement as set out in Schedule H. [15]

5. CHARGES

5.1 In consideration of CloudTV supplying the Core Services you shall pay to CloudTV in cleared funds the fees set out in Schedule G (the **Charges**) plus any VAT or equivalent tax which shall be payable in addition.

5.2 In consideration of CloudTV supplying the Bespoke Services (if any) you shall pay to CloudTV the fees set out in Schedule G, plus any VAT or equivalent tax which shall be payable in addition.

5.3 You must issue CloudTV with a purchase order (which shall quote a purchase order number) or equivalent signed by your Authorized Representative immediately after signature of this Agreement specifying the relevant staged payments. NO CORE SERVICES SHALL BE PROVIDED BY CLOUDTV UNDER THIS AGREEMENT PRIOR TO RECEIPT OF THE PURCHASE ORDER.

5.4 CloudTV may agree to provide further services and products to you from time to time and where applicable such services and products shall be invoiced separately.

5.5 At each relevant date, CloudTV shall issue an invoice for each payment due under this Agreement (which shall quote any relevant purchase order number) to the address for invoices indicated on the Front Sheet. You must pay each invoice within fourteen (14) days of receipt of such invoice from CloudTV.

5.6 Without prejudice to any other rights or remedies CloudTV may have,

15 As discussed in further detail at Chapter B9.

if you fail to pay any invoice by the due date CloudTV shall be entitled to:

(a) charge interest at the rate of four per cent over the base rate of Barclays Bank plc from the date that the payment fell due until the date of actual payment; and

(b) suspend your access to the Core Services and/or suspend any further work on any Bespoke Services and extend timescales for delivery of the Bespoke Services accordingly.

6. INTELLECTUAL PROPERTY RIGHTS

6.1 As between you and CloudTV, all intellectual property and related rights in the Client Services (with the exception of your Material and the Service Content) are owned by CloudTV. You are granted a non-exclusive, non-transferable licence of such rights to the extent that this is reasonably necessary for your normal and lawful use of the Client Services in accordance with this Agreement only. Any APIs provided to you as part of the Client Services are provided for your use in connection with the Site(s) and the Client Digital Media only and for no other purpose. All underlying development know-how, tools and technology shall remain the property of CloudTV's and its suppliers. Decompiling, reverse engineering, disassembling, or otherwise reducing the code used in any software in the Client Services into a readable form to examine the construction of such software and/or to copy or create other products based (in whole or in part) on such software, is prohibited except to the extent permitted by law.

6.2 Certain programming coding routines that CloudTV uses are open source and although these are industry standard and widely used throughout the web CloudTV is only able to provide these in accordance with the limited terms upon which they have been made available (the **Non-Proprietary Code**).

6.3 All goodwill and other intellectual property or related rights generated or subsisting in the logos, domains, branding and marks used by CloudTV shall, as between the Parties, vest in CloudTV and you agree not to use or register any confusingly similar names, logos, domains, branding or marks during or after the term of this Agreement.

7. WARRANTIES AND LIABILITY

7.1 CloudTV warrants and undertakes to you that the Client Services and all its obligations under this Agreement shall be performed by competent persons with appropriate levels of qualification and experience and with reasonable diligence, skill and care in a professional manner, subject always to the SLA.

7.2 CloudTV agrees to fully indemnify you and keep you fully indemnified from and against all losses, damages, claims and costs of whatever nature (including but not limited to legal costs) incurred by you as a result of any claim by a third party that the provision of the Client Services infringe any third party intellectual property or related rights [16] (except in relation to your Materials and Service Content and any use of the Non-Proprietary Software [17]) PROVIDED THAT you must notify CloudTV immediately of any claim made or action brought against you in relation to the

16 Note that the service provider has not offered a warranty for this, ie it will not be in breach if there is a problem even though it will trigger the indemnity. Some agreements try to limit infringement liability, especially of patents, to 'knowledge and belief'.

17 This is an increasingly standard inclusion—although it does trigger the question whether either side is able to identify easily which elements are open source?

Client Services and that CloudTV shall have the conduct of any defence of that claim or action and you shall provide any assistance that CloudTV may reasonably request and you may not make any settlement of admission regarding that claim or action without CloudTV's prior written consent.

7.3 If in CloudTV's reasonable opinion the Client Services (or any portion thereof) is likely to infringe any third party intellectual property or related rights [18] CloudTV may suspend provision of the Client Service (or any portion thereof) and CloudTV will either procure the right for Client to continue using the Client Services (or any portion thereof), or will replace or modify the same to be non-infringing; if neither of the forgoing options is reasonably available, either Party may immediately terminate this Agreement.

7.4 Except as expressly provided in this Agreement, all conditions, warranties and terms and undertakings express or implied statutory or otherwise are expressly excluded to the fullest extent permitted by law. This Agreement is the entire and only agreement between the Parties concerning its subject matter and supersedes any and all prior agreements, arrangements and understandings (whether written or oral) relating thereto. Neither Party has relied upon any statement, representation or warranty of any person other than as expressly set out in this Agreement but nothing in this Agreement shall limit or exclude either Parties' liability for fraud

7.5 CloudTV does not exclude or restrict its liability for death or personal injury resulting from its own negligence or any liability the exclusion or restriction of which is prohibited by law.

7.6 Subject to paragraph 7.5:

(a) CloudTV shall not be liable to you for direct loss or damage whether in contract, tort (including negligence or breach of statutory duty) or otherwise including under any indemnity for any claims arising out of or in connection with this Agreement exceeding an amount equal to [the sums paid by the Client to CloudTV in the 12 months before the date that the claim arose]; and

(b) CloudTV shall not be liable to you in contract, tort (including negligence or breach of statutory duty) or otherwise including under any indemnity for any indirect, special or consequential loss or damage whatever including profits, business, wasted management time or anticipated savings.

7.7 Paragraphs 7.4 to 7.7 inclusive are to be construed as a separate provisions applying and surviving even if for any reason one or the other of them is held inapplicable or unreasonable in any circumstances and shall remain in force following termination of this Agreement.

7.8 You acknowledge and agree that the limitations and exclusions set out above represent a reasonable allocation of risk between the Parties taking into account the circumstances of the Parties, the fees payable and the nature of Client Services offered.

8. CONFIDENTIAL INFORMATION

8.1 Each Party undertakes to the other that, subject to paragraph 8.2 below, it

18 The suspension could be an issue for the Client—with the need for swift action.

will treat as confidential the terms of this Agreement together with all information whether of a technical nature or otherwise relating to the business or affairs of the other Party as may be communicated to it under or otherwise in connection with this Agreement and will not disclose such information to any person (other than to its auditors and other professional advisers under similar terms of confidentiality) and will not use such information other than for the purposes of this Agreement subject always to any proper specific authorization in writing by the disclosing Party to such disclosure or use.

8.2 The provisions of paragraph 8.1 above shall not apply to any information which:

(a) is in the public domain other than by default of the recipient Party;
(b) is obtained by the recipient Party from a bona fide third party having no apparent restraint on its free right of disposal of such information; or
(c) is required to be disclosed by law (or applicable regulation) or the valid order of a court of competent jurisdiction, or the request or direction of any governmental or other regulatory authority or agency.

8.3 CloudTV shall have the right to be able to refer to the public domain information aspects of the Client Services after they have been delivered, for use in general marketing. CloudTV shall be able to refer to you as a client on its website and promotional materials and refer to the work CloudTV carried out. Unless CloudTV notifies you otherwise, CloudTV shall be credited in its role in the support of the Client Digital Media credits section with a branded link to the CloudTV.com website.

8.4 The provisions of this paragraph 8 shall survive termination of this Agreement.

9. RESOLVING DISPUTES

9.1 If the Services Managers, Authorized Person and Account Manager fail to resolve any dispute (except than a dispute which relates solely to the non-payment of fees to CloudTV under this Agreement) (a **Dispute**) the matter shall be referred to the Parties' respective managing directors who shall attempt to settle the Dispute.

9.2 If the managing directors fail to settle the Dispute within 30 days, the Parties shall liaize in good faith for a period of not more than fourteen (14) days (or such shorter period as the Parties agree) with a view to agreeing the identity of a suitably qualified mutually acceptable expert to be appointed to resolve the Dispute.

9.3 If the Dispute has not been resolved by the expert within 30 days of his appointment, or if either Party does not wish to participate in the procedure, the Dispute may be resolved under paragraph 13.1.

10. TERM AND TERMINATION OF THIS AGREEMENT

10.1 This Agreement shall take effect from the Start Date and shall continue for the Initial Period (as detailed on the Front Sheet) and shall continue thereafter unless and until terminated:

(a) by either you or CloudTV on at least three months prior written

notice to the other such notice not to be given before the end of the Initial Period; or

(b) at any time in accordance with this paragraph 10.

10.2 Either you or CloudTV may terminate this Agreement on immediate written notice to the other:

(a) if the other resolves to go into a voluntary liquidation (including any voluntary arrangement as described in the Insolvency Acts 1986 and 2000 or amendments made to the same, but other than a members' voluntary winding up for the purposes of a reconstruction of its affairs), presents or has presented against itself a winding up petition, makes a composition with its creditors, has a receiver, manager or administrative receiver appointed over to the whole or any part of its assets or property, presents or has presented against itself a petition for the making of an administrative order or becomes unable to pay its debts within the meaning of section 123 of the Insolvency Act 1986, or an analogous event occurs in any other jurisdiction; or

(b) if the other is in material breach of any of its obligations under this Agreement which is capable of remedy and has not remedied such breach or agreed to a satisfactory course of action within thirty (30) days of having received written notice of the breach from the notifying Party; or

(c) if the other is precluded by a force majeure event in accordance with paragraph 11 from performing its obligations for a period more than sixty (60) days.

10.3 Upon the termination of this Agreement in accordance with its terms for whatever reason:

(a) CloudTV shall cease to provide the Client Services and CloudTV shall be under no further obligation to support the Client Digital Media;

(b) all rights granted to the Client hereunder shall immediately and automatically revert to CloudTV and the Client shall cease any further use of the Client Services and shall not directly or indirectly refer to or associate itself with CloudTV;

(c) all sums payable by either Party to the other under this Agreement relating to the period up to termination shall become immediately due and payable; and

(d) the Client shall, at the Client's cost, permanently delete and/or deliver to CloudTV all copies of CloudTV materials and any confidential information then in the Client's possession or control. As soon as reasonably possible following such termination and in any event within 21 days thereof the Client shall issue a certificate signed by the a duly authorized signatory of the Client confirming that the Client has fully complied with its obligations under this paragraph 10.3(d).

10.4 The termination of this Agreement in accordance with the terms for whatever reason shall be without prejudice to any rights or remedies which either Party may be entitled to hereunder or at law,

any accrued rights or liabilities of either Party and/or the coming into or continuance in force of any provision of this Agreement which is expressly or by implication intended to come into or continue in force on or after such expiry or termination.

11. EVENTS BEYOND THE PARTIES' CONTROL

Each Party shall not be liable to the other if it is unable to perform or is late in performing its obligations under this Agreement due to circumstances over which it has no control (eg failure, interruption or degradation of any third party telecommunications network or system or the Internet or any part of it, industrial action, government action, interruptions in public order, accidents, epidemics, extremes of weather or event of nature, unavailability of raw materials or of normal means of transport or act of God).

12. ADDITIONAL PROVISIONS

12.1 Any notice which is given by you or CloudTV under this agreement can be sent by e-mail, fax or recorded delivery to the contact address on the Front Sheet. If its contact details change during the agreement CloudTV shall let you know and you should let CloudTV know if your contact details change. Unless you or CloudTV can prove otherwise, the notice shall be deemed to have been received, if sent by e-mail on the day it was sent; if sent by fax on receipt of an error free transmission report or if sent by recorded delivery, two days after the date on which it was posted.

12.2 Nothing contained in this Agreement creates any form of association, partnership, joint venture or the relationship of principal and agent between you and CloudTV. You and CloudTV each agree that the provisions of this Agreement have been the subject of discussion and negotiation and are fair and reasonable.

12.3 If you breach this agreement and CloudTV do not take any action against you, CloudTV may still take action against you if you breach the same term on another occasion or if you breach a different term.

12.4 This Agreement cannot be changed or terminated orally, and no changes or amendments to this Agreement requested by the Client shall be binding upon the Parties until accepted in writing by a duly authorized representative of both Parties.

12.5 CloudTV shall be entitled to propose changes or amendments to this Agreement by notifying the you via the Dashboard. If you object to any changes or amendments, you will be given a period of 30 days in which to terminate this Agreement before the changes or amendments take effect. After such period, your continued use of the Client Services will constitute your acceptance of the changes or amendments.

12.6 A person who is not a Party to this Agreement has no right under the Contracts (Rights of Third Parties) Act 1999 to enforce the benefit of any term of this Agreement and to the extent permitted by law the Parties hereby exclude the application of such Act to this Agreement.

12.7 You shall not assign, sub-license, sub-contract, share or part with in whole or in part or transfer by any means any of the rights or any other benefit or obligation contained in this Agreement without CloudTV's prior written consent.

12.8 In this Agreement:

(a) headings are for convenience only and shall not affect the interpretation of this Agreement;

(b) references to any **paragraph** or **Schedule** are to those contained in this Agreement and all Schedules are an integral part of this Agreement;

(c) references to a **Party** are references to a party to this Agreement including that party's successors in title and assigns or transferees permitted in accordance with the terms of this Agreement;

(d) all references to statutory provisions shall be construed as references to those provisions as they may be amended or re-enacted;

(e) references to one gender shall include the others; and to the singular shall include the plural, and vice versa;

(f) the words include, including and in particular shall be construed as being by way of illustration or emphasis only and shall not be construed as, nor shall they take effect as, limiting the generality of any preceding words; and

(g) references to a **person** include an individual, firm, governmental authority, unincorporated association or body corporate.

13. GOVERNING LAW AND JURISDICTION

13.1 This agreement is subject to English law and the English courts shall have non-exclusive jurisdiction for its interpretation and enforcement.

Schedules A–H

A7

WEBSITE DESIGN AND BUILD AGREEMENT

Introduction

Experience suggests that, like many projects and activities on which lawyers are asked to advise, the development of a website may often be well under way before anyone looks for legal input. There are, however, so many different elements that need to be drawn together successfully to create a website that the sooner guidance on the contractual framework in place to control those elements comes, the better.

The owner of the website, in this agreement the 'Website Client', could potentially be looking for strategic planning, different types of design work, hosting and maintenance services, site management and ancillary support, software licensing or a combination of the above from completely separate advisers and suppliers. And that is without looking further into the range of domain name, e-commerce, content delivery and advertising products and services that might also be added.

Different suppliers might be more effective and/or cost-efficient at providing certain services and the Website Client's own in-house abilities and experience will influence what might be seen as the optimum deal. By contrast, however, from a contractual point of view it might be preferable to buy an all-in-one solution from a single (reliable) entity responsible for all elements of the project—even if that prime contractor sub-contracts certain elements to others—to avoid obligations and liability falling between suppliers.

As with suppliers from any industry, the standard terms offered by website developers, design houses, hosts and others can often be inappropriate and inadequate. If the Website Client is working on a major online presence, it should certainly consider drawing up its own contractual documentation—which is what is presented here—even if the Website Client uses technical material prepared by its supplier (as agreed) in schedules, and as supporting documents. This form of document could also be easily adapted for similar design and build projects.

Designing and building a website involves both traditional design skills as well as technical support. As discussed above, if the two aspects are not provided by the same supplier linking the separate legal relationships together will be important. As with any design project reviewing previous work which a potential supplier has produced for other clients is a standard starting point. Potential suppliers are often asked to prepare an initial proposal for the Website Client to review and even if that is not part of a formal request for proposals (RFP) and tender process it is always helpful to try to ensure key legal and commercial terms are also discussed, not just the creative and technical approach.

Developers can be wary about cost, confidentiality and ownership issues even at pitch stage, especially for smaller projects—seeking to avoid presenting ideas for free to a Website Client who uses the ideas with a rival or an in-house team. Some may therefore encourage the Website Client to purchase an initial package or consultancy advice and the Website Client then needs to take care to ensure that such services are actually of value. Costs vary enormously; from a few thousand pounds for a whole (if very limited) website to several thousand pounds per day over several months work on a far more serious online presence.

As with any long-term creative project the Website Client needs to build in some protection over the payment process with the usual range of options—ring-fencing money, setting agreed milestones and delivery controls. Some developers are prepared to take a deferment of fees in return for a share of revenue from the website but clearly this still has to be managed carefully from the Website Client's side. Either way the Website Client will usually look for the security of a fixed-price deal rather than open-ended payment or recoupment of costs on a time and material basis.

Control of intellectual property rights is obviously very important and different suppliers may take different approaches. Traditionally, suppliers from the design/advertising sector may be more comfortable with assignment than those with an IT/software background more used to licensing structures. The Website Client needs to think carefully to ensure that it receives all the appropriate rights, particularly on termination of its relationship with the relevant supplier. A different approach to ownership and use will often be applied to different elements of a website.

Some items will be more important, technically and commercially, than others. A website will be made up of a range of different elements sourced from different origins and a uniform rights position is seldom practical. In very broad terms the bespoke elements may be separated from the generic underlying applications. The former involving overall branding or 'look and feel', specific design features and even perhaps individual elements of functionality, the latter including both standard 'off-the-shelf' software as well as proprietary applications. Each needs to be discussed separately.

Design services are also likely to be necessary on an ongoing basis, as the website is updated, amended and rebranded, so it is also necessary to deal with how further work will be requested, priced and supplied. This 'content maintenance' is just as important as the operational hosting and maintenance of the website as a whole (see Chapter A8). The document below focuses on the design and build of a website before launch but clearly where the supplier has ongoing involvement those services could also be built into it—with associated service level commitments (see Chapter A9).

PROJECT MANAGEMENT CHECKLIST

1. A common problem with suppliers' standard terms is that they will fail to establish any kind of formal management process for the performance of the relevant services. The Website Client should remedy this by ensuring that one of the first clauses added to any contract is one establishing a clear project management procedure explaining how the Website Client will monitor, liaise and control the delivery of the relevant services, setting out which personnel will be involved, whether and how they will be deputized or replaced, who will report to whom, when and what will happen when there is disagreement and how any dispute procedure will operate.
2. Defining the controls the Website Client has over the delivery process is important. This can ensure that the talented technical and creative team the Website Client saw at pitch stage actually stay with the project and that any access to the Website Client's content, business, technology, and/or premises is properly regulated.
3. The supplier will often stress the partnership relationship required to make the project work, and it is not unreasonable for the Website Client to accept some responsibility for this. In legal terms, however, the Website Client should ensure that this does not actually involve accepting too many potential liabilities toward its supplier if it is the one in practice that has problems implementing the project.
4. Part of the project management process is agreement and implementation of a proper testing and acceptance procedure. Wherever possible some clear contractual obligations need to be established and a proper delivery specification—both as to design and functionality, and a binding but appropriately flexible timescale—should be set.
5. The project should be broken down into phases with the emphasis on successful testing of each element not mere delivery. With both creative and technical input involved, the potential for, and impact of, delays is obviously significant. Realistic remedies for late delivery and failure to achieve service levels need to be considered.

Website Design and Build Agreement

WEBSITE DESIGN & BUILD AGREEMENT

DATED [ ]

BETWEEN:

(1) [**WEBSITE CLIENT**] (the **Website Client**) a company incorporated under the laws of [ ] and registered under number [ ] whose registered office is at [ ]; and

(2) [**DEVELOPER**] (the **Developer**) a company incorporated under the laws of [ ] and registered under number [ ] whose registered office is at [ ]

INTRODUCTION:

The Website Client wishes to engage the Developer to [re-]develop (1) the Website, and the Developer wishes to accept such work, subject to and in accordance with the terms and conditions of this Agreement.

IT IS AGREED:

1. DEFINITIONS AND INTERPRETATION

1.1 In this Agreement, the following definitions apply and related expressions shall be construed accordingly:

Charges means the charges payable to the Developer by the Website Client under this Agreement as set out in Schedule 1;

Content means all content of whatever nature and form including text, graphics, photographs, audio and audio-visual material which is created by or on behalf of the Developer and/or supplied by or on behalf of the Website Client to the Developer (including by a Website Partner) for inclusion within or otherwise in relation to the Website [but expressly excluding the Website Client Marks]; (2)

Data means any information, data or other material generated by or in relation to use of the Website including user registration, transaction data, usage report and statistics, user-generated content and other submissions (whether or not containing personally identifiable information); (3)

Deliverables means those documents, manuals, data files or other materials of whatever nature and in whatever form which the Developer shall create for or supply to the Website Client in the performance of the Services as more fully set out in the Specification and including the Front End and the bespoke elements of the Platform; (4)

1 For the purposes of this agreement it is assumed there is no current site to be replaced but clearly some development projects will involve building upon an existing online presence.

2 In this Agreement the website is effectively divided up into its constituent parts of the Front End, ie the bespoke user-facing elements, through which the site's Content (defined broadly here) is delivered, which sits on the Platform, ie the underlying software, and potentially hardware, that effectively operates the site. There is clearly the potential for overlap between these elements and further detail and delineation can be provided by the Specification. Obviously additional or alternative elements can be identified as necessary to match the actual operational or ownership breakdown.

3 A broad definition of data and information generated by users from registration data to user-generated content. This may well be more important where the Developer has an on-going role with the operation of the website. See the data protection provisions at Clause 7.

4 The Specification would provide detail but it is assumed that while all the Front End will be created specifically for the Website Client only limited aspects of the Platform would be bespoke.

Final Acceptance means full and final approval of the Website by the Website Client in accordance with Clause 6.5;

Front End means the page templates, format, layout, look-and-feel and all other elements of the Website's user interface as more fully set out in the Specification;

Key Team Members means those individuals set out in Schedule 2; 5

Nominated Third Parties means those third parties listed in Schedule 3 who have been nominated by the Developer and approved by the Website Client to provide the Third Party Services; 6

Platform means the content management and delivery system and other underlying infrastructure for the Website as more fully set out in the Specification; 7

Progress Report means the Developer update report in the form set out in Schedule 4;

Project Plan means the timetable for the [re]development of the Website and the performance of this Agreement as set out in Schedule 5; 8

Rights means all present and future copyrights as well as all computer code or scripts, whether compiled or not in any computer language or program form, patents, petty patents and utility models, trade marks and service marks, trade names, domain names, rights in get-up, inventions, all rights in computer software and data, database rights, confidential information, trade secrets and know-how, design rights, registered designs and semi-conductor topographies, synchronization rights, publishing rights, performance rights, rights in sound recordings and all rights, privileges and forms of protection similar or related to above including all registrations and applications to register any of the above, and all renewals, revivals, reversions, extensions, continuations, divisions and re-issuances which may subsist anywhere in the world with the right to sue for past infringements; 9

Services means the Website [re]development services to be provided by the Developer to the Website Client under this Agreement; 10

Specification means the detailed functional, technical and design specification for the [re]development of the Website as set out in Schedule 6; 11

Start Date means [ ];

Style Guidelines means the Website Client's brand, design, tone and style guidelines as set out in Schedule 7; 12

Term shall have the meaning set out in Clause 11.1;

Third Party Services means those services listed in Schedule 3;

5 Very often the supplier will have key personnel whom the client will want to ensure are involved.

6 It is rare for any supplier to be able to provide all elements of any technical project in-house so provision is made here for specified pre-approved sub-contractors to be named, which also assists confirm ownership issues—see Clause 9 below.

7 It is assumed that there is a largely proprietary underlying platform from which the website will operate.

8 Ideally the timetable is agreed upfront but there could be provision for this to be an initial deliverable.

9 An 'everything and the kitchen sink' long-form definition—with particular emphasis around technical and media related rights.

10 As discussed in the introduction the Developers are not taking responsibility for hosting the site or continuing content administration services—but see Clause 7.

11 Clearly a crucial document and if necessary this may need to be a deliverable itself if the parties cannot settle the document ahead of signature. It may be appropriate to divide it between technical and content sections.

12 These might have been produced as part of the project or more likely will be provided by the Website Client's separate brand advisers.

Virus means any computer code, programming instruction or set of instructions that is intentionally and specifically constructed with the ability to damage, interfere with or otherwise adversely affect computer programmes, data files or hardware without the consent or intent or knowledge of the computer set;

Website means [ ]; [13]

Website Client Marks means the names, branding, logos and trade marks of the Website Client [including those set out in Schedule 8]; and

Website Partner means any person whom the Website Client engages to supply content and/or other services for the Website. [14]

1.2 In this Agreement, unless otherwise stated:

(a) words in the singular shall include the plural and vice versa and use of any gender shall include the others;
(b) the headings in this Agreement are for convenience only and shall not affect its interpretation;
(c) references to Clauses and Schedules relate to this Agreement and all Schedules to this Agreement are an integral part of this Agreement;
(d) references to a **Party** shall mean a party to this Agreement and (subject to Clauses 2.2, 12 and 21) include references to their respective successors in title and permitted assigns, transferees and novatees and references to a **person** include an individual, firm, unincorporated association or body corporate;
(e) references to **writing** does [not] include e-mail, SMS or other electronic communication [other than fax]; and
(f) references to **include** and **including** shall be for illustrative purposes and not be construed to limit the sense of the preceding words; and
(g) unless otherwise stated references to the **approval**, **agreement** or **consent** of the Website Client shall be to such approval, agreement or consent being given, withheld or delayed at the Website Client's sole discretion and obtained in writing and in advance.

2. APPOINTMENT

2.1 The Website Client appoints the Developer, and the Developer agrees, to provide the Services to the Website Client from the Start Date subject to and in accordance with the terms and conditions of this Agreement. [15]

2.2 No element of the Services may be provided by any person other than the Developer without the approval of the Website Client save that the Website Client acknowledges and agrees that the Third Party Services may be provided by the Nominated Third Parties subject always to Clause 12. The cost of the Third Party Services is included within the Charges, and subject only to Clause 8 below, no additional cost shall be charged to the Website Client as a result of the engagement of the Nominated Third Parties.

13 At the minimum a simple reference to the intended URL (which someone has hopefully remembered to register—see Chapter A10 and which may be more appropriate where an existing site is being re-developed) or ideally some more descriptive overall background.

14 Specific partners and contact information could be listed in a schedule.

15 In some cases the Website Client will look for some form of exclusivity from the Developer—if only over confidentiality concerns where competitors use the same supplier. Conversely the fact that the Developer has experience in the Website Client's sector may be a comfort factor. At the same time the Website Client may want to clarify that it may use other suppliers.

3. PROJECT MANAGEMENT

3.1 Each Party has appointed an individual to be their designated project manager with a named deputy, for the purposes of this Agreement as follows:

Website Client:	Developer:	
Project Manager:	[ ]	[ ]
Deputy:	[ ]	[ ]

or, subject to Clause 4, such other persons as the Website Client or the Developer may notify to each other. [16]

3.2 The Developer shall meet (physically or via remote conference call) with the Website Client in accordance with the schedule of meetings (and procure the attendance of the relevant personnel including any Key Team Members) as set out in the Project Plan and at such further meetings as either Party deems reasonably necessary for the proper performance of the Services and to ensure that the provision of the Services and the Deliverables occurs on time and in accordance with the terms and conditions of this Agreement.

3.3 The Developer shall also meet (physically or via remote conference call) with the Website Partners and/or such other person(s) as may be involved with the Website in accordance with the schedule of meetings (and procure the attendance of its relevant personnel including any Key Team Members) as set out in the Project Plan or as the Website Client may reasonably direct from time to time for the purposes of liaison and ensuring compatibility between the different elements of the Website. [17]

3.4 The Developer shall on a [weekly] basis provide the Website Client with the Progress Report. [18]

4. PERSONNEL

4.1 The Developer acknowledges that the identity of the personnel engaged in the provision of the Services is regarded by the Website Client as essential to the successful implementation of the Website.

4.2 The Developer shall not remove any of the Key Team Members from their designated roles in Schedule 3 without the Website Client's prior written consent, such consent not to be unreasonably withheld or delayed. [19]

4.3 If at any time during the performance of the Services the Website Client reasonably believes that any of the Key Team Members or any other person engaged by the Developer is not performing to a standard commensurate with the performance level required under this Agreement or is otherwise having a detrimental impact upon the Services and/or the implementation of the Website, then the Website Client shall be entitled to require the Supplier to

16 As the Introduction makes clear, with both technical and creative design elements to marry together the need for co-ordination and strong project management is usually reflected in clear contractual roles and procedures.

17 Again as stressed in the Introduction, further detail should be provided on the necessary liaison requirements if there are other elements of the site that are separate to the Developer's performance.

18 This will usually be an online process.

19 Job changes and illness must be taken into account.

remove such person from their involvement with the Website and the Developer agrees to consult with, and give meaningful consideration to the wishes of, the Website Client with regard to the identity of any proposed replacement. [20]

5. PROJECT PLAN

5.1 The Developer shall provide the Services in accordance with the Project Plan. As soon as the Developer becomes aware that the provision of any element of the Services is not in accordance with the Project Plan and is therefore likely to be or is being delivered later than required by the Project Plan (a **Project Delay**), then the Developer must inform the Website Client either in the next Progress Report or in the case of a material Project Delay by immediate written notice.

5.2 If the Website Client is informed of a Project Delay or the Website Client itself has reasonable grounds for suspecting a Project Delay, the Developer shall discuss with the Website Client at either the next scheduled project meeting provided for in Clause 3, or in the case of a material Project Delay an emergency meeting convened by the Website Client, the circumstances and implications of and the reasons for the relevant Project Delay.

5.3 Once the existence of a Project Delay is identified the Developer shall provide at or within a reasonable period after any meeting referred to in Clause 5.2 above (within 48 (forty-eight) hours in the case of any emergency meeting) a report specifying the impact and consequences of and remedial actions in response to the Project Delay. The Developer shall always act reasonably and diligently in seeking to mitigate the effects of any Project Delay.

5.4 To the extent that a Project Delay is directly attributable to any act or omission of the Website Client or a Website Partner (other than when such act of omission was in reliance upon the instructions of or otherwise caused by the Developer) or due to a force majeure event (subject always to Clause 16), then the Developer shall not be liable for such Project Delay provided always that the Developer has complied with the provisions of this Clause 5. To the extent that the Developer has not so complied the Developer shall be deemed to have contributed to the relevant Project Delay. [21]

6. [RE]DEVELOPMENT OF THE WEBSITE [22]

6.1 The Developer shall [re]develop the Website in accordance with the Specification, the Style Guidelines and the reasonable directions of the Website Client in accordance with the terms and conditions of this Agreement.

6.2 The Website Client shall have final editorial, design and technical approval over all aspects of the Website and the provision of the Services having regard (where relevant) to the Specification.

20 The Website Client will often want to have it both ways and demand personnel are removed if they believe it necessary. The Developer, especially if a smaller supplier, may want to avoid these personnel commitments, preferring to keep internal flexibility as to how it resources the project. Indeed the Developer may look for protection from the Website Client poaching Developer staff to work in-house.

21 Delays are often inevitable so some form of procedure for reporting and responding to them is usually important—provided what is agreed contractually can and will be reflected in practice. What is not tackled here is whether specific sanctions or costs implications should be triggered. These can be difficult to agree upfront and will be project specific but ideally they would prevent argument later when a problem has arisen.

22 A suggested delivery, testing and acceptance procedure. For more complex projects it may be necessary to include additional provisions in a schedule detailing individual testing activities and severity reporting procedures.

6.3 Without prejudice to the general right of approval in Clause 6.2 certain aspects of the Services will require a written notice from the Website Client to the Developer indicating that a given Deliverable or other task has been satisfactorily completed and signed off. Those elements requiring such approval have been or shall be clearly marked as requiring approval in the Project Plan and/or the Specification itself.

6.4 Each element of the Services which requires written approval in accordance with Clause 6.3, including the final version of the Website as a whole, shall be submitted to the Website Client in accordance with the Project Plan for testing and review. The Website Client shall accept each element or (as the case may be) the final version of the Website as a whole immediately after the Developer has demonstrated to the Website Client's satisfaction that it is in substantial conformity with the Specification by issuing a written notice.

6.5 If the Developer is unable to demonstrate such substantial conformity of any element or (as the case may be) the final version of the Website as a whole, the Website Client shall promptly notify the Developer of any modifications it requires to ensure substantial conformity with the Specification within the time set out in the Project Plan or, if no time is set out in the Project Plan, within [five (5) working days] of the Developer's submission. The Developer shall then (at its cost) redeliver to the Website Client the relevant element of the Services, or (as the case may be) the final version of the Website as a whole, incorporating the modifications. Such redelivery shall take place within the time set out in the Project Plan or, if no time is set out in the Project Plan, within five (5) working days of the Website Client's notification.

6.6 If such modifications are incorporated satisfactorily to ensure substantial conformity with the Specification or if no modifications are required, the Website Client shall issue a written notice to the Developer confirming that its written approval has been given. If such modifications are not incorporated satisfactorily to ensure substantial conformity with the Specification within the time set out in the Project Plan or specified in this Clause, the Website Client may either:

(a) require the Developer to redeliver the relevant element of the Services or (as the case may be) the final version of the Website as a whole in accordance with this Clause 6.4 and a revised timescale; or

(b) [deem the Developer to have committed a material and irremediable breach of this Agreement and terminate this Agreement in accordance with Clause 11]. [23]

6.7 When the final version of the Website as a whole has been delivered by the Developer and:

(a) the Website Client has issued written confirmation that such final version has been accepted by the Website Client in accordance with Clause 6.4;

23 Alternatively an intermediate step before termination could be included.

(b) the Developer has procured from third parties all waivers in favour of, and all licences of Rights to, the Website Client in compliance with Clause 9 of this Agreement; and

(c) [the Developer has successfully completed the provision of knowledge transfer services and an agreed number of training sessions to the Website Client and Website Partners.] [24]

(together, Final Acceptance). [25]

6.8 Provided always that the Developer has materially complied with the Progress Report and Project Delay provisions in Clauses 4 and 6, the Developer shall not be liable for any failure to provide the Services in accordance with this Agreement to the extent and in so far as it is due to the Website Client failing to provide, or failing to procure that the Website Partners provide, such information and assistance as is necessary, and has been reasonably requested by the Developer, to enable the Developer to provide the Services provided always that the Developer shall ensure that the Website Client is notified immediately of such failure to supply and the Developer acts reasonably and diligently in seeking to mitigate the effect of such failure.

7. [CONTENT AND DATA OBLIGATIONS] [26]

7.1 The Developer shall at all times during the Term remain responsible for the Content [27] and any Material in the Developer's possession or control until its return to the Website Client's possession or its delivery to another location designated by the Website Client in writing or destruction pursuant to the Website Client's specific written instructions. The Developer shall establish and employ at its cost security procedures (providing such further details as the Website Client may reasonably request) sufficient to prevent any theft or unauthorized access, copying, exhibition, transmission or removal of the Content and any Material, and co-operate with the Website Client to implement such additional security measures and policies (including utilizing additional personnel) as the Website Client may reasonably require from time to time.

7.2 The Developer shall not (and shall not permit or authorize any third party to) copy, sub-license, part with possession of, or allow third party access to, the Content and any Material in its possession or control except as necessary to perform applicable obligations under this Agreement, nor remove or modify any burn-in warnings or watermarks included on such materials. The Developer shall:

(a) advise each of its employees, contractors and other individuals under the Developer's control or supervision (in writing) of the criminal and civil liability that may arise by reason of the piracy, theft, unauthorized copying or unauthorized exhibition of such materials;

(b) maintain a record of all employees or contractors who have access to such materials and shall provide such information to the Website Client on request; and

24 This may or may not be required and if important to the Website Client might even be the subject of a separate schedule.

25 Ideally the Website Client is looking to accept a supplier's deliverables only if they are all in accordance with the agreed specification and timetable. Thus even if the first elements of the project were in order, where the later deliverables were unacceptable the Website Client reserves the right to reject the project as a whole as having no economic value ie either the full specification is delivered or it is not. Developers may resist this but the contract does need to set a clear procedure for rejection and/or redelivery.

26 With the Developer having no ongoing role the commitments here may be limited. Obviously if the Developer were providing content administration services or indeed hosting and other operational support these additional services would be included here.

27 Assuming the Developer will have access to valuable Content even without ongoing operational activity, the Website Client would usually want some protection as set out here. There may be the need to include access to a separate Content archive separate from the site and specific back-up procedures.

(c) immediately notify the Website Client by telephone and e-mail or fax of any loss, theft, injury, unauthorized access, copying, distribution or use of such materials. Notwithstanding any other provisions of this Agreement, if such instance occurred in whole or in part due to the Developer's lack of establishment and/or execution of security procedures required by this Agreement, the Developer shall be liable for any and all damages arising from such unauthorized activity. The Developer shall use best efforts, at its cost, to recover or procure the permanent destruction of such materials.

7.3 Notwithstanding the above, the Developer acknowledges that under the Data Protection Act 1998 (the 'Act'), the Website Client is the Data Controller and the Developer is the Data Processor of any Personal Data (as such capitalized terms are defined in the Act) within the Content and the Materials. The Developer shall only process the Personal Data to the extent and in such manner as is necessary for the proper performance of the Services in accordance with this Agreement and the Website Client's instructions from time to time and not for any other purpose. The Developer must comply with any request from the Website Client to correct, amend, transfer or delete the Personal Data. The Developer shall take appropriate technical and organizational measures against the unauthorized or unlawful processing of the Personal Data and against the accidental loss or destruction of, or damage to, the Personal Data. [The Parties will enter into a data controller agreement before execution of this Agreement]; 28

7.4 The Website Client is entitled, on giving at least ten (10) working days notice to the Developer to inspect or appoint representatives to inspect all facilities, equipment, documents and electronic data relating to the processing of the Content and the Materials including any Personal Data by the Developer.

8. ADDITIONAL REQUIREMENTS

8.1 If at any time during the provision of the Services the Website Client decides in its absolute discretion that there is an additional service, document or other deliverable not falling within the specification of the Services or the Deliverables in accordance with this Agreement that the Website Client would like the Developer or one of the Nominated Third Parties to supply (an **Additional Requirement**), then the Website Client shall provide the Developer with a written request specifying the nature of the Additional Requirement and the manner in which, and the timetable within which, the Website Client would like it to be supplied and delivered (a **Change Request**). Within ten (10) working days of receipt by the Developer of any Change Request (or within such time limit as the Developer may request and to which the Website Client gives its consent (such consent not to be unreasonably withheld or delayed) where the Developer requires more time to undertake a more detailed analysis of such

28 Again some data protection provisions will be needed as a minimum if there is any potential access provided to personal data. With an ongoing role the Developer and Website Client probably ought to execute a separate data controller agreement—perhaps attached as a schedule.

Change Request) it shall provide to the Website Client a written document setting out:

(a) the cost of supply of the Additional Requirement (an **Additional Fee**), the time frame in which the Additional Requirement could be supplied and details of who would supply such Additional Requirement along with any other information reasonably requested by the Website Client in its Change Request which is relevant to the Additional Requirement including the Rights ownership and/or licensing terms for its supply (a **Change Quote**); or

(b) rejection of the opportunity to perform the services in the Change Request or, where possible, changes to the Additional Requirement that the Website Client may wish to consider so as to enable the Developer to deliver the Additional Requirement in accordance with (so far as possible) the Change Request (a **Change Rejection**); or

(c) a request for further information regarding the Change Request (provided the Developer has not previously made such a request) to which the Website Client may respond within a reasonable period by re-submitting the Change Request with additional information to be re-considered on the terms of this Clause 8.1.

8.2 Within ten (10) working days of receiving a Change Quote the Website Client shall provide the Developer with a written notice either:

(a) confirming that the Additional Requirement is required subject to and in accordance with the provisions of this Agreement and at the level of Additional Fee specified in the Change Quote, and if the Website Client so wishes imposing further conditions as may he agreed by the Developer on the delivery of the Additional Requirement; or

(b) indicating that the Website Client does not wish to pursue the Additional Requirement.

8.3 Following receipt of a Change Rejection in respect of any Additional Requirement, the Website Client shall not be entitled to require the Developer to supply such Additional Requirement in accordance with its original Change Request unless it modifies such Change Request and repeats the process described in Clause 8.1 in relation to such modified Change Request.

8.4 Following receipt by the Developer of a notice of acceptance of a Change Quote from the Website Client in accordance with Clause 8.2(a), the Developer shall proceed to deliver the relevant Additional Requirement in accordance with the timetable, budget, specification and Rights terms set out in the Change Quote relating to such Additional Requirement.

9. INTELLECTUAL PROPERTY [29]

9.1 Subject to Clauses 9.3, 9.4 and 9.5, the Developer hereby assigns absolutely and irrevocably to the Website Client (where relevant by present assignment of future rights) with full title guarantee all Rights in and to the Deliverables throughout the world absolutely for the full period or periods of protection conferred by law including all renewals, extensions and revivals of such period(s).

9.2 The Developer hereby undertakes to procure in favour of the Website Client the irrevocable and unconditional waiver of all rights relating to the Deliverables to which any person is or are now or may in the future be entitled pursuant to the provisions of Sections 77, 80, 84 and 85 of the Copyright Designs and Patents Act 1988 and, in so far as and to the extent permitted by law, any other so-called moral rights or analogous rights to which any person may be entitled in any part of the world and all other permissions and consents necessary in so far as and to the extent permitted by law for the Website Client's unrestricted use of the Deliverables throughout the world in any and all media (whether now known or hereafter invented) at no cost to the Website Client.

9.3 [All the Developer's pre-existing and intangible skills and know-how shall remain the property of the Developer but the Developer hereby grants to the Website Client a non-exclusive irrevocable licence, throughout the world and in perpetuity (to the fullest extent permitted by law), of all Rights in such Developer know-how to the extent necessary for the Website Client's unrestricted use of the Deliverables in the operation and exploitation of the Website throughout the world at no cost to the Website Client.] [30]

9.4 The Developer has identified in the Specification (and shall in any Change Quote accepted by the Website Client) any third party Rights in the Deliverables (including in any material produced and/or provided by the Nominated Third Parties) which the Developer cannot assign to the Website Client under Clause 9.1 and the Developer shall procure that the Website Client is granted by the owners of such third party Rights a non-exclusive irrevocable licence, in perpetuity (to the fullest extent permitted by law), of all such third party Rights to the extent necessary for the Website Client's unrestricted use of the Deliverables in the operation and exploitation of the Website throughout the world at no cost to the Website Client.

9.5 For the avoidance of doubt the assignment in Clause 9.1 and the waiver in Clause 9.2 only extends to the Deliverables and therefore not to the non-bespoke elements of the Platform as such elements are identified in the Specification (and in any Change Quote accepted by the Website Client). The Developer hereby grants to the Website Client a non-exclusive irrevocable worldwide licence, with effect from the final day of the Term and continuing

29 The starting point for the lawyer is to discuss the specification with the Website Client's technical and commercial team to try to identify all relevant elements, hopefully without descending into too much technical detail. The aim is to agree on which items to take a strong line over ownership and use rights and which the Website Client can be more relaxed about. The developer cannot be expected to offer ownership in major third party software components (and while licences might be easy to obtain in such elements, competitive fees from suppliers re-selling in bulk may not) and it is not unreasonable for it to seek to protect its right to re-use know-how, provided this does not allow wholesale repetition. This clause sets out a model where bespoke items are assigned to the Website Client but the proprietary platform is retained by the Developer.

30 Developers will usually push hard for such a clause—although further definition of 'know-how' may well be necessary.

thereafter in perpetuity to the fullest extent permitted by law, of all Rights owned by the Developer in those elements to the extent necessary for the Website Client's unrestricted use of the Platform in the operation and exploitation of the Website at no cost to the Website Client. [31]

9.6 The Developer agrees and acknowledges that, as between the Parties, the Website Client is the owner of all Rights in:

(a) the Website Client Marks;
(b) the Content;
(c) the Style Guidelines;
(d) the Data;
(e) any domain names or equivalent identifiers used for the Website; and
(f) any other materials created or supplied by or on behalf of the Website Client in connection with the Website;

(together, the **Material**). The Website Client hereby grants to the Developer during the Term a non-exclusive licence (at no cost to the Developer) of the Rights in and to the Material and the Rights in and to the Deliverables assigned to the Website Client in Clause 9.1, and the Developer undertakes not to use or authorize any third party to use any of the Material or the Deliverables other than, to the extent and for so long as is reasonably necessary for the performance of the Developer's obligations under this Agreement. The Developer undertakes to comply with all such guidelines for the usage of the Website Client Marks and any other Material as are issued by the Website Client or its licensors from time to time and which are notified to the Developer. All goodwill arising from such use shall accrue to the Website Client and Section 30(2) of the Trade Marks Act 1994 is expressly excluded by the parties.

9.7 The Developer shall at no cost to the Website Client promptly provide to the Website Client a complete, accurate and up-to-date copy of the Deliverables (including any source code) upon (a) the approval of each element of the Deliverables in accordance with Clause 6, (b) the creation of any enhancement or amendment of any such element and (c) any termination of this Agreement. The Developer shall at no cost to the Website Client procure that a complete, accurate and up-to-date copy of the source code and development notes for the elements of the Platform are at all times during the Term lodged in escrow with such escrow agent as is reasonably approved by the Website Client on terms subject to the reasonable approval of the Website Client including provision for the release of the lodged materials if the events set out in Clause 11.2(d) to (g) are suffered by the Developer or the Website Client terminates this Agreement for any reason pursuant to Clause 11.2. [32]

31 There may be further practical limitations here eg if open source software is used or third party licences are required.

32 The Website Client will need some protection against the Developer not being around—for whatever reason: insolvency, breach, force majeure. The more involved and ongoing the role of the Developer the more important this becomes perhaps requiring a detailed the continuity plan attached as a schedule.

10. FINANCIAL TERMS [33]

10.1 Subject to and in consideration of the provision by the Developer of the Services in accordance with the terms and conditions of this Agreement and the assignment and grant of Rights to the Website Client under Clause 9, the Website Client shall pay to the Developer the Charges adjusted to reflect any service credits applicable pursuant to the provisions of Schedule 1.

10.2 Subject to the proper performance of this Agreement by the Developer, and subject to any bona fide dispute regarding the amounts shown, the Charges shall be payable on the dates and in the instalments as set out in Schedule 8 on the receipt by the Website Client of an appropriate VAT invoice.

10.3 Unless any Additional Fees become payable by the Website Client to the Developer in accordance with the provisions of Clause 8, no further costs or fees shall be payable to the Developer under this Agreement.

10.4 The Charges and any Additional Fees are exclusive of and subject to the addition of VAT at the rate from time to time in force but are inclusive of party and all fees which may be required to be paid by the Developer to any third party in connection with this Agreement and/or the provision of the Services.

11. TERMINATION

11.1 This Agreement shall commence on the Start Date and continue in force until [ ] [34] subject always to any earlier termination in accordance with the provisions of Clause 7.2 or this Clause 11 (the **Term**).

11.2 In addition to (and not in substitution for) any other right or remedy, either party may terminate this Agreement immediately by notice in writing to the other if:

(a) the other commits any breach of any material term of this Agreement which if capable of remedy it fails to remedy within five (5) working days of receiving written notice from the terminating party requiring such remedy;

(b) the other commits any irremediable breach of any material term of this Agreement or repeats any breach of any material term which has previously been the subject of a notice under Clause 11.2(a) above;

(c) the other is precluded by a force majeure event in accordance with Clause 16 from performing its obligations for a period in excess of ten (10) working days;

(d) any meeting of creditors of the other party is held or any arrangement or composition with or for the benefit of its creditors (including any voluntary arrangement as defined in the Insolvency Acts 1986 and 2000) is proposed or entered into by or in relation to the other party;

33 As discussed in the Introduction, the Website Client will normally break the project down into several delivery milestones to ensure that the Developer is on the right track throughout the project. Ideally the Website Client should avoid paying on each delivery milestone (both for cash-flow and to avoid arguments over partial acceptance) or at least weight payments toward final acceptance with perhaps some upfront payment as a sign of goodwill. The Developer will, of course, often seek quite the reverse. What is important, however payment is split, is that where the Website Client establishes a right to reject all the deliverables, even if only some parts were not in order, it will then be repaid/have no liability for payment, in addition to any further rights it may have, if it rejects the whole project.

34 The end of the contract may vary according to delivery so this may simply reference 'proper delivery of the Services' rather than a specific date.

(e) a supervisor, receiver, administrator, administrative receiver or other encumbrancer takes possession of or is appointed over or any distress, execution or other process is levied or enforced (and is not discharged within five working days) upon the whole or any substantial part of the assets of the other party;

(f) the other party ceases or threatens to cease to carry on business or is or becomes unable to pay its debts within the meaning of Section 123 of the Insolvency Act 1986; or

(g) a petition is presented, or a meeting or a court hearing is convened for the purpose of considering a resolution or application, for the making of an administration order in respect of or for the winding-up, bankruptcy or dissolution of, the other party.

11.3 On termination of this Agreement the Developer shall immediately: [35]

(a) deliver to the Website Client the latest version of the Deliverables in accordance with Clause 9.8;

(b) cease any further use of the Deliverables except as specifically directed by the Website Client to allow for the orderly transfer of the operation of the Website;

(c) having complied with (a) above, at the Website Clients election destroy or deliver to the Website Client or as the Website Client directs all copies of the Deliverables and the Material in the Developer's possession or control at the date of termination; and

(d) provide all reasonable assistance which may be required for the orderly transfer of the operation of the Website and which the Website Client may request;

and the Developer shall cease to be entitled to any further payment from the Website Client under this Agreement provided that the Website Client shall remain under an obligation to pay any moneys properly due under this Agreement up to and including the date of termination subject always to the Developer refunding (on a pro rata basis where relevant) any element of the Charges which have been paid in advance by the Website Client but which should remain unspent at the date of termination in accordance with the production budget in Schedule 1.

11.4 Termination of this Agreement shall be without prejudice to any other rights or remedies to which a party may be entitled under this Agreement or at law as a result of or in relation to any breach or other event which gives rise to such termination, and shall not affect any other accrued rights or liabilities of either party as at the date of termination.

11.5 Clauses [1, 11.3, 11.4, 11.5, 18, 20, 23 and 24] shall survive the termination of this Agreement.

35 Obviously both rights and physical access need to be safeguarded—see note 32 above.

12. SUB-CONTRACTORS

If the Website Client provides its written consent to the Developer in respect of any sub-contractor in accordance with Clause 2.2 of this Agreement, such written consent shall be given, and shall at all times remain, subject to the following terms and conditions and the Developer shall:

(a) at all times remain liable for the performance of its obligations under this Agreement and the engagement of a sub-contractor shall not in any way relieve the Developer from such liability;
(b) indemnify the Website Client in respect of any claims, costs, expenses, damages and/or losses (including reasonable legal fees) incurred or suffered by the Website Client as a result of any act or omission of the sub-contractor and/or as a result of any circumstance(s) affecting the sub-contactor which has or have an adverse effect on the provision of the Services; and
(c) procure that such sub-contractor complies, where appropriate, with the terms of this Agreement.

13. WARRANTIES AND UNDERTAKINGS [36]

13.1 The Developer hereby warrants and undertakes with and to the Website Client that:

(a) the Developer shall ensure that all the Services and the Deliverables are provided, produced and delivered in compliance with the Style Guidelines, the Specification, the Project Plan and other terms and conditions contained in this Agreement, with reasonable diligence, skill and care by competent personnel with appropriate levels of experience for the tasks which they are required to perform, to the best of its ability and in a professional, lawful and timely manner;
(b) the Developer is wholly free to enter into and perform its obligations under this Agreement and its performance hereunder shall not be impaired, restricted or interfered with by any other contract or obligations it may have or by any outstanding litigation or dispute in which it or any of its personnel is or are involved;
(c) the Developer is or shall be the owner of the Rights assigned or licensed to the Website Client by the Developer, has or shall obtain prior to inclusion in the Website all releases, licences and consents (at its cost) necessary for the provision and use of the Deliverables in accordance with the terms and conditions of this Agreement which shall in no way whatever be a violation or infringement of any third party Rights, right of privacy or publicity and shall not be obscene, libellous or defamatory or otherwise illegal or unlawful and shall not in any way inhibit, restrict or impair the free and/or unrestricted operation or exploitation of the Website or any other exercise by the Website Client of the Rights assigned or granted to it in this Agreement;

36 As usual warranties and indemnities need to give comfort to the Website Client as to the Developer's right to assign, license and supply the Deliverables; in particular, to make clear which elements if any the supplier is expecting the Client to clear itself. There may of course be other additional warranties added to this —or indeed any of the agreements featured (particularly the longer form contracts)—whether specific to a particular deal or a particular jurisdiction and as relevant legal and regulatory changes develop. One general example in the UK is in relation to anti-corruption law. The Bribery Act 2010 received Royal Assent in April 2010 and will come into force in April 2011. It replaces existing laws with a comprehensive code, comprising a number of offences: a general offence of paying and receiving a bribe, particular offences of bribing foreign officials, and the failure of a commercial organization to prevent bribery. Some commentators have suggested that while the Act may change little from an individual's perspective, it puts significant pressure on companies to ensure that they install appropriate anti-corruption rules.

(d) the Deliverables shall comply with all applicable laws and regulations including those relating to e-commerce, accessibility and consumer protection; [37]

(e) the Developer shall comply with the content and the principles of the Data Protection Act 1998 and any subsequent or associated legislation or regulations regarding personal data including those requirements relating to data security and shall provide the Services, and only use the Data, in accordance with the Website Client's instructions and Clause 7; and

(f) the provision of the Services shall be free from any Virus. [38]

13.2 The Website Client warrants and undertakes that:

(a) the Website Client is wholly free to enter into and perform its obligations under this Agreement and its performance hereunder shall not be impaired, restricted or interfered with by any other contract or obligations it may have or by any outstanding litigation or dispute in which it or any of its personnel are involved; and

(b) the Website Client has or shall obtain all licences and consents necessary for the use of the Content, the Materials and the Website Client Marks and all other materials provided to the Developer by the Website Client (or those authorized by it) in the provision of the Services in accordance with the terms and conditions of this Agreement and that such use shall in no way whatever be a violation or infringement of any third party Rights, right of privacy or publicity and shall not be obscene, libellous or defamatory or otherwise unlawful; and

(c) the Website Client shall comply with the content and the principles of the Data Protection Act 1998 and any subsequent or associated legislation or regulations regarding personal data including those requirements relating to data security.

14. INDEMNITY

14.1 Each party shall indemnify and hold harmless the other party (the **Indemnified Party**) against all third party claims, actions, proceedings, losses, damage, injury, costs or expenses suffered or incurred by the Indemnified Party, and against a final award of damages made against the Indemnified Party by a court of competent jurisdiction, as a result of any breach of any of its obligations, warranties and/or undertakings contained in this Agreement provided that the Indemnified Party complies with Clause 14.2 below.

14.2 The Indemnified Party shall:

(a) notify the other party if any claim or action by a third party is made or threatened against the Indemnified Party to which the other party's indemnity under Clause 14.1 is likely to extend; and

37 Developers are often wary of wide commitments but it is not unreasonable to seek comfort on relevant legal and regulatory requirements. Often these issues, especially accessibility, are dealt with at Specification level.

38 Developer may only be willing to commit to the use of industry-standard protection.

(b) make no admission nor attempt to settle or compromise any such claim or action without the other party's consent.

14.3 Nothing in this Agreement shall be deemed to limit or restrict the liability of any party hereto for death or personal injury caused by the negligence of the other or for liability arising from a party's fraud or any other illegal act.

14.4 Subject to Clause 14.3 no party shall be liable under this Agreement for any special, punitive, indirect or consequential losses whatsoever provided that this shall not exclude or limit the Website Client's right to claim under the indemnity in Clause 14.1 or otherwise to claim under this Agreement for any of the following which result from a breach by the Developer:

(a) additional operational costs and expenses which would not otherwise have been incurred by the Website Client;
(b) expenditure or charges paid by the Website Client which would not otherwise have been incurred or would have ceased or would not have occurred;
(c) costs, expenses and charges resulting from the loss or corruption of the data or software owned by or under the control of the Website Client. In the case of data or software which can be recovered or reconstituted, liability shall be limited to costs, expenses and charges associated with reconstituting of the data or software and returning it to a fully operational state, but shall not otherwise be limited; or
(d) infringement of any Rights or breach of any obligations of confidence.

14,5 Subject to Clause 14.4 the liability of the Developer to the Website Client except under the indemnity in Clause 14.1, and the liability of the Website Client to the Developer, for loss or damage occasioned to the other arising out of or in connection with this Agreement (inclusive of costs and expenses incurred) shall not exceed [ ]. 39

15. DISPUTE RESOLUTION

15.1 If there is a dispute between the parties in relation to any matter arising from or in connection with this Agreement, then the parties agree to follow the procedures set out in this Clause as follows:

(a) if a party reasonably believes that there is a dispute which has not been resolved at an operational level, then that party (for the purposes of this Clause known as the **Escalating Party**) shall bring the existence of such dispute to the attention of the Escalating Party's Project Manager as identified in Clause 3 of this Agreement;
(b) having been notified of the dispute, the Escalating Party's Project Manager shall provide written notice setting out all the details of the alleged dispute to the other party (the **Recipient Party**)'s Project Manager to enable adequate consideration of the dispute;

39 The liability position will always be subject to discussion and negotiation but here the Website Client is looking for broad protection subject to an overall limit—probably in practice linked to the insurance position of the Developer, which might then be set out expressly too.

(c) following receipt by the Recipient Party of the notice of dispute from the Escalating Party, the Project Managers of both parties shall meet and shall use their reasonable endeavours to resolve the dispute within three (3) working days of the date of receipt of the notice of dispute;

(d) if that the dispute is still unresolved after three (3) working days, each party shall on the fourth working day following receipt of the dispute notice by the Recipient Party inform its chief executive of the existence of the dispute and provide them with sufficient detail to enable them to give proper consideration to the dispute;

(e) the chief executive of each party shall then meet and shall use their reasonable endeavours to resolve the dispute within seven (7) working days from the date on which they are informed of the existence of the dispute by their respective Project Managers or such longer period as may be agreed.

15.2 If such dispute has not been satisfactorily resolved after the parties have followed the procedures set out in Clause 15.1 above or, notwithstanding the provisions of Clause 15.1(e) above, in any event within a period of five (5) working days (prior to Final Acceptance) or twenty (20) working days (after Final Acceptance) from the date of receipt by the Recipient Party of the notice of dispute, either party may, subject to the terms and conditions contained in this Agreement, enforce any right or pursue any remedy it may have at law or in equity.

16. FORCE MAJEURE

Neither party shall be liable to the other if it is unable to perform or is delayed in performing its obligations under this Agreement due to circumstances over which it has no control (such as extremes of weather or nature, government action, war, terrorism, civil unrest or act of God but excluding default of its Developers or contractors and provided that:

(a) it takes all practical and appropriate steps to minimize the impact of and to overcome those circumstances;

(b) it gives the other party immediate written notice of the circumstances and the steps it is taking under (a) and otherwise complies with the reporting and project management provisions of this Agreement; and

(c) any payment obligation of the other party shall be suspended and if such circumstances prevents performance for a period of more than ten (10) working days, the other party may terminate this Agreement by giving immediate written notice to the party unable to perform (for the avoidance of doubt, where the Developer is the affected party, the Website Client shall be free at all times to seek alternative supply of the Services).

17. FURTHER ASSURANCES

The Developer undertakes that it shall at its own cost and at the Website Client's reasonable request do all such acts and execute such further documents as may be necessary to give effect to the terms of this Agreement.

18. CONFIDENTIALITY

18.1 Each party undertakes to the other that, subject to Clause 18.2 below, it will treat as confidential the terms of this Agreement together with all information whether of a technical nature or otherwise relating in any manner to the business or affairs of the other party as may be communicated to it hereunder or otherwise in connection with this Agreement and will not disclose such information to any person, firm or company (other than to its associated companies, auditors and other professional advisers, shareholders and funders) or to the media and will not use such information other than for the purposes of this Agreement subject always to any proper specific authorization in writing by the disclosing party to such disclosure or use.

18.2 The provisions of Clause 18.1 above shall not apply to any information which:

(a) is in the public domain other than by default of the recipient party;
(b) is obtained by the recipient party from a bona fide third party having no apparent restraint on its free right of disposal of such information; or
(c) is required to be disclosed by law (or applicable regulation) or the valid order of a court of competent jurisdiction, or the request or direction of any governmental or other regulatory authority or agency.

19. NOTICES

Any notice to he given hereunder shall be duly given if:

(a) delivered personally;
(b) mailed by first-class pre-paid mail to the address stated in this Agreement of the party to be served which notices shall be deemed to have arrived in the ordinary course of post; or
(c) sent by facsimile to the addressee's number notified to the sender by the addressee or (if not so notified) recorded in any official index of facsimile numbers which notices shall be deemed to have arrived on the date of transmission if sent not later than one hour before close of business on a business day or otherwise on the next business day and provided that the sender does not within 24 hours after sending such notice receive any indication that the message is incomprehensible.

20. ANNOUNCEMENTS AND MARKETING

Neither party to this Agreement shall make any public announcement, press release or other external communication in relation to the existence or contents of, or the Developer's appointment under, this Agreement without the prior written consent of the other party to the text and content of any such announcement, release or communication save and except that the Developer shall be permitted to:

(a) refer to the Developer's appointment under this Agreement in marketing materials in accordance with such guidelines as the Website Client may issue from time to time; and
(b) issue to the public on or after the date of signature of this Agreement a press release in the form previously agreed to in writing by the Website Client.

21. NO ASSIGNMENT

The Developer shall not have the right to assign or (save as expressly contemplated in, and in compliance with, Clauses 2 and 12 of this Agreement) sub-license the benefit of or subcontract any of the obligations under this Agreement (or any part thereof) without the prior written consent of the Website Client, which may be given or withheld in its absolute discretion. The Developer may assign or grant all or any part of its rights pursuant to this Agreement to any person who is, and for so long as such person remains, an Associated Company of the Developer provided that no such assignment or grant shall relieve the Developer of any of its obligations under this Agreement.

22. SEVERABILITY

If any provision of this Agreement shall he adjudged by a Court of competent jurisdiction to be unlawful, void or unenforceable, such provision shall to the extent required be severed from this Agreement and rendered ineffective as far as possible without modifying the remaining provisions of this Agreement and shall not in any way affect the validity or enforceability of this Agreement.

23. GENERAL

23.1 A waiver by either party of any of the terms or conditions of this Agreement in any instance shall not be deemed or construed to be a waiver of such term or condition for the future, or of any subsequent breach thereof. All remedies, rights, undertakings, obligations and agreements contained in this Agreement shall be cumulative and none of them shall be in limitation of any other remedy, right, undertaking, obligation or agreement of either party.

23.2 This Agreement constitutes the entire agreement between the Developer and the Website Client with respect to the subject matter herein contained. This Agreement cannot be changed or terminated orally, and no changes or amendments to this Agreement shall (save as provided in Clause 8) be binding upon the parties until accepted in writing by a duly authorized representative of both parties.

23.3 No terms, obligations, representations, promises or conditions oral or written, express or implied, have been made or relied upon by either party other than those expressly contained herein. For the avoidance of doubt, each party irrevocably waives any right it may have to seek a remedy for:

(a) any misrepresentation which has not become a term of this Agreement; or
(b) any breach of warranty or undertaking (other than those expressly contained in this Agreement) whether express or implied, statutory or otherwise;

unless such misrepresentation, warranty or undertaking was made fraudulently.

23.4 A person who is not a party to this Agreement has no right under the Contracts (Rights of Third Parties) Act 1999 to enforce the benefit of any term of this Agreement and to the extent permitted by law the parties hereby exclude the application of such Act to this Agreement.

23.5 Nothing contained in this Agreement shall in any way create any association, partnership, joint venture or the relationship of principal and agent between the parties hereto or be construed as evidencing the intention of the parties to constitute such a relationship.

24. GOVERNING LAW AND JURISDICTION

This Agreement shall be governed by and construed in all respects in accordance with English law and the parties agree to submit to the non-exclusive jurisdiction of the English Courts as regards any claim or matter arising in relation to this Agreement.

Schedule 1—The Charges

Schedule 2—Key Team Members

Schedule 3—Nominated Third Parties

Schedule 4—Progress Report

Schedule 5—Project Plan

Schedule 6—Specification

Schedule 7—Style Guidelines

Schedule 8—Website Client Marks

A8

HOSTING AGREEMENT

Introduction

All talk of cyberspace, virtual worlds and 'the cloud' for a lawyer is, ultimately, an illusion. Somewhere there is a computer or set of computers sitting in the real world hosting and operating the digital service in question. This has two important legal consequences.

The contractual arrangements for the provision of those computers and the associated services needed to link them to the Internet or to any other distribution network are vital. The service levels of that service are dependent on this contract; and whatever questions might arise as to how digital media services can be regulated—in particular the jurisdictional issues that arise when a service is received or has other connections across a range of territories—the physical presence of these host computers clearly falls within the jurisdiction of the territory in which they are located. That territory's laws, and their ability to regulate, control, gain access and otherwise monitor the server, will certainly apply (see the Introduction).

So the selection and operation of the servers hosting and delivering any digital media service is key. Obviously for many entities that selection process will merely involve the identification of the nearest and cheapest option. But for others it is a more complex consideration linked to the jurisdiction of the operational entity. Online gambling operations locate in certain territories to benefit from offshore licensing regimes. A key consideration for those regimes is tax. Tax considerations are also relevant for many other services; for example, many operators in the EU select Luxembourg as their base as it currently has the lowest VAT rates. We have worked with other clients, selecting territories on the regimes for data retention and liability for hosting content of third parties.

This 'regulatory arbitrage' that international operators now look to benefit from will be reflected in the contractual arrangements they put in place with their suppliers and in particular the party providing hosting and operational services. This chapter focuses on that hosting contract. The reality for most digital media companies is that they will not draft their own hosting agreements. They will be presented with the terms of service of the provider or providers they select. Even bigger players with more negotiating clout may still work from the documents of their supplier. Accordingly we have presented here a sample agreement that should reflect the type of document that is likely to be used. It is a generic document and as such is simplified without the detail used by specific suppliers; but it should give a sense of what to expect.

In very simple terms to get a website online its owner (here, 'the Customer') has a range of options. For a small website the Customer might simply rent a certain amount of server space as any individual user may. A more serious website might be allocated to a specific server at a carefully selected site. Equipment may or may not be provided by the Customer and the supplier may offer different levels of support from full managed hosting to mere 'remote hands' button pushing. Alternatively the Customer may consider it more appropriate to develop and operate at least some of the necessary facilities in-house and obtain connectivity between its own premises and the supplier's network. The commercial reality is that service providers will be keen to sell additional services, such as security protection, to a Customer wherever possible.

SERVICES

The services will vary:

- provision of site to host equipment
- provision of access to the Internet and telecoms services
- provision of equipment
- maintenance services
- provision of equipment and services at the customer's sites
- security services
- special services, eg e-commerce or cloud computing.

The services may be defined in great detail with the technical specification and specific contractual terms effectively forming an agreement in itself—see the Service Order Form concept in the document below.

The service provider host will usually be keen to make clear what does not fall within its responsibility. The room for negotiation, especially where an individual Customer requires only capacity for a single website, may often be limited. Where a Customer is looking to develop a major online presence it may be able to improve upon those standard terms. Larger service providers will usually be better placed to host bigger, more sophisticated websites and offer better functionality, support and performance on an international basis. The larger service providers actually own the telecommunications infrastructure (the backbone, which is often leased to the smaller providers—like wholesaler to retailer) and have the capacity to establish the large-scale operations needed for international digital media services. They are more able to invest in the necessary bandwidth and interconnection arrangements to establish and offer high performance services.

Whilst it is fair to say that the supplier should not be responsible for those parts of the Internet outside its control, there is no reason a supplier should not be liable for the performance of its own systems. Service Providers will also seek to limit or restrict liability extensively, which the Customer may have to reflect in its own end-user agreements, in so far as it can when, for instance, dealing with consumers. It is very important that the Customer should discuss performance guarantees with the supplier. Issues to consider include:

- **Stability**—What and when are the scheduled/unscheduled server down-times?
- **Scalability**—How many users accessing the website can the server support and how is performance affected?
- **Usability**—What response times will users experience when accessing or searching the website and how will that vary?
- **Statistics**—What reporting information on access and use will the Customer receive?

Suppliers may be reluctant to offer much in the way of service guarantees if the Customer is only buying a small amount of server space and connectivity, and they may also be concerned that heavy traffic levels to the Customer's website might affect the performance of the rest of their service. The Customer must be prepared to negotiate and suggest their own service level agreement and reporting mechanism (see Chapter A9). What happens on termination or if the service provider is prevented from continuing to perform is important—how the transfer from one supplier to another is to be handled should if possible be agreed in a specific exit plan.

Some service providers may offer particular services geared toward e-commerce and the use of websites for online sales, pay-per-views and other transactions. They may also seek to charge on a per-transaction basis. (The service provider may then also have the necessary financial elements in place, eg accounts set up with selected financial institutions or it may be left to the Customer to establish that separately.) There are of course a range of contractual, consumer and sales law issues to be considered with e-commerce and any compliance requirements resulting from them, eg incorporation of terms, transaction and fulfilment procedures, merchant agreements, data protection notices, etc need to be considered during the implementation process—and not as an afterthought.

Hosting Agreement

BIG HOSTING COMPANY

BHC HQ, BHC Business Park, New City 10035

MASTER SERVICES AGREEMENT [1]

MSA Contract Date		MSA Contract Number	

Customer Name	
Customer Address	
Customer Billing Address	
Customer Account Manager	Name: Phone: Fax: Email:
Customer Technical Contact	Name: Phone: Fax: Email:

Big Hosting Company Account Manager	Name: Phone: Fax: Email:
Big Hosting Company Technical Contact	Name: Phone: Fax: Email:

1 Most of the larger suppliers use the format set out here. A main set of terms—a master services agreement—under which specific services are agreed in specific Service Order Forms. The order forms may set out further provisions that vary the main terms and care is often needed to ensure that negotiated provisions in the main terms are not overridden by the specifics. Generally the Service Order Forms will take precedence unless otherwise agreed. The terms are unashamedly protecting the service provider and the Customer should be willing to negotiate over the standard terms or agree specific protections in each Service Order Form.

THE PARTIES HEREBY AGREE that they have read the attached **Master Services Agreement Terms & Conditions** (the **MSA T&Cs**) and the documents referred to in the MSA T&Cs including:

- **Appendix 1—Acceptable Use Policy** 2
- **Appendix 2—Data Protection & Privacy Policy** 3 **and**
- **Appendix 3—Service Level Agreement** 4

along with the provisions of each **Service Order Form** accepted by Big Hosting Company (together, the **Agreement**) and by signing below they agree to be bound by the terms of the Agreement.

ACCEPTED BY CUSTOMER:	
Name and Title	
Signature	
Date	

ACCEPTED BY BIG HOSTING COMPANY:	
Name and Title	
Signature	
Date	

BIG HOSTING COMPANY

MASTER SERVICES AGREEMENT TERMS AND CONDITIONS

v.101 dated 01.10

TOGETHER WITH THE SERVICE ORDERFORM(S) ACCEPTED BY BIG HOSTING COMPANY THESE MSA T&CS INCLUDING THE DOCUMENTS REFERRED TO IN THESE MSA T&CS SET OUT THE BASIS UNDER WHICH BIG HOSTING COMPANY SHALL PROVIDE THE SERVICES (AS DEFINED BELOW) TO THE CUSTOMER IDENTIFIED IN THE ATTACHED FRONT SCHEDULE.

1. DEFINITIONS AND INTERPRETATION

1.1 In the MSA T&Cs the following words and phrases shall have the following meanings, unless the context otherwise requires:

2 The Customer must expect the service provider to be concerned about its liability for the Customer content that it is hosting. The obligations of the Customer will usually be set out in an 'acceptable use policy'. This always needs careful review—in essence how wide is the definition of 'acceptable use': clearly illegal material or anything that is 'unsuitable' and in whose opinion is non-acceptability judged? The Customer will want to know in what circumstance the service provider can block access to the content and provide information to third parties.

3 Data protection and privacy issues may be covered in the acceptable use policy or set out in a separate policy. The Customer will in any case want to ensure that the agreement deals appropriately with the obligations of the service provider as the Customer's data processor to ensure the Customer's compliance with data protection law (see data protection provisions in Chapter A7).

4 The service level agreement will be a key aspect of the contract and the operational document that the technical teams must take a role in negotiating (see Chapter A9).

Acceptable Use Policy means the Big Hosting Company policy set out in Appendix 1 as amended from time to time;

Charges means the set-up fees, network charges, rental fees and/or other charges payable in respect of the Services and set out in each Service Order Form as amended from time to time in accordance with Clause 6.1;

Customer Equipment means the hardware, software, facilities, systems, cabling and other equipment provided by or on behalf of the Customer for the purposes of receiving the Services;

Customer Premises means the locations identified in the relevant Service Order Form;

Data Protection and Privacy Policy means the Big Hosting Company policy set out in Appendix 2 as amended from time to time;

Equipment means the hardware, software, facilities, systems, cabling and other equipment provided by or on behalf of Big Hosting Company for the purposes of delivering the Services;

IPR means patents, petty patents, utility models, rights in trade secrets and other confidential or undisclosed information such as inventions or know-how, registered and unregistered designs, copyright including authors' and neighbouring or related rights, database rights, trade and service marks, business and trade names, branding, get-up, logos, domain names, URLs and equivalent identifiers, rights in unfair competition and rights to sue for passing off and all rights having equivalent or similar effect to, and all registrations or applications and the right to apply to register, any of the preceding items referred to in this definition in any jurisdiction for the full period of protection and all renewals, revivals, reversions and extensions;

Network means the telecoms services and systems owned, operated or provided by or on behalf of Big Hosting Company for the purposes of delivering the Services including Internet points of presence, exchanges and network hubs;

Services means the particular services to be provided by Big Hosting Company to the Customer as set out in each Service Order Form to facilitate the operation of the Customer's Internet website(s) or other applications and/or the provision of other telecoms products and services;

Service Level Agreement means the Big Hosting Company service level agreement set out in Appendix 3 as amended from time to time;

Service Order Form means a specific order for services requested by the Customer and accepted by Big Hosting Company;

Service Period means the period for which a Service will be provided to the Customer by Big Hosting Company as set out in its applicable Service Order Form; and

Service Start Date has the meaning set out in Clause 3.2.

1.2 In these MSA T&Cs words in the singular shall include the plural and vice versa; the headings are for convenience only and shall not affect

interpretation; references to *Clauses* and *Appendices* relate to these MSA T&Cs; references to a *person* include an individual, firm, government body or authority, unincorporated association or body corporate; reference to a *Party* is to a party set out in the attached Front Schedule and reference to *including* or *include* shall not be construed to limit the sense of the preceding words.

2. SERVICE ORDER FORMS

2.1 Each Service Order Form shall constitute a separate contract between the Parties for the provision of the applicable Services from the Service Start Date for the Service Period in accordance with these MSA T&Cs and the specific provisions of that Service Order Form. If there is any conflict or inconsistency between the Service Order Form and these MSA T&Cs the Service Order Form shall take priority.

2.2 Each Service Order Form must be in such written form as is authorized from time to time by Big Hosting Company and shall be binding on the Parties only after acceptance in writing by Big Hosting Company.

2.3 Big Hosting Company reserves the right at all times without notice to: (a) sub-contract the performance of any of its obligations hereunder to its Group Companies or to any other persons; and (b) reconfigure, replace, alter or amend any element of the Equipment or the Network; provided this does not impact materially on the Services. [5]

2.4 Big Hosting Company shall use reasonable endeavours to ensure that each of the Services will conform to the Service Level Agreement any service descriptions and/or service levels as set out, or referred to, in the applicable Service Order and/or any applicable ancillary service level agreement. [6]

3. TESTING

3.1 Big Hosting Company (and/or any other person it may nominate) shall carry out such tests as appear reasonable or necessary to confirm the successful completion of any preparatory work before the provision of any Services and shall issue a ready-for-service notice to the Customer in writing when such tests have been passed.

3.2 Customer shall be deemed to have accepted the Services on receipt of the above ready-for-service notice or the date the Customer first uses the Services (the **Service Start Date**). [7]

4. SERVICE LEVELS

4.1 The remedies set out in the Service Level Agreement or any applicable Service Order Form shall be the sole and exclusive remedy of Customer, and Big Hosting Company's entire liability, for a failure to meet the Service Level Agreement or any service-specific service levels set out in any applicable Service Order Form.

4.2 Big Hosting Company may immediately suspend any or all of the Services if any of the suspension trigger events set out in the Service Level Agreement or in any applicable Service Order Form occur at any time. Big Hosting Company shall endeavour to provide prior notice of such suspension to Customer. Customer shall be responsible

5 The service provider standard terms will look to allow the service provider maximum flexibility in the performance of the Services.

6 Standard terms will also try to limit the commitment levels given by the service provider. The Customer will usually seek to obtain absolute contractual obligations to comply with agreed service levels and then include in the service level agreement any specific margin for error.

7 The Customer should be careful with this sort of provision. If presented with sub-standard services the Customer may have no choice but to still use them to operate the Customer's business. The Customer should ensure that it is not deemed to have accepted those services as a result.

for all costs and expenses incurred by Big Hosting Company in suspending the Services where the trigger events are due to the act or omission of the Customer. 8

5. CUSTOMER OBLIGATIONS 9

5.1 The Customer shall provide and shall procure that its employees, agents and suppliers shall provide Big Hosting Company with all information, facilities and assistance which Big Hosting may reasonably require to enable Big Hosting Company and/or its permitted contractors to provide the Services and to comply with Big Hosting Company's other obligations hereunder.

5.2 The Customer warrants, represents and undertakes that it:

5.2.1 shall hold all necessary licences, permissions, authorizations and consents in order to operate the Customer Equipment and receive the Services and that it shall do so in compliance with all applicable law and regulation and in accordance with the Acceptable Use Policy and the Data Protection and Privacy Policy;

5.2.2 ensure that the Equipment is used solely for the purpose of receiving the Services in accordance with Big Hosting Company's reasonable instructions and/or any applicable third party licences, permissions, authorizations and consents and not nor attempt to (nor authorize or permit any other person to or to attempt to) amend, modify, tamper with, repair, service, move, relocate, sell, convey, assign, transfer or otherwise deal with or dispose of any Equipment, the Services or any interest therein and shall keep the Equipment and its rights and interests under this Agreement free and clear of all liens, security interests, encumbrances, charges or adverse claims;

5.2.3 permit Big Hosting Company and/or its permitted contractors to safely and effectively access (in accordance with all applicable health and safety legislation) the Equipment held at the Customer Premises at all reasonable times in order to inspect, test, reconfigure, replace, alter or amend any element of the Equipment and otherwise maintain the Equipment and audit Customer's compliance with this Agreement; and

5.2.4 maintain adequate insurance of the Equipment held at the Customer Premises as approved by Big Hosting Company from time to time. Title to the Equipment shall at all times remain with Big Hosting Company and/or its permitted contractors.

5.3 The Customer shall, at all times during and after the term of this Agreement, on demand, indemnify, keep indemnified and hold Big Hosting Company harmless against all claims, demands, actions, proceedings, losses, damages, costs and expenses (including all legal fees incurred) by Big Hosting Company including any damage to the Equipment and/or the Network as result of any breach by the Customer of the its warranties, representations or undertakings above.

6. PAYMENT

6.1 Customer shall pay the Charges which shall accrue and may be invoiced in accordance with the applicable provisions of the Service Order Form.

8 There will usually be a long list of technical and operational matters listed by the service provider that will allow it to suspend services. Some will link back to the acceptable usage policy and specific—and legitimate—concerns arising from the Customer's content. Some will be more debatable—such as the service provider designating certain 'emergency' suspension triggers to effectively provide additional operational flexibility.

9 The service provider standard terms can often include extensive obligations for the Customer. Clearly where the service provider is using equipment supplied by the Customer and/or physically accessing the Customer premises the service provider should expect the Customer to accept responsibilities under the agreement. The Customer will, however, want to avoid undertaking unreasonable obligations regarding those elements of the arrangements on which it is expecting the service provider's expert guidance and where the Customer should be relying upon the service provider's contractual commitment.

The Customer agrees to such minimum use commitments as are set out in the Service Order Form. Big Hosting Company may amend the Charges on 30 days' notice at any time. 10

6.2 All invoices issued by Big Hosting Company shall be payable within 30 days of issue. All monetary amounts and payments referred to in this Agreement are calculated exclusive of VAT and any similar tax which shall be payable in addition to such amounts. If invoices are not paid within such thirty day period, the Vendor shall notify the Customer of the same, and if the Customer does not pay such invoices within 2 weeks from the date of such notice, notwithstanding and in addition to any other right or remedy with the Customer may have, the Customer shall be liable for payment of interest at the rate equal to one (1) per cent per month for payments which are delayed beyond the expiry of such 2 week period.

7. INTELLECTUAL PROPERTY 11

7.1 The Customer agrees and acknowledges that:

7.1.1 all IPR in the Equipment and otherwise in the delivery of the Services are reserved to and retained by the Big Hosting Company;

7.1.2 any IP addresses assigned to the Customer are solely for use in connection with the applicable Services;

7.1.3 the Customer is responsible for transferring any domain names registered by Big Hosting Company following termination of the relevant Services and Big Hosting Company shall have no obligation to transfer or maintain such registrations;

7.1.4 the Customer grants a non-exclusive, non-transferrable, revocable, royalty-free licence for the term of this Agreement to use any IPR of the Customer to the extent reasonably necessary to develop the provide the Services.

7.2 The Customer shall, at all times during and after the term of this Agreement, on demand, indemnify, keep indemnified and hold Big Hosting Company harmless against all claims, demands, actions, proceedings, losses, damages, costs and expenses (including all legal fees we reasonably incur) in relation to any infringement or alleged infringement of any third party IPR or any other rights Big Hosting Company suffers as a result of Big Hosting Company use or possession of the Customer Equipment, the Customer's IPR and any other data, materials or equipment provided by or on behalf of the Customer.

8. LIABILITY 12

8.1 Big Hosting Company shall have no liability to the Customer whether in contract, tort (including negligence or breach of statutory duty) or otherwise, arising out of or in connection with this Agreement for loss of profits, business, production, revenue, goodwill or anticipated savings and for any kind of indirect, special or consequential loss or damage. Subject to Clause 8.2 Big Hosting Company's entire liability to Customer, whether in contract, tort (including negligence or breach of statutory duty) or otherwise, arising out of or in connection with this Agreement

10 Specific pricing details will usually be set out under each Service Order Form but the Customer must take care over default provisions relating to price increases and payment provisions.

11 Here the intellectual property rights provisions are one-way. The Customer may be concerned that valuable content hosted by the service provider require additional commitments from the service provider (see content provisions in Chapter A7).

12 This is a typical stance on liability with the service provider attempting to exclude liability for business loss and indirect loss and limiting overall liability to the Charges paid or payable. Clearly the impact on the Customer's business of failures by the service provider could be considerable so these limits may well be insufficient. Service providers will, however, often be reluctant to be seen to be providing guarantees for online business—or at least seek to balance liability risk (and recover the costs of insurance protection from the Customer) in the form of increased Charges.

shall be limited to the total of the Charges Big Hosting Company has been paid or which may be payable under this Agreement.

8.2 Nothing in this Agreement shall exclude or limit:

8.2.1 either Party's liability for death or personal injury caused by its (or its agent's or sub-contractor's) negligence or for fraud or fraudulent misrepresentation;

8.2.2 any breach of obligations implied by section 12 of the Sale of Goods Act 1979 or section 2 of the Supply of Goods and Services Act 1982;

8.2.3 Customer's liability to Big Hosting Company, whether categorized as direct or indirect losses, arising out of any claim under any indemnity in this Agreement; or

8.2.4 any other liability that cannot, as a matter of law, be limited or excluded.

9. CONFIDENTIALITY

The Parties hereby individually undertake that they shall, and shall procure that their employees, agents and sub licensees keep secret and treat as confidential all documents and information relating to this Agreement and the business affairs of the other Party and shall not disclose any such documents or information to any third party except as is required by law or by statutory or regulatory authority or as otherwise permitted by this Agreement. If a Party is required to disclose confidential material, the Party obliged to so disclose shall give the other Party prompt written notice of such requirement before such disclosure and such assistance as is reasonable in obtaining an order protecting the information from public disclosure. The obligations of this clause shall survive the variation, renewal or termination of this Agreement but shall not apply to any information which is in or subsequently comes into the public domain through no breach of this Clause 9 by the disclosing Party.

10. DATA PROTECTION

Each Party shall ensure that in the performance of its obligations under this Agreement it complies at all times with the Data Protection & Privacy Policy.

11. TERMS AND TERMINATION [13]

11.1 Unless otherwise agreed between the Parties this Agreement shall commence on the Start Date of the first Service Order Form accepted by Big Hosting Company and shall continue in force unless and until terminated by either Party in accordance with this Clause 11.

11.2 Either Party may terminate a Service Order Form on immediate written notice:

11.2.1 after expiry of the relevant Service Period;

11.2.2 if the other Party has committed a material breach which is incapable of remedy in respect of the applicable Services;

11.2.3 if the other Party has committed a material breach capable of remedy, but which it fails to remedy within fifteen (15) business days of having been notified of such breach in respect of the applicable Services; or

13 As with suspension rights the service provider will usually seek to provide for a range of termination triggers in its favour.

11.2.4 if a Force Majeure Event subsists for a continuous period exceeding four (4) months in respect of the applicable Services.

11.3 Either Party may terminate this Agreement on immediate written notice:

11.3.1 if the other Party has committed a material breach which is incapable of remedy which has application to all the Services then provided under this Agreement;

11.3.2 if the other Party has committed a material breach capable of remedy, but which it fails to remedy within fifteen (15) business days of having been notified of such breach remedy which has application to all the Services then provided under this Agreement;

11.3.3 if the other has a receiver or an administrative receiver appointed over it or over any part of its undertaking or assets or passes a resolution for winding up (other than for the purpose of a bona fide scheme of solvent amalgamation or reconstruction) or a court of competent jurisdiction makes an order to that effect or if the other becomes subject to an administration order or enters into any voluntary arrangement with its creditors or ceases or threatens to cease to carry on business, or undergoes into suspension of payments or bankruptcy or is subject to any analogous acts or proceedings under any foreign law;

11.3.4 if a Force Majeure Event subsists for a continuous period exceeding four (4) months in respect of the applicable Services which has application to all the Services then provided under this Agreement; or

11.3.5 after expiry of all relevant Service Periods, no Services are being provided under this Agreement.

11.4 The Big Hosting Company may terminate this Agreement or the relevant Services on immediate notice if a suspension of a Service pursuant to Clause 4.3 has continued for a period of at least one (1) month.

11.5 If Big Hosting Company has reasonable grounds to consider that there has been a violation of:

11.5.1 the Accpetable Use Policy; or

11.5.2 the Data Protection & Privacy Policy it shall require the Customer to remedy the violation and if the remedy has not been effected within twenty-four (24) hours the Big Hosting Company may terminate this Agreement or the relevant Services on immediate written notice to the Customer.

11.6 The Big Hosting Company may terminate this Agreement or the relevant Services on five (5) business days' notice if the Customer fails to make any payment, when due, in accordance with the terms of this Agreement.

11.7 Without prejudice to accrued rights or obligations, upon termination of this Agreement:

11.7.1 all Service Order Forms and accompanying Services shall terminate immediately;

11.7.2 notwithstanding the provisions of Clause 6, all accrued Charges not yet invoiced shall become due and shall be paid by the Customer immediately on receipt of an invoice; and

11.7.3 each Party shall promptly return to the other Party all copies of the other Party's Confidential Information and, if requested, verify to the other Party that it has done so.

11.8 Termination of this Agreement shall not affect the continuation, to the extent necessary, of Clauses 1, 2.2, 4.1, 5.3, 6, 7, 8, 9, 10, 11.8–11.10, 13 and 14.

11.9 Upon termination of a Service, the Customer shall allow Big Hosting Company immediate access to the Customer Premises to remove the Equipment. Should any changes have been made to the Customer Premises in order to host such Equipment or otherwise to receive any Services, Big Hosting Company has no obligation in respect of maintaining or reversing those changes following termination.

11.10 Termination in accordance with clause 11 shall not prejudice or affect any right of action or remedy which accrued or thereafter accrues to either Party. All provisions which survive this Agreement (expressly or impliedly) shall remain in force and in effect following this termination.

12. FORCE MAJEURE

12.1 If either Party's performance of any of its obligations under this Agreement is delayed or impaired by reason of any act of God, war, act of terrorism, civil disturbance, strike, adverse weather conditions, inability to arrange for or delays in transportation, inability to obtain or delays in obtaining any permits or any law, rule or order of any government agency or official or any other cause not reasonably within such Party's control (a '**Force Majeure Event**'), then the Party prevented from performing its obligations under this Agreement by a Force Majeure Event shall be excused performance of such obligations from that date of the occurrence of the Force Majeure Event for so long as the Force Majeure Event continues.

13. ENTIRE AGREEMENT

13.1 Each Party confirms that this Agreement sets out the entire agreement and understanding between the Parties regarding its subject matter and that it supersedes all previous agreements, arrangements and understandings (whether written or oral) between them relating thereto. Except as expressly set out in this Agreement, all warranties, representations or agreements, with respect to the provision of a Service or otherwise, whether oral or in writing and whether express or implied, either by operation of law, statute or otherwise, are excluded to the extent permitted by law. Neither Party has relied upon any statement, representation or warranty of any person other than as expressly set out in this Agreement but nothing in this Agreement shall limit or exclude either Parties' liability for fraud.

14. GENERAL

14.1 Any provision of this Agreement may be amended or varied by agreement of the Parties in writing, provided always that such amendment or variation is duly signed by the Parties' Account Managers (details of which are set out in the Order Form).

14.2 Any notice or other document required to be given under this Agreement or any communication between the Parties with respect to any of the provisions of this Agreement shall be in writing and sent to the address of the Party receiving such notice as set out in the attached Front Schedule or relevant Service Order Form.

14.3 Big Hosting Company shall be entitled freely to assign and/or sub-license Big Hosting Company's rights and obligations under this Agreement to any third party. This Agreement is personal to the Customer and the Customer shall not be entitled to assign, subcontract or sub-license any of its rights and/or obligations under this Agreement to any third party.

14.4 The Agreement is subject to and shall be deemed to incorporate the Service Order Forms and these MSA T&Cs to the exclusion of any terms and conditions which Customer may seek to impose under any quotations, confirmation of order, delivery note, invoice or similar document. Any other terms or conditions (whether or not inconsistent with the terms of this Agreement) implied by custom, practice or course of dealing shall not apply. The rights and remedies in this Agreement are cumulative and not exclusive of any rights or remedies provided by law.

14.5 No failure or delay by the Parties in the exercise of any right power privilege or remedy provided under this Agreement shall operate as a waiver.

14.6 Each Party shall (at its own cost) sign, execute and deliver all such documents as may be reasonably required by the other and shall do all such other acts and things as may be necessary to give full effect to this Agreement.

14.7 This Agreement shall be governed by and construed in accordance with the law of England and Wales and any dispute hereunder shall be subject to the exclusive jurisdiction of the English courts.

Appendices 1–3

A9

SERVICE LEVEL AGREEMENT

Introduction

While the Service Level Agreement is a key component of many commercial arrangements, it is perhaps the least purely 'legal' agreement that we cover in this book, in the sense that it is intended to record the parameters within which a 'supplier' will provide a service to a 'client', and these parameters will be discrete and keyed to the specifics of the exact service relationship contemplated by the parties.

As such, a sample agreement can only hope to set out the key areas that one would expect an SLA to cover, with the detail necessarily left open. We list below some of the key components that would be likely to be included.

Think about the provision of a service, perhaps a website. What will be the key concerns of the customer of that service? That the website is up and running, available to be used. From a customer perspective, the website should presumably be up and running twenty-four hours a day, seven days a week, 365 days a year. 24/7/365 availability of the website therefore is a possible service level—a level of service provision that can be monitored and that the parties might contractually commit to. From the service provider point of view, however, it is a big commitment. How realistic is that level of performance? What about maintenance, planned downtime? What about software error, equipment malfunction?

In the context of digital media it is important to stress that it is not just the performance of the underlying technology that can be measured. Where a service provider is delivering or dealing with large amounts of content or data it is possible to use an SLA to assess the quality of that supply. Clearly some parameters, eg typographical errors, broken links, word count etc, lend themselves to quantification better than more subjective assessments, but the two are often linked and an SLA can help maintain overall creative standards.

This therefore is the dynamic of a service level negotiation. The client's expectations for service performance balanced against the service provider's view of what is technically possible and, often more importantly, commercially realistic, in both cases set against a background of how far any of the parameters are easily measurable and whether the time spent in recording, reporting and reviewing the results is an efficient use of resources given the overall importance to the project.

A service level agreement will also then generally cater for what happens if something does go wrong. How quickly will the service provider respond and resolve faults that occur? Should there be other consequences if the service provider does not meet the agreed level of performance? Rather than leave the issue to the complexities and uncertainties of a legal debate over (even legal proceedings for) breach of contract, a service level agreement may contain express rights for the client in such circumstances, whether these are in the nature of monetary credits, discounts from the agreed fees, or even rights of termination in particular circumstances. By their nature, these provisions are very specific to the agreed deal.

An SLA may also cover monitoring and reporting obligations on the service provider; fail-over or back-up requirements; security obligations; the list is, if not exactly endless, then only bounded by the commercial importance of the service to be provided, and the technical details of the service.

As can be seen from the above, certain service level agreements can be so important for a project that they become detailed stand-alone documents, negotiated separately from the main commercial agreement.

Service Level Agreement

SERVICE LEVEL AGREEMENT 1

This service level agreement ('SLA') applies to Service Provider's provision of the Services to Client.

'**Business Days**' refers to Monday through Friday, measured by reference to GMT.

Service Availability 2

Service Provider shall ensure that the Services are available to Customers for at least [x] per cent of the available uptime in each calendar month.

'Available uptime' means the total time in a month less any time during which the Services are unavailable due to: (1) scheduled or emergency maintenance by Service Provider or (2) causes outside of the Service Provider's reasonable control.

Service Provider shall use commercially reasonable efforts to provide at least [x days] notice by email of the date and time of any planned outages to the Services and shall use reasonable endeavours to ensure that planned outages shall take place at a time suitable to ensure the smooth operation of the Services.

Security 3

Service Provider will maintain its servers and other hardware related to its service in a secure environment, exercising all reasonable skill and care and at least the standard of care customary for services of this nature.

Fail-Over 4

Service Provider will use reasonable endeavours to provide back-up or alternate servers and hardware as is required to enable it to fulfill its obligations under this SLA.

Monitoring 5

Service Provider will monitor the availability of the Services [24/7/365].

Helpdesk 6

For non-emergency technical support and other queries relating to the Services, Service Provider shall make a telephone helpdesk available to the Client between the hours of [x am and y pm on UK business days] and shall respond to email queries within [z hours].

1 General—Our sample agreement serves as an overview of the kinds of issues that an SLA may be generally expected to cover. You will need to adapt it to suit your specific perspective and requirements, whether this is from a supplier or client standpoint. The sample agreement is drafted from a supplier perspective.

2 Service Availability—This is often expressed as a percentage of overall time, less scheduled downtime. The client may want to limit scheduled downtime to a set number of minutes or hours, and perhaps require that this downtime takes place in 'off peak' times of low traffic or usage of the service to minimize disruption.

3 Security—A client who is procuring service provision from a supplier may have very detailed and specific requirements upon that supplier in terms of the security of its service. This is likely to be especially true where the supplier handles sensitive data on behalf of the client, whether that is financial data or Personal Information (as defined by the Data Protection Act). In addition to obligations and warranties in the main agreement on these issues, specific requirements might be set out in the SLA. It is possible to conceive of objective, measurable performance metrics that might also be agreed here.

4 Fail-Over—Again, an important consideration where the service provided is of a critical nature to the client, who may require a full-scale off-site replication of necessary infrastructure to ensure that service downtime is minimized or obviated completely. Service levels might be constructed that apply to the time lag between the primary system going down and the back-up system going live, for example.

5 Monitoring—If service levels should be objective and measurable, then clearly someone needs to measure them. The Supplier should be under an obligation to monitor the service at all times to ensure it acts promptly in the event of any issue arising. Of course this does not prevent the client from taking its own precautions here.

6 Helpdesk—This covers non-critical service issues, and is drafted here in terms of support to the client by the service provider's technical team. If the Service Provider is expected to have a customer-facing support role, then this will need to be defined. Metrics to consider are: time to answer calls; number of dropped calls; number of calls that require escalation versus issues resolved in-call.

Incident Resolution [7]

Service Provider will respond to issues in accordance with the table below. The Service Provider will aim to resolve issues in accordance with the target timetables set out below.

Error Code	Description
Category 1	An error which causes a complete (100 per cent) loss of service for which a workaround has not been made available
Category 2	An error that causes a greater than [50] per cent degradation of performance and which constitutes a material failure of the Services, but which does not constitute a Category 1 Error.
Category 3	An error has a material impact on the Services but which does not constitute a Category 1 or Category 2 Error.
Category 4	an error that has a non material impact on the Services.

Error Category	Response Time (Email or call returned)	Target Time for Resolution of Error
1	[a] minutes	[b] hours
2	[c] hour	[d] hours
3	[e] hours	[f] Business Days
4	[g] Business Day	Next Update

[**Termination** [8]

[As its sole and exclusive remedy,] the Client may terminate this Agreement if any of the following events occurs:

[There are 3 or more Category 1 Errors in any period of [1 calendar month] etc]]

7 Incident Resolution—If something does go wrong, these provisions set out the parties' agreement as to what effort will be placed in resolving the problem.

Typically the degree of effort expected will vary dependent upon the seriousness of the problem. If the site is offline, the client will expect a far greater commitment to resolution by the supplier than if, say, certain media are loading more slowly than they should be.

The parties are then likely to categorize faults in terms of seriousness. An issue here that might be dealt with is who gets to determine which category any given error falls into. The client may wish to do so; the supplier may wish to have a right to dispute this categorization.

There will follow typically the commitment levels in terms of response time and time to resolution, varying in length of time by the category of error. The key issue here is whether or not the resolution time periods are binding commitments by the Supplier, or simply targets. Clearly from the client perspective, the preference will be for the former.

8 Service Credits/Termination—This section is really a place holder; the issue being—what is the consequence if the supplier fails to meet its service level requirements?

The answer to that question is likely to vary by the nature of the deficiency and the importance of the particular service level that the supplier is in default of.

The parties may agree a framework under which the client receives credits on any monies paid for the service in the event of default, these credits being perhaps on a sliding scale of severity, quantified perhaps against length of downtime, or number of issues within a specified time period.

In certain cases a right of termination may be considered appropriate, if the service is of a critical nature, or if the level of performance over a period of time is suitably poor, whether in seriousness of individual issues, or in the aggregate total of incidents that in themselves are of less importance, but which add up to a level of defective performance that the client might consider to be material.

Notification Process 9

The Client shall notify the Service Provider of any error, including which Category the Client deems the Error to belong in, in accordance with the following:

Email: operations@[service provider.com]

or

Telephone: [ ]

Escalation Process

In the event of Category 1 or Category 2 Error remaining unresolved for a period in excess of the relevant target incident resolution time specified above, the Client shall be entitled to escalate the matter by using the guidelines detailed below.

Category 1 Error

Duration Open Error	Escalation contact within Service Provider
2 hours	[Helpdesk]
4 hours	[Head of Operations]
8 hours	[CTO]
12 hours	[CEO]

Category 2 Error

Duration Open Error	Escalation contact within Service Provider
4 hours	[Helpdesk]
8 hours	[Head of Operations]
16 hours	[CTO]
24 hours	[CEO]

Reporting and Reviews 10

On a [monthly] basis the Service Provider will provide to the Client a report [in the [attached/agreed] format] detailing Service unavailability and response/resolution times metrics.

9 Notification/Escalation Process—These provisions speak for themselves, establishing a mechanism for the reporting of faults by the client to the supplier (to avoid a timing dispute over a particular fault); and providing for an escalation path for ongoing faults.

10 Reporting and Reviews—Providing for the parties to generate reports of performance under the service levels, and a regular meeting for this performance to be discussed. A client may wish to build upon this with an ongoing requirement for period-on-period performance improvements by the supplier, or benchmarking exercises.

The Service Provider and the Client shall, unless otherwise agreed, meet every [three (3) months] to review the Service Provider's performance against this Service Level Agreement, to discuss possible improvements to the service performance and any other related matters at the discretion of the parties.

A10

DOMAIN NAME AGREEMENT

Introduction

Obviously for any online business—but particularly a branded digital media service—it is crucial that a suitable domain name is available for use. A digital media service will usually want to use and promote a primary domain name featuring its chosen brand but will often also seek to obtain potentially confusing or similar names to maximize traffic and as a defensive measure. The need for defence against others registering those domains remains as important now as when the first edition of this book appeared in the 1990s. Back then domain name piracy and so-called 'cyber-squatting' was one of the earliest legal problems to arise for businesses online (see the box below).

Domain name disputes

Domain name disputes have arisen in a range of circumstances but in practice we have found they broadly fall into three scenarios:

- **Non-Bona Fide Use**—where A registers a domain name featuring B's brand and uses it to trade upon, ridicule or denigrate B, its trade marks and its reputation: there have been many examples of websites established as part of a campaign against the activities of a business and intended to promote grievances and act as a magnet for supporters or disgruntled customers. In these situations other legal issues such as defamation or copyright will be relevant.
- **Grabbing or Warehousing**—where A registers domain name featuring B's brand with no intention of use but to try to prevent B from establishing a site under that name, simply for B's reaction, or, most commonly, to force B to pay to acquire the name. The sheer scale of such activity was one of the primary reasons for the ICANN/WIPO reforms mentioned below.
- **Bona Fide Dispute**—where A and B are in dispute over a domain name incorporating a common trade mark because although A and B may be able

to co-exist in different markets and territories with the same brand only one can have a given domain name. The increase in the range of top and country level domain names has helped but the importance of key top level domains, especially*.com* names, remains.

Since then much has been done to try to improve the position for brand owners seeking to prevent or recover registrations by third parties of domain names featuring their brand. Suspension and dispute procedures run by the domain name registries now allow trade mark rights to be recognized within the registration process (alongside of course any court action—domain name use is subject to trade mark law just as any other brand use is). Further, the relevant body with overall responsibility for Internet domains, ICANN—the Internet Corporation for Assigned Names and Numbers—continues to work closely with the global intellectual property rights body, WIPO—the World Intellectual Property Organization—including on the current proposal for a trade mark clearing house.

Despite these steps it is important to note that the process of obtaining a domain name in the first place is still a separate process, run by separate registration entities, to obtaining any trade mark registration. Accordingly, in practice, any programme for selecting and registering trade marks for a digital media project should also take account of a similar process in respect of domain names. Increasingly trade mark registration advisers (in the UK the distinct profession of trade mark agent, in other territories specialist lawyers) will also advise on domain names. There are also specialist domain name advisers who are able to provide specific searching and registration guidance (see box below).

Dealing with domains

In 1991, there were just 165 .com domains. By 1999, this number had grown to 4.25 million .com domains. At the end of 2010, there were almost 100 million .coms and a further 96 million registrations under other domain extensions. In 1999 registration was only possible in ASCII (the Roman Alphabet). Now it is possible in scripts such as Katakana, Cyrillic, Arabic. In 1999 if you wanted to tackle a domain infringer who had taken what you regarded as your dot com, you went to the courts or took out your cheque book. By 2010, the World Intellectual Property Organisation had decided 17,000 administrative cases at a cost of around $1,500 each involving over 31,000 infringing domains, 87 per cent of which were decided in the complainants favour. During this time, the business of domain name management has matured. Large corporations now register domains across the 21 gTLDs (generic Top Level Domain registries such as .com, .org and .net that are open to anyone anywhere) and as many of the 253 ccTLD 253 country code domain registries which match where they trade like .au for Australia, .be for Belgium, .cn for China. Even the smallest companies may have a package of domain names including .com, .uk, .eu and .asia all of which could be managed for a total of around £100 a year. Domain names may be subordinate to trade marks in the minds of traditional businesses but for companies born of the Internet age, they are vital assets to be cherished. After all, without domain names websites cannot be found and email does not work—so make sure you manage your renewal process.

Nick Wood, Managing Director, Com Laude—<nick.wood@comlaude.com>

Notwithstanding the improvements for brand owners and the assistance of specialist advisors it can still be necessary for someone wanting to use a particular domain name to buy that registration from another person. It may be that the suspension or dispute procedure of the relevant registration entity does not cover the particular scenario or because the costs and publicity associated with such a procedure are prohibitive or simply because the buyer has insufficient legal rights to enforce. As a result, some form of domain name agreement by which the selling registrant agrees to transfer the domain to the buyer will be needed and a suggested form or agreement is set out below.

CHECKLIST

1. There are two sides to any selection and registration programme. First, the defensive need to ensure that use of the brand selected cannot be prevented by others and, secondly, from an offensive perspective being able to enforce rights in the brand to be able to stop others. Both are important in building a successful and valuable online brand.
2. Searching the relevant trade mark and domain name registers is a standard way of clearing use of a perspective brand (although it is also sensible to make checks for non-registered marks, ie by reviewing the relevant market both on and offline in trade directories and websites etc). Applying for trade mark registrations is in many territories the best way to protect and enforce rights in that brand.
3. Both searching and registration costs can involve significant expenditure so at the early stages of a project, where budgets are limited, it makes sense to be cautious. Some checking can be done for free online using public sources but reliability maybe limited. Domain name costs will be lower than those for registered trade marks but with multiple names and defensive registrations costs can still add up.

4. Trade mark applications are traditionally made on a national basis save that under the Community Trade Mark (CTM) procedure pan-EU protection can be obtained and under the Madrid Protocol procedure it is possible to create a bundle of registrations using a 'base' national application. Both can help to reduce the total costs. Madrid has the advantage of allowing a brand owner to register in just one territory to begin with but then extend to other territories as the business and budgets allow.
5. In some cases within the EU a national application can provide a quicker and more reliable base mark for a possible subsequent Madrid application than a CTM since the CTM process is much longer and many more CTMs are opposed (as it covers many countries not one).
6. Trade mark registrations cover specific classes of goods and services from an internationally agreed list so the scope of coverage must be selected to match the intended business activities. For example, social networking services would likely cover the following: Twitter is registered for classes 38 (telecoms), 42 (Internet services) and 45 (personal services) and Facebook has registrations in class 35 (advertising) and class 41 (entertainment). Costs will increase with the scope of the application.
7. Further costs will arise along the registration process. These include the registration agent's and official fees and the cost of dealing with any objections, either from the register itself or other parties, which may arise during the application. The value of searching is also to alert as to possible objections.
8. Registered trade marks often appear with the '®' symbol, unregistered marks often appear with just the '™' symbol. There is no legal requirement to use such symbols in the UK, although to represent a trade mark to be registered, when it is not, is illegal. It is, however, a sensible notice of ownership. Renewals of both trade marks and domain names need to be attended to promptly.

If someone has registered a domain name you want, or if someone is trying to reclaim a domain name from you, think carefully before you take action:

- The application of trade mark law to domain names is not certain in all jurisdictions and anti-threats provisions in trade mark legislation (particularly in the UK) may mean that ill-judged responses can prejudice your position. Always be ready to take specialist advice on your rights.
- Accurate information is vital to anyone involved in a domain name dispute and the swift collation of appropriate information will help you and your advisers resolve disputes quickly and effectively. It is often useful to hire a private investigator to assist in this process.

- Different domain name registries have different registration and allocation procedures and different approaches to disputes. Check the latest version of the relevant registries dispute policy as well as the registration, renewal and transfer procedures as these can change frequently—you need to ensure that you know which set of rules you are playing by!
- The approach at different registries can vary enormously—some have much more effective and informal ways of dealing with matters than others.
- Identify the registrant (use a whois server) and their trading activities. Find out how long they have had the registration, whether they have used it with a site or service and if so what that site or service is. Have they registered other names? Are other businesses in dispute with them?
- There are essentially three options, which may be adopted simultaneously: (a) issue relevant proceedings (eg in the UK for passing off and trade mark infringement: this may be necessary to avoid falling foul of anti-threats legislation); (b) invoke the registry's dispute resolution procedure. These often allow for *suspension* but not the *transfer* of the domain names in question and are often only effective where the parties genuinely want to reach agreement but they can be useful in putting pressure on the other side; (c) attempt a settlement deal: in many circumstances the quickest and cheapest way forward may still be to reach a financial settlement with the other party.

Domain Name Agreement

THIS ASSIGNMENT is made the day of 20

PARTIES

(1) THE ASSIGNOR of ('the Assignor'); and
(2) THE ASSIGNEE of ('the Assignee')

INTRODUCTION

(A) The Assignor entered into an assignment with [ ] ('the Original Proprietors') on [ ] under which the Original Proprietors assigned to the Assignor, acting as agent for Assignee, all their rights in the domain name registration [ ] ('the Domain Name') and the trading name [ ] ('the Trading Name').
(B) The parties have agreed that the Assignors shall confirm the assignment to the Assignee of all its rights under the Assignment. 1

DEFINITIONS

Agreed Terms

1. In consideration of the sum of [ ], payable as provided for in Clause 4, the Assignor with full title guarantee hereby assigns to the Assignee:
   (a) all rights, title and interest of the Assignor in the Domain Name; and
   (b) all rights, title and interest of the Assignor in the Trading Name [but excluding any goodwill hitherto derived from the operation of the [ ] (the 'Business')]. 2
2. The Assignor agrees that, by no later than [ ] hours on [ ], it will:
   (a) delete or remove from all titles, text, graphics and other material on or accessible [through the websites listed in the attached schedule] [*add other*] any reference to the Trading Name or any substantially, confusingly or colourably similar name;
   (b) destroy any stocks of written material of any type that would or might otherwise have been sent to customers of the Business which contain reference to the Trading Name, or any substantially, confusingly or colourably similar name;
   (c) provide to [*add name of relevant registry*] formal authorization to the transfer of the registration of the Domain Name into the name of [the Assignee] or its nominee [in the form set out in the attached Schedule]; and 3
   (d) [*other*] [eg remove from any business bank account any reference to the Trading Name.] 4

1 To be filled in setting out the sequence of events that has led to the agreement. Here the transfer is taking place through an intermediary, which can often be the case, and the buyer is looking to obtain not just the domain name but any rights in an associated trading name.

2 This envisages an entity that has both registered as a domain and is trading under the required name but with some separate undisputed business activity; if only the former is in question, then the agreement can be simplified accordingly.

3 The correct form of transfer documentation can be attached or with transfers performed online a suitable reference to the relevant procedure may be sufficient; but clearly whatever formality is necessary to effect the domain name transfer needs to be undertaken for the deal to have any value.

4 Add any other practical steps that the Assignor will need the Assignee to take, dealing with the removal of the name from the public eye.

3. The Assignor agrees, whether acting by themselves, their partners or agents and whether in their own capacity or as employees or directors of any other company, or otherwise howsoever, not after the date of this Assignment to register or use or to permit the use of the Trading Name or any substantially, confusingly or colourably similar name:

   (a) in relation to any business or on-line activity whatsoever whether in the UK or elsewhere;
   (b) as a domain name, URL/URI or as part of or in connection with any website or other internet or on-line resource; or
   (c) as a trade or service mark. [5]

4. The consideration shall be paid:

   (a) as to one half (being [ ]) on execution of this Assignment, the receipt of which is acknowledged; and
   (b) as to the other half (being [ ]) immediately on the Assignee being satisfied from making a Web search and such other checks as are reasonably necessary, that the Assignor has complied with their obligations under Clause 2 (a), (b) and (d). [6]

5. The Assignor acknowledges that the Assignee may carry on any business under the Trading Name or any substantially, confusingly or colourably similar name free from any claim from the Assignor, or any person claiming under or in trust for them.

6. The Assignor warrants that:

   (a) they are the sole proprietors of the Business and that no other person has any interest in the Business;
   (b) the Domain Name is registered in the name of [ ];
   (c) none of [ ] have, and no other person has, any interest in the Business, the Trade Name, the Domain Name or the Website;
   (d) the Assignor has not registered or applied to register the Trading Name or any substantially, confusing or colourably similar name as a trade or service mark or part of a domain name in any part of the world;
   (e) they are free to enter into this Assignment; and
   (f) no claim has been made against them or is pending in respect of the Website, the Domain Name or the Trading Name. [7]

7. Each of the assignors undertakes to sign any further documents and do any further acts that the Assignee or its client may reasonably require to give effect of the terms of this Agreement, and each Assignor appoints the Assignee as his or her agent to do such acts or execute such documents on their behalf should either of them fail to do so. The Assignors acknowledge that this appointment is made to secure the performance of an obligation owed to the Assignee and is irrevocable. [8]

5 This inhibits the Assignor causing difficulties in the future.

6 Half the payment is to be held back until the Assignee has satisfied himself of the Assignor's compliance.

7 This provides the Assignee with protection against third party claims or interest or litigation.

8 A further assurance provision to simplify the carrying out of any formalities that may prove necessary to accomplish the transfer.

8. Each party confirms that this Agreement sets out the entire agreement and understanding between the parties regarding its subject matter and that it supersedes all previous agreements, arrangements and understandings (whether written or oral) between them relating thereto. Neither party has relied upon any statement, representation or warranty of any person other than as expressly set out in this Agreement but nothing in this Agreement shall limit or exclude either parties' liability for fraud.

9. No failure or delay by any party in exercising its rights under this Agreement will operate as a waiver of that right nor will any single or partial exercise by either party of any right preclude any further exercise of any other right.

10. The rights and remedies of the parties under this Agreement are cumulative and in addition to any rights and remedies provided by law.

11. The parties do not intend that any term of this Agreement shall be enforceable solely by virtue of the Contracts (Rights of Third Parties) Act 1999 by any person who is not a party to this Agreement.

12. Any variation to this Agreement must be in writing and agreed by the parties.

13. Any notice given under this Agreement will be in writing and may be delivered to the other party or sent by pre-paid post or facsimile transmission to the address or transmission number of that party specified in the Terms Sheet or such other address or number as may be notified under this Agreement by that party from time to time for this purpose.

14. This Agreement will be governed by and construed in all respects in accordance with English law and the parties agree to submit to the non-exclusive jurisdiction of the English Courts as regards any claim or matter arising in relation to this Agreement.

EXECUTED as a Deed by	)	
THE ASSIGNOR	)	....
in the presence of	)	....

EXECUTED as a Deed by	)	
THE ASSIGNEE	)	....
in the presence of	)	....

B1

INTERACTIVE ENTERTAINMENT SOFTWARE DISTRIBUTION AGREEMENT

Introduction

In the original incarnation of this book we included a suite of contracts for developing, manufacturing and distributing digital media products by disc. Even at that time, however, the market for CD-Rom and similar proprietary disc products like CD-I, outside of very specific types of content, was not developing as had once been expected. Indeed, mainstream print publishers soon retreated from electronic publishing pretty much until the appearance of popular e-book platforms in the last few years. For other content providers it was also clear that with the rise of the web, notwithstanding the bursting of the dotcom bubble, electronic publishing opportunities would move online.

It was therefore primarily interactive entertainment software products, otherwise known as computer games, that continued to be distributed in physical form—and still are, even though online delivery grows. Accordingly we have updated the original contracts to reflect that, although the basic format provided here could be used for any type of physical distribution: from USB sticks to proprietary devices. Computer games agreements, like video film distribution arrangements, themselves grew out of music industry structures—indeed they have often been sold using the same retail channels, wholesalers and distributors.

This agreement is a licensing or replication deal where the publisher of the products supplies master materials to the distributor which the distributor uses to manufacture stock for distribution. Our original contracts, however, presented two other forms of distribution arrangement:

1. Sale and purchase—where the publisher manufactures stock and sells that to the distributor, which the distributor owns and holds for distribution; and

2. Consignment—where the publisher manufactures stock and supplies that to the distributor but in which the publisher retains ownership until the distributor sells on.

There may in fact be limited commercial difference between 2 and 3 above if the purchase made by the distributor is qualified to some extent. For example contracts might include provisions such as 'sale or return' or, more popular in computer games, 'price protection', where if sales are disappointing the publisher agrees to buy back certain stock or there will be some other facility for effectively sharing that downside. Of course, whether or not ownership in the stock passes from one party to another can make a big difference in legal terms. The publisher could be exposed where it retains ownership in stock held by a distributor: for instance if the stock is damaged, stolen or destroyed or it becomes subject to third party claims in the event of the distributor becoming insolvent.

Accordingly the publisher should try to make very clear in such distribution agreements as to when ownership and, separately, risk in the stock passes. The publisher will usually include provisions in the contract that aim to assist, as far as is possible under the local insolvency law applicable where the stock is held, in establishing that ownership is retained by the publisher, eg keeping stock separately identified (and with the publisher checking in practice that these are implemented). The publisher will also usually look for the distributor to implement secure storage measures (and again taking steps to audit contractual obligations) to avoid problems with stock arising and also put in place insurance provisions that, again as far as local law allows, will protect the publisher's position even if they do.

A possible fourth arrangement is where the distributor acts as sales agent—with ownership never passing to them but the publisher in effect selling direct to the counter-parties in the relevant sales channels. In fact, it is not always clear in many distribution arrangements whether or not an agency actually exists. Legally, this is very important. It has an impact on competition/anti-trust law issues and in particular whether the publisher is able to set the price at which the counter-parties purchase the stock (something that has arisen in the context of online distribution: see Chapter B6). Also in certain territories there are specific provisions relating to agency contracts that do not apply to distributorships. For example in the EU, as a result of a specific harmonization legislation, compensation payments may be due to an agent on termination of their contract with a publisher that would not be due to a distributor. These are mandatory and their precise scope varies between member states, so great care is needed with agency agreements, certainly with physical goods.

Each of the above options hold different benefits for both publisher and distributor and the sample agreement below could be adapted to reflect those alternatives if needed. This is a relatively simple form of agreement and the commentary suggests areas where further detail might be included.

Interactive Entertainment Software Distribution Agreement

INTERACTIVE ENTERTAINMENT SOFTWARE DISTRIBUTION AGREEMENT **dated** [ ] 1

BETWEEN:

(1) [PUBLISHER] of [ ] ('**Publisher**'); and
(2) [DISTRIBUTOR] of [ ] ('**Distributor**').

INTRODUCTION:

PUBLISHER publishes interactive entertainment software products. PUBLISHER agrees to grant to DISTRIBUTOR, and DISTRIBUTOR agrees to accept, certain distribution rights relating to certain of those products subject to and in accordance with the terms and conditions set out below.

IT IS AGREED AS FOLLOWS:

1. DEFINITIONS

1.1 In this Agreement the following expressions shall have the following meanings:

'Commencement Date': [ ];

'Distribution Date': in respect of each Title the relevant launch date(s) in the Distribution Territory as set out in the relevant Supply Order or as otherwise agreed in writing in advance by PUBLISHER; 2

'Distribution Term': in respect of each Title the authorized period of distribution as set out in the relevant Supply Order or as otherwise agreed in writing in advance by PUBLISHER;

'Distribution Territory': in respect of each Title the authorized countries of distribution as set out in the relevant Supply Order or as otherwise agreed in writing in advance by PUBLISHER;

'Intellectual Property Rights': all present and future copyrights as well as all computer code or scripts, whether compiled or not in any computer language or program form, patents, petty patents and utility models, trade marks and service marks, trade names, domain names, rights in get-up, inventions, all rights in computer software and data, database rights, confidential information, trade secrets and know-how, design rights, registered designs and semiconductor topographies, synchronization rights, publishing rights, performance rights, rights in sound recordings and all rights, privileges and forms of protection similar or related to above including all registrations and applications to register any of the above, and all renewals, revivals, reversions, extensions, continuations, divisions

1 General—Overall the agreement protects the position of the Publisher who, in handing over the materials necessary to produce his products, is placing a high degree of trust in the distribution partner—more so that if it were a sale and/or supply of stock (as discussed in the Introduction). This is a simplified document and the Publisher may well look to add further detail and levels of protection.

2 Distribution Date/Term/Territory—The structure of this agreement is based on individual Supply Orders that will be entered into by the parties from time to time—probably around specific titles as they are released—with the specific commercial details included: in particular the term and territory.

and re-issuances which may subsist anywhere in the world with the right to sue for past infringements;

'**Licensed Materials**': in respect of each Title: (i) a 'gold' disc or equivalent master recording, including any localized versions; (ii) product artwork, packaging and promotional material; and/or (iii) any other materials set out in the relevant Supply Order or as otherwise provided by or on behalf of PUBLISHER;

'**Supply Channels**': any and all means of physical distribution channels including all retail store distribution channels; 'bundling' or other OEM distribution; third party wholesalers or distributors; and retail and direct sales for physical delivery but not including online product delivery; [3]

'**Titles**': those interactive entertainment software products in the relevant languages and platforms/formats as listed with relevant SKU number in each Supply Order or as otherwise agreed in writing in advance by PUBLISHER; [4] and

'**Trade Marks**': the following trade and service marks: [ ] and such other marks, names, logos, domain names and branding of PUBLISHER as otherwise agreed in writing in advance by PUBLISHER;

1.2 In this Agreement: (a) headings are for convenience only and shall not affect the interpretation of this Agreement; (b) references to any **Clause** or **Supply Order** are to those contained in this Agreement and all Supply Orders are an integral part of this Agreement; (c) references to a **Party** are references to a party to this Agreement; (d) all references to statutory provisions shall be construed as references to those provisions as they may be amended or re-enacted; (e) references to one gender shall include the other and to the singular shall include the plural, and vice versa; (f) the words **include** and **including** shall be construed as being by way of illustration or emphasis only and shall not be construed as, nor shall they take effect as, limiting the generality of any preceding words; and (g) references to a **person** include an individual, firm, governmental authority, unincorporated association or body corporate.

2. APPOINTMENT

2.1 PUBLISHER hereby appoints DISTRIBUTOR as its [sole and exclusive] distributor of the Titles in the Supply Channels only in the Distribution Territory during the relevant Distribution Term subject to and in accordance with the terms and conditions set out in the Agreement. [5]

2.2 All other rights in relation to the Titles including distribution rights for online product delivery systems via any means whether now known or to be devised are expressly reserved to PUBLISHER.

2.3 DISTRIBUTOR may appoint sub-distributors for some or all the Titles in the Supply Channels within some or all the Distribution Territory for the

3 Supply Channels—This effectively grants rights to all physical channels—including the right to sell physical products online—but retains the right to distribute in digitally delivered form (which might be the subject of perhaps a download deal as set out in Chapter B6). A Publisher may however look to be more restrictive about the way in which, say, bundling deals are done. So even if wide rights are granted the Publisher would include approval rights or other ways of maintaining more control.

4 Titles—The agreement might include an obligation that specific titles would be included or that there is overall generic commitment, eg for the Publisher's AAA (top-rated) releases. Clearly with a non-exclusive arrangement this is particularly important.

5 Appointment—The other common way to structure the arrangements is to refer to the distribution services that will be provided and indeed reflect that in the payment details with reference to a service fee. That allows for some measurable performance element beyond the basic concept of royalties.

Distribution Term subject in each case to the agreement in writing in advance of PUBLISHER and otherwise in accordance with the terms and conditions set out in the Agreement provided that:

(a) the foregoing does not relieve DISTRIBUTOR of any of its obligations under this Agreement;
(b) DISTRIBUTOR must ensure that each such sub-distributor complies with the applicable terms and conditions of this Agreement; and
(c) DISTRIBUTOR remains fully responsible for the acts and/or omissions of such sub-distributors in connection herewith.

3. LICENSED MATERIALS

PUBLISHER shall deliver, in such medium and format set out in the relevant Supply Order or as otherwise agreed in writing in advance by PUBLISHER, the Licensed Materials for each Title to DISTRIBUTOR or directly to DISTRIBUTOR'S authorized replication and/or warehousing, delivery and shipment suppliers in accordance with the timetable or other delivery requirements set out in the relevant Supply Order or or as otherwise agreed in writing in advance by PUBLISHER. [6]

4. DISTRIBUTOR OBLIGATIONS

4.1 DISTRIBUTOR shall undertake the manufacture, sale, distribution, advertising, marketing and exploitation of the Titles in accordance with this Agreement and such other guidelines, requirements or directions as PUBLISHER may from time to time provide. [7]

4.2 Without limitation to the above, DISTRIBUTOR agrees that it shall:

(a) use its best endeavours to maximize distribution of the Titles in the specified countries in the Distribution Territory in the Supply Channels, during the relevant Distribution Term, using appropriate sales methods and otherwise in accordance with good industry practice;
(b) procure the manufacture, replication (including where relevant the agreed localization and bespoke (if any) development for the Territory) and maintenance of an adequate stock of the Titles; [8]
(c) develop, maintain and operate: an appropriate sales network and support facilities; customer and end-user support; advertising and promotional campaigns including point of sale, press and public relations and trade shows; and other services required to satisfy market demand;
(d) enter into appropriate agreements in relation to the above including: authorized console publisher status; for manufacture, replication and/or warehousing; with delivery and shipment suppliers and proprietary platform/format owners and other third party licensors; [9]
(e) submit the Titles to the relevant ratings agencies having jurisdiction in the Distribution Territory and comply with such agencies rules and regulations for the marketing and distribution of the Titles; [10]

6 Delivery—Clearly this is incredibly valuable material. The Publisher may want additional comfort as to the reliability of not just the Distributor but also its chain of production—replication, warehousing and delivery. Where these products are for proprietary games consoles the console manufacturers themselves will have their own requirements and approvals process.

7 Distribution—These further requirements of the Publisher might well be set out here or included in schedules. In particular, and as in feature film distribution, the importance and cost of advertising and marketing a title on release should not be underestimated. Accordingly the distribution agreement may include significant detail on the process of buying media and approving localized advertising. There may be provision for the costs of this to be shared but with the Publisher maintaining sufficient control over the process. Indeed any of the elements in the following list of activities at 4.2 could be further defined and specified for the benefit of the Publisher.

8 Replication—See above re the security concerns.

9 Licensing and contractual—The Publisher might want to review these as part of a commercial due diligence or at least include further information or evidence of them here.

10 Ratings—Many territories have statutory or self-regulatory requirements for the classification of computer games—in a similar way to feature films and commercial home video. Indeed in many territories the same authorities deal with all forms of audiovisual products. In the EU there is encouragement for member states to adopt the Pan European Game Information (PEGI) classification system: <http://www.pegi.eu>.

(f) launch the Titles in the Distribution Territory by the Distribution Dates;
(g) provide a regular report to PUBLISHER (in such detail, format and medium as agreed in writing in advance by PUBLISHER) listing stock levels, expected and actual sales and demand and such other information at PUBLISHER may from time to time request; [11]
(h) punctually pay to PUBLISHER all moneys owing to PUBLISHER under this Agreement;
(i) give full particulars to PUBLISHER as DISTRIBUTOR becomes aware of any actual or threatened claim by any third party in connection with the Titles or the Licensed Materials or the Trade Marks and not by any act of omission impair or prejudice PUBLISHER's or its licensors' rights therein;
(j) comply at its own expense with all laws, regulations and requirements relating to the manufacture, sale, distribution, advertising, marketing and exploitation of the Titles in the Supply Channels in the Distribution Territory including those relating to consumer and data protection, the classification and distribution of audiovisual works and codes of conduct or other standard industry practice for entertainment software adopted within the Territory;
(k) in all dealings in relation to the Titles indicate that it acts as principal on its own account and not as agent for PUBLISHER;
(l) not, nor license others to copy, alter, translate or modify the Titles or the Licensed Materials except as necessary to perform its obligations under the terms of this Agreement except as agreed in writing in advance by PUBLISHER;
(m) obtain insurance for all stock of the Titles manufactured by or on behalf of DISTRIBUTOR or under its possession or control for such amount and on such conditions as are appropriate as agreed in writing in advance by PUBLISHER; [12] and
(n) not actively distribute the Titles outside the Supply Channels in the specified countries in the Distribution Territory. [13]

5. FEES [14]

5.1 DISTRIBUTOR shall pay to PUBLISHER in respect of each Title an amount equal to:

(a) the non-recoupable licence fee (if any) as set out in the relevant Supply Order and payable as set out in the relevant Supply Order;
(b) the recoupable advance(s) against Royalties as set out in the relevant Supply Order and payable as set out in the relevant Supply Order (the **Advances**); and
(c) the percentage of Net Receipts as set out in the relevant Supply Order and payable in accordance with this Clause 5 or as otherwise set out in the relevant Supply Order (the **Royalties**).

11 Reporting—Increasingly this will be in online format and in great detail, probably measured against previously agreed sales forecasts and targets.

12 Insurance—Even where stock is not being delivered by the Publisher it still has a significant commercial stake in ensuring maintenance of stock and successful sales, so insurance protection remains important. The Publisher may demand more detail of the insurance and explicit extension of the coverage to itself.

13 Active Sales—Under EU law limitation of distribution rights to any territory cannot prohibit passive sales eg where a buyer requests that the distributor supply outside of the territory. Note that this can become complicated where online sales are involved as the European Commission is keen to avoid that channel being treated any differently.

14 Fees—This assumes that there will be three-fold fee structure of licence fee, advance and royalties: the first two providing committed levels of return, and therefore maximum financial protection for the Publisher, even if the latter were to be low due to poor sales.

5.2 In this Agreement, unless specified to the contrary in any relevant Supply Order **Net Receipts** shall mean 'all moneys actually received by or on behalf of DISTRIBUTOR from its sales or other permitted exploitation of the Titles hereunder less only (i) any VAT, excise, sales or similar taxes; (ii) returns, discounts, allowances or credits (to a maximum per cent specified in writing in advance by PUBLISHER from time to time); and (iii) third party shipping or handling charges (to a maximum per unit amount specified in writing in advance by PUBLISHER from time to time)'.

5.3 No Royalties shall be payable on Titles provided on a 'free goods' basis (to a maximum specified by PUBLISHER from time to time) or as otherwise set out in the relevant Supply Order.

5.4 All Advances are recoupable on a fully cross-collateralized basis against all Royalties payable hereunder.

6. ACCOUNTING

6.1 Subject to the other provisions of this Clause 6, or as otherwise set out in the relevant Supply Order, DISTRIBUTOR shall send a statement (in such detail, format and medium as agreed in writing in advance by PUBLISHER) as to moneys payable to PUBLISHER in accordance with Clause 5 within 30 days of the end of each calendar quarter in respect of that quarterly period. Such statement shall be accompanied with payment of the moneys due by electronic transfer to such account as notified to DISTRIBUTOR by PUBLISHER from time to time.

6.2 DISTRIBUTOR shall be entitled to retain, as a reserve against charges, credits or returns such portion of the moneys due in respect of each quarter as shall be as agreed in writing in advance by PUBLISHER provided that each such reserve shall be paid within four further accounting periods after it is first established.

6.3 DISTRIBUTOR shall keep complete, accurate and up-to-date books and records of account in relation to the moneys payable hereunder and provide statements in accordance with Clause 6.1 both during the term of this Agreement and after as required in accordance with Clause 9.3(d).

6.4 PUBLISHER shall have the right to audit (or designate a third party to audit) DISTRIBUTOR's records and books of account relating to the Titles at any time both during the term of this Agreement and for a period of two years thereafter. If the audit reveals any discrepancy this shall be immediately rectified and if this is more than 5 per cent of the total moneys due DISTRIBUTOR shall refund PUBLISHER's reasonable costs of audit. DISTRIBUTOR shall maintain such records and books of account and PUB's audit right shall continue.

6.5 DISTRIBUTOR may make any withholding in respect of any moneys due to PUBLISHER hereunder where required by law and supported by appropriate

documentation and DISTRIBUTOR shall provide on a timely basis all reasonable assistance and other documentary evidence requested by PUBLISHER in any attempts to reclaim or set off such withholdings.

6.6 All moneys due hereunder shall be payable in GBP sterling with no deductions for currency conversion or payment charges at an exchange rate designated by PUBLISHER from time to time.

7. INTELLECTUAL PROPERTY RIGHTS

7.1 The Parties agree and acknowledge that all Intellectual Property Rights in the Titles and the Licensed Materials are owned by PUBLISHER and/or its licensors. DISTRIBUTOR is granted an exclusive licence of the above rights to the extent and in so far and so long that this is necessary to distribute the Titles in the specified countries in the Distribution Territory through the Supply Channels for the Distribution Term and perform its other obligations subject to and in accordance with the terms and conditions of this Agreement.

7.2 DISTRIBUTOR may sub-license such rights only to the extent and in so far as is necessary for the appointment of any sub-distributors in accordance with Clause 2.3. All underlying development know-how, tools and technology shall remain the property of PUBLISHER and/or its licensors. Reverse engineering including the decompilation, decrypting, simulating, disassembling, or otherwise reducing into readable form the microcode, object code or source code used in any software in the Titles and the Licensed Materials, is prohibited except to the extent agreed in writing in advance by PUBLISHER or permitted by law. DISTRIBUTOR shall not remove or obscure any copyright notices and other proprietary rights notices within the Titles and the Licensed Materials.

7.2 DISTRIBUTOR shall at all times during the term of this Agreement remain responsible for the protection of the Intellectual Property Rights in the Titles and any Licensed Materials including any stock and other physical manifestations thereof in DISTRIBUTOR's possession or control. DISTRIBUTOR shall establish and employ, and where appropriate procure its permitted sub-distributors, replication and/or warehousing, delivery and shipment suppliers and any other commercial counter-party employs, security procedures (providing such further details as PUBLISHER may reasonably request) sufficient to prevent any theft or unauthorized access, copying, exhibition, transmission, use or exploitation and shall co-operate with PUBLISHER to implement such additional security measures and policies (including utilizing additional personnel) as PUBLISHER may reasonably require from time to time.

7.3 PUBLISHER hereby grants to DISTRIBUTOR the non-exclusive royalty-free right, as from the Commencement Date during the term of this Agreement, to use the Trade Marks (subject, if so required by PUBLISHER, to DISTRIBUTOR entering into a long-form licence agreement with

PUBLISHER comprising reasonable standard and customary protections in favour of PUBLISHER and assisting with any formal registration of this licence as PUBLISHER deems necessary or appropriate) and such other third party marks, names, logos, domain names and branding contained within the Titles for the purposes of the performance of this Agreement provided that DISTRIBUTOR hereby acknowledges and agrees that it: (a) shall comply with such brand guidelines, requirements or directions (including pre-approval procedures) as PUBLISHER or its licensors may from time to time provide; (b) shall not (other than as licensed under this Agreement) acquire any title or interest in and to the Trade Marks and/or those third party brands (including any goodwill therein) which shall remain vested in and shall enure solely for the benefit of PUBLISHER and its licensors; and (c) section 30 of the Trade Marks Act 1994 shall not apply to this licence. DISTRIBUTOR may sub-license such rights only to the extent and in so far as is necessary for the appointment of any sub-distributors in accordance with Clause 2.3.

7.4 PUBLISHER may at its sole discretion commence or prosecute and effect the disposition of any claims or actions relative to the imitation, infringement and/or unauthorized use of the Titles and the Licensed Materials and, if legally necessary to protect all Intellectual Property Rights in the Titles and the Licensed Materials, to prosecute such claim or action in DISTRIBUTOR's name, subject to DISTRIBUTOR's prior written approval, such approval not to be unreasonably withheld or delayed. DISTRIBUTOR agrees to co-operate with PUBLISHER in the conduct of all proceedings. DISTRIBUTOR shall promptly notify PUBLISHER in writing of any such imitations, infringements or unauthorized uses by others of the Titles and the Licensed Materials of which DISTRIBUTOR becomes aware. PUBLISHER shall in its sole discretion have the right to settle such claim or action unless where prosecuted in DISTRIBUTOR's name it shall be subject to DISTRIBUTOR's prior written approval, such approval not to be unreasonably withheld or delayed. DISTRIBUTOR shall not institute any claim or action in respect of the imitation, infringement and/or unauthorized use of the Titles and the Licensed Materials without PUBLISHER's prior written consent and/or direction.

7.5 All rights not expressly granted by PUBLISHER in this Agreement are reserved by PUBLISHER.

8. WARRANTIES AND INDEMNITY

8.1 Each Party warrants and undertakes to the other that it is wholly free to enter into and perform its obligations under this Agreement and its performance shall not be impaired, restricted or interfered with by any other contract or obligations it may have or by any outstanding litigation or dispute in which it or any of its personnel are involved.

8.2 PUBLISHER warrants and undertakes to DISTRIBUTOR that it shall be the owner of or otherwise authorized to grant the Intellectual Property Rights licensed to DISTRIBUTOR under this Agreement and the manufacture, sale, distribution, advertising, marketing and exploitation of the Titles in accordance with this Agreement shall in no way be a violation or infringement of any third party Intellectual Property Rights, or be obscene, libellous or defamatory or in any other way unlawful.

8.3 DISTRIBUTOR warrants and undertakes to PUBLISHER it shall only use, license and/or permit the use of the Intellectual Property Rights licensed to PUBLISHER under this Agreement and manufacture, sell, distribute, advertise, market and exploit the Titles and otherwise perform its obligations at all times in accordance with this Agreement.

8.4 Each Party agrees to fully indemnify the other (the '**Indemnified Party**') and keep the Indemnified Party fully indemnified from and against all losses, damages, claims and costs of whatever nature (including but not limited to reasonable legal costs) incurred by the Indemnified Party as a result of any breach by the former Party of its warranties and undertakings above *provided* that the Indemnified Party must notify the former Party immediately of any claim made or action brought against it and that the former Party shall have the conduct of any defence of that claim or action and that the Indemnified Party shall provide any assistance that the former Party may reasonably request and the Indemnified Party may not make any settlement of admission regarding that claim or action without the former Party's prior written consent.

8.5 Except as expressly provided in this Agreement, all conditions, warranties and terms and undertakings express or implied statutory or otherwise are expressly excluded to the fullest extent permitted by law.

8.6 Neither Party excludes or limits its liability for death or personal injury resulting from its own negligence or any liability the exclusion or restriction of which is prohibited by law.

8.7 Subject to Clause 8.6:

(a) with the exception of any liability under each Party's warranties and undertakings and respective indemnity above, neither Party shall be liable to the other Party for direct loss or damage whether in contract, tort (including negligence or breach of statutory duty) or otherwise for any claims arising out of or in connection with this Agreement exceeding an amount equal to the fees paid hereunder; and

(b) neither Party shall be liable to the other in contract, tort (including negligence or breach of statutory duty) or otherwise for any loss of actual or anticipated profits, loss of business opportunity, loss of anticipated savings, wasted management time, loss of goodwill, injury to reputation or any

indirect, special or consequential loss or damage howsoever caused even if the Party was advised of the possibility of them in advance.

9. BEGINNING AND ENDING THIS AGREEMENT

9.1 This Agreement shall commence on the Commencement Date and, unless terminated earlier at any time in accordance with the terms of this Clause 9, shall continue unless and until terminated by PUBLISHER by 45 days' written notice to DISTRIBUTOR. [15]

9.2 Either Party may terminate this Agreement immediately by notice in writing to the other if:

(a) the other commits any material breach of this Agreement which is capable of remedy and fails to remedy the same within 30 days of notice from the other Party requiring the remedy; or
(b) the other commits any material and irremediable breach of this Agreement or repeats any breach which has previously been the subject of a notice under Clause 9.2(a) above; or
(c) if any meeting of creditors of the other Party is held or any arrangement or composition with or for the benefit of its creditors (including any voluntary arrangement as defined in the Insolvency Acts 1986 and 2000 or amendments made to the same) is proposed or entered into by or in relation to the other Party; if a supervisor, receiver, administrator, administrative receiver or other encumbrancer takes possession of or is appointed over or any distress, execution or other process is levied or enforced (and is not discharged within 7 days) upon the whole or any substantial part of the assets of the other Party; if the other Party ceases or threatens to cease to carry on business or is or becomes unable to pay its debts within the meaning of Section 123 of the Insolvency Act 1986; if a petition is presented, or a meeting is convened for the purpose of considering a resolution, for the making of an administration order, the winding-up, bankruptcy, or dissolution of the other Party; or if an event which is analogous to any of the foregoing under the laws of any country in which the other Party is incorporated or established shall occur in relation to such other Party.

9.3 On termination of this Agreement for any reason DISTRIBUTOR shall immediately:

(a) cease any further manufacture, sale, distribution, advertising, marketing and exploitation of the Titles except as specifically directed by PUBLISHER to allow for the orderly transfer of such activities;
(b) having complied with (a) above, at PUBLISHER's election, destroy or deliver to PUBLISHER or as PUBLISHER directs all copies of the Licensed Materials in DISTRIBUTOR's possession or control at the date of

15 Term—Obviously the Distributor may want a more mutual provision although the key time period may well be the per title licence terms agreed in each Sales Order. The post-termination arrangements may be negotiated to allow the Distributor a sell-off period or protection that existing Sales Orders can continue even if the overall agreement has been terminated.

termination and (unless otherwise specified in the relevant Supply Order) it is agreed that PUBLISHER shall have the right but not the obligation to purchase and collect from DISTRIBUTOR all copies of the Titles within the possession or under the control of DISTRIBUTOR at a unit cost equal to the actual cost of manufacture and, to the extent PUBLISHER does not exercise this right, DISTRIBUTOR shall procure the destruction of all copies in its possession or under its control and provide certificates of destruction in such form as may be satisfactory to PUBLISHER;

(c) provide all reasonable assistance which may be required by PUBLISHER for the orderly transfer of the manufacture, sale, distribution, advertising, marketing and exploitation of the Titles in the Supply Channels in the Territory; and

(d) PUBLISHER shall cease to be entitled to any further payment from DISTRIBUTOR under this Agreement provided that DISTRIBUTOR shall remain under an obligation to pay any moneys properly due under this Agreement up to and including the date of termination.

9.4 Termination of this Agreement for any reason shall be without prejudice to any other rights or remedies a Party may be entitled to under this Agreement or at law and shall not affect any accrued rights or liabilities of either Party.

10. CONFIDENTIALITY

Each Party undertakes to the other that it will treat as confidential the terms of this Agreement together with all information whether of a technical nature or otherwise relating in any manner to the business or affairs of the other Party as may be communicated to it hereunder or otherwise in connection with this Agreement and will not disclose such information to any person (other than to its auditors and other professional advisers under an equivalent obligation of confidence) and will not use such information other than for the purposes of this Agreement subject always to any proper specific authorization in writing by the disclosing Party to such disclosure or use. The provisions of this Clause shall not apply to any information which is in the public domain other than by default of the recipient Party or is obtained by the recipient Party from a bona fide third party having no apparent restraint on its free right of disposal of such information or is required to be disclosed by law (or applicable regulation) or the valid order of a court of competent jurisdiction, or the request or direction of any governmental or other regulatory authority or agency.

11. NOTICES

Any notice given under this Agreement shall be in writing and signed by or on behalf of the Party giving it and shall be delivered to the other Party by hand or

by pre-paid post or fax transmission to the address or transmission number of that Party specified above or such other address or number as may be notified by time to time for this purpose. Any notice given or made under this Agreement shall be deemed to have been received as follows: (a) if delivered by hand, at the time of actual delivery; or (b) if posted on the 2nd clear working day following the day on which it was dispatched by pre-paid post; or (c) if sent by fax transmission, with a confirmed receipt of transmission from the receiving machine, on the day on which transmitted if that day is a working day and if that day is not a working day, the next working day.

12. GENERAL

Neither Party shall be liable to the other if it is unable to perform or is delayed in performing its obligations under this Agreement due to circumstances over which it has no control (such as extremes of weather or nature, government action, war, terrorism, civil unrest or act of God but excluding default of its suppliers or contractors) and provided that that it takes all practical and appropriate steps to minimize the impact of and to overcome those circumstances, it gives the other Party immediate written notice of those circumstances and if such circumstances prevent performance for a period of more than 14 days, the other Party may terminate this Agreement by giving immediate written notice to the Party unable to perform. Each Party confirms that this Agreement sets out the entire understanding between the Parties regarding the Title and neither Party has relied upon any statement, representation or warranty of any person other than as expressly set out in this Agreement but nothing in this Agreement shall limit or exclude either Parties' liability for fraud. Any variation to this Agreement must be in writing and signed by both Parties. No failure or delay by any Party in exercising its rights under this Agreement shall operate as a waiver of that right. No term of this Agreement is enforceable pursuant to the Contracts (Rights of Third Parties) Act 1999 by any person who is not a Party. DISTRIBUTOR may not nor attempt to assign or transfer this Agreement without the prior written consent of PUBLISHER. DISTRIBUTOR shall do all such acts and execute such further documents as may be necessary to give effect to the terms of this Agreement as reasonably requested by PUBLISHER and DISTRIBUTOR hereby appoints PUBLISHER as its agent to perform such acts or executes such documents on its behalf.

13. LAW

This Agreement shall be governed by English law and the Parties agree to submit to the exclusive jurisdiction of the English Courts.

AS WITNESS the hands of the duly authorized representatives of the parties the day and year first above written

SIGNED by	)
duly authorized	)
for and on behalf of	)
PUBLISHER	)

SIGNED by	)
duly authorized	)
for and on behalf of	)
DISTRIBUTOR	)

SUPPLY ORDER(S)

B2

ONLINE INFORMATION SUPPLY AGREEMENT

Introduction

The law surrounding data and its protection (both from the intellectual property angle and from the question of its integrity and its security) is complex. The precise scope of intellectual property right protection for information, especially real time data, may differ from territory to territory and not be clear in certain territories.

The Anglo-Saxon tradition has been to grant copyright protection for databases and similar works on the simple basis that effort had been put into the compilation (the so-called 'sweat of the brow test'). Civil law jurisdictions have tended to look for a minimum level of originality before allowing protection, and have never been able to conceive that a corporation could have the necessary level of intellectual creativity to be an author (whereas the common law has not had trouble with that concept).

Within the EU, the differences, irreconcilable it seemed, between civil and Anglo-Saxon law led eventually to the creation of the database right, designed to provide a specific form of protection for structured forms of aggregated information. The relevant harmonizing legislation defines a database as a 'collection of works, data or other independent material arranged in a systematic or methodical way and capable of being individually accessed by electronic or other means'.

Essentially, the right allows a database publisher to prevent the 'extraction' or 're-utilization' of a substantial part of the database *and* the repeated and systematic extraction and re-utilization of insubstantial parts of the database if that conflicts with normal exploitation of the database or unreasonably prejudices the publisher's legitimate interests. Thus many online activities, especially those involved in aggregating small amounts of third party content, like linking, framing, scraping, searching etc, could involve an infringement of database rights even if there is no infringement of copyright. Certainly some initial cases (mainly in Europe not UK) suggest that publishers could use their database rights where rivals are deep linking or otherwise using a site or service for unfair advantage.

Whatever the state of the law, the distributor will want comfort that the provision of the information and its use will not result in liability. Equally the supplier will seek protection against misuse. This agreement gives an idea of what is involved and the issues to be confronted in dealing with the supply of data (generally) and how its value can be protected. Many suppliers insert what are known as 'sleepers' into the data supply; these deliberately incorrect pieces of information allow for a modicum of tracking of any misuses. But the important thing is to ensure that the licence and the warranties are tightly drawn.

CHECKLIST

1. In the EU it is necessary to think about database rights and copyright when considering online data especially where commercial benefits are being obtained by one supplier from another supplier's site or service.
2. Note that fair dealing defences of the type available for copyright do not apply to database rights.
3. Unlike copyright, the database right is a relatively new right and there have been a limited number of conflicting cases to determine just what its true scope and application is.
4. The US does not have a database right but has developed alternative areas of law that may be relevant, eg hot news doctrine, trespass.
5. Database makers should keep an audit trail of:
    - the work done in obtaining, verifying and presenting the database;
    - the criteria used to determine selection, arrangement and presentation; and (separately)
    - the investment made on putting it all together.

Online Information Supply Agreement

THIS AGREEMENT is made on [ ]

BETWEEN:

(1) **INFORMATION SUPPLIER** registered in [England] with number [ ] whose registered office is at [ ] (the 'Supplier'); and
(2) **ON-LINE DISTRIBUTOR** registered in [England] with number [ ] whose registered office is at [ ] (the 'Distributor').

BACKGROUND:

A The Supplier collates and supplies the Information.
B The Distributor is in the business of making information available to Customers via the Service.
C The Supplier wishes to license the Distributor to make the Information available to Customers via the Service in accordance with the terms of this agreement.

IT IS AGREED:

1. DEFINITIONS

The following definitions shall apply in this agreement:

'**Brand**' means [ ] ;

'**Business Day**' means any day during the Term when both the Supplier and the Distributor are open for business;

'**Commencement Date**' means [ ] or any other date agreed by the parties in writing;

'**Customers**' means existing customers of the Distributor at the date of execution of this Agreement and any additional customers to whom the Distributor agrees to make the Information available;

'**Customer Contracts**' means contracts between the Distributor and Customers the terms of which shall be determined by the Distributor providing that terms relating to restrictions on Customer's use of the Information and intellectual property infringement are first approved by Supplier; [1]

['**Customer Details**' means [ ] ; [2]]

'**Data Feed**' means [ ] ; [3]

'**Information**' means [ ] ; [4]

'**Location**' means [ ] or any other location agreed from time to time by the parties in writing;

1 The Supplier may well want notice, even approval, of existing and future Customers

2 This may be needed if the Supplier does want visibility as to existing or future Customers. Clearly confidentiality and wider commercial issues as to what the Supplier could do with that information would then come in to play. To the extent this involves the provision of personal data then more detail on data protection would be needed than currently stated in Clause 7.5.

3 There are clearly a wide range of ways that the information could physically be supplied. Specific point-to-point data links are now likely to be replaced by Internet-based distribution but depending on the information and its importance there may be need to include further detail here or eg password access, update times etc.

4 The Distributor will presumably want sufficient detail here to make clear what it is to receive and the Supplier will often have standard descriptions to include here or add in a schedule. The assumption with this form of agreement is that information supplied is some form of regularly updated data to which the distributor requires continuous access—but obviously any form of content might be included here.

['**Permitted Purpose**' means [ ] ;] [5]

'**Quarters**' means three-month periods calculated from the date of execution of this agreement and Quarterly shall be construed accordingly;

'**Royalties**' means the payments set out in the Schedule;

'**Service**' means [ ] ; and

'**Term**' means the period specified in Clause 8.

2. GRANT OF LICENCE

Supplier grants to the Distributor a non-exclusive licence to make the Information available to Customers under the Brand during the Term in accordance with the terms of this agreement. [6]

3. SUPPLY OF THE INFORMATION

On each Business Day from and including the Commencement Date, the Supplier will supply updated Information via the Data Feed to the Distributor at the Location. [7]

4. OBLIGATIONS OF DISTRIBUTOR

4.1 The Distributor shall, at its cost, establish and maintain appropriate technical facilities to enable the Distributor to reformat in real time the Information received via the Data Feed without corruption or error into a form suitable for on-line access by Customers via the Service at all times during the Term. [8]

4.2 [The Distributor] shall, at its cost provide a telephone help desk [for Customers] operating between 9am and 5pm on Mondays to Fridays excluding Bank Holidays. [9]

4.3 The Distributor undertakes to make the Information available via the Service only to Customers who have entered into current and valid Customer Contracts, to enforce the termination provisions of the Customer Contracts in relation to any breach of those terms and to use reasonable endeavours to obtain appropriate remedies.

4.4 The Distributor undertakes that while the Information is provided on the Service during the Term The Distributor shall not [ ] [10]

4.5 [The Distributor undertakes that the Information is supplied only for the Permitted Purpose. the Distributor shall not disclose the Information to any other persons and the Information will not be recorded, reproduced or further communicated or transmitted except as necessary for the Permitted Purpose.]

4.6 The Distributor undertakes only to use the Brand in connection with the Information only in ways that have previously been approved in writing by the Supplier. The Distributor shall not use the Brand or any other Supplier

5 It may be appropriate to further define the scope of the access licence granted by the Supplier by limiting the way in which the Information may be presented, re-formatted, re-used or otherwise exploited.

6 A specifically non-exclusive licence—so therefore less of a concern for the Supplier that the rights are fully exercised, ie no inclusion of a must-carry obligation by the Distributor with a commitment to generate revenue. The Distributor is also granted the right to use the Brand subject to the provisions of Clause 4.7.

7 If appropriate additional provisions as to access and use of the Information at the Location could be included.

8 As mentioned above this could be developed into a wider commitment to ensure that the Information was carried within the Service in a specific manner with obligations as to prominence and updating. This might be presented as something more akin to a service level agreement. Equally of course the Distributor might seek an equivalent level of commitment in terms of the delivery of the Information.

9 For a sophisticated high value service the Distributor may place this obligation on the Supplier. Equally of course, the Supplier may look for this to be provided by the Supplier whether as support to the Distributor itself or directly to the Customers.

10 Two possible forms of restriction that the Distributor might seek to impose on the Supplier, given this is a branded supply arrangement, could be a restriction on the Distributor including a competing supplier's information within the Service or else that particular forms of content or advertising do not also appear.

trade mark in any other way including, but not limited to, use or registration as a business or Internet domain name. Use of the Brand by the Distributor shall inure to the benefit of the Supplier and the Distributor shall not he deemed to acquire any right, title or interest in or to the Supplier's trade marks. Section 30(2) of the Trade Marks Act 1994 shall not apply. [11]

4.7 When the Information is made available to Customers, the Distributor undertakes to include appropriate copyright and trade mark notices acknowledging the Supplier's rights in the Information and the Brand as approved in writing by the Supplier.

4.8 The Distributor shall use its reasonable endeavours to ensure that the availability of the Information shall appear prominently in response to relevant user requests on all leading search, index and other content aggregation sites. Both parties agree to monitor and discuss regularly during the term of this agreement how to improve visibility of the Information on such sites.

4.9 The Distributor shall at all times act as principal on its own account and not, nor purport to act, as agent for the Supplier.

5. **FEES** [12]

5.1 The Distributor shall pay to the Supplier:

5.1.1 a licence fee of £ [ ] per calendar week from the date of signature of this agreement until the Commencement Date; and

5.1.2 the Royalties for the remainder of the Term.

5.2 Royalties shall he accounted for by the Distributor within 30 days of the end of each Quarter and paid within 30 days of receipt of a corresponding invoice from the Supplier.

5.3 The Royalties shall be reviewed annually by the parties with effect from [the first anniversary of the Commencement Date]. Unless otherwise agreed in writing by the parties, the Supplier may increase the Royalties for any year by a rate no higher than the increase in the UK Retail Price Index over the 12 months ending on 1 January of the previous year.

5.4 The Distributor shall keep full and proper books of account relating to the Service and the Royalties payable under this agreement. Supplier or its representative shall have the right during normal business hours and on not less than 30 days' prior written notice to inspect and audit and take copies of these books of account. This right shall exist for three years after termination of this agreement. If the audit or inspection reveals a deficiency of more than five per cent of monies paid to the Supplier then the Distributor shall immediately pay the amount to the Supplier and pay any reasonable costs incurred by the Supplier in carrying out the audit.

11 A separate branding agreement might even be agreed separately from this document.

12 Here there is a fixed licence fee in addition to a royalty that will presumably take a share of revenue generate through actual use. The former effectively functions as a minimum guarantee for the Supplier.

5.5 All sums are expressed to be exclusive of Value Added Tax at the rate then applying for any other applicable sales tax or duties which shall additionally be paid by the Distributor.

5.6 All sums payable by the Distributor shall be paid without any deduction, withholding, counter-claim or set off and if the Distributor is compelled by law to make any deduction or withholding from any payment the Distributor shall provide the Supplier with such documentary evidence as the Supplier may reasonably require to obtain a tax credit.

6. RIGHTS [13]

6.1 The Supplier warrants that it has acquired (and will continue to hold throughout the Term) all rights necessary for the supply of the Information by the Distributor to Customers on the terms of this agreement. The Supplier shall indemnify the Distributor for the amount of any award of damages made against the Distributor by a court of competent jurisdiction as a result of any claim arising out of any breach of this warranty.

6.2 The Distributor acknowledges that no rights in the Information are or will be acquired by the Distributor or by any Customer or other person other than as specifically set out in this agreement. All copyright and related rights, including unfair extraction rights and any other intellectual property rights throughout the world in the Information, whether or not registered or capable of registration, remain owned by and vested in the Supplier to the fullest extent possible.

6.3 If the Distributor becomes aware, or is notified by the Supplier, that any Customer is breaching the terms of his Customer Contract or is otherwise infringing the Supplier's rights in the Information, the Distributor will terminate the supply of the Information to the Customer immediately.

7. WARRANTIES AND LIABILITY

7.1 No warranty is given that the Information will be error free but the Supplier warrants that the Information has been compiled, classified and updated using reasonable skill and care and that the Information will be supplied via the Data Feed with reasonable skill and care.

7.2 Except as expressly provided in this agreement, all conditions, warranties and terms and undertakings express or implied statutory or otherwise in respect of the Information are expressly excluded.

7.3 In no event, subject to clause 0, shall the Supplier be liable to the Distributor in contract, tort or otherwise for loss of profits, business, goodwill or anticipated savings or for any indirect or consequential loss whatever.

7.4 The Supplier does not exclude or restrict liability for death or personal injury resulting from its own negligence.

13 The precise scope of intellectual property right protection for information especially real time data may not be clear in certain territories. Traditionally common law territories have been more readily prepared to grant copyright protection for databases and similar works than civil law jurisdictions that have looked for a minimum level of originality. Within the EU, this has led to the creation of the database right, designed to provide a specific form of protection for structured forms of aggregated information. The interpretation of the relevant implementing legislation has proved controversial with key decisions both at member state and European level setting limitations both on what will qualify for protection and the scope of that protection. Whatever the state of the law, the Distributor will want comfort that the provision of the Information and its use will not result in liability. Equally the Supplier will seek protection against misuse.

7.5 Each party undertakes to comply with the provisions of the Data Protection Act 1998 and all associated legislation and regulations.

8. TERM AND TERMINATION

8.1 This agreement shall commence on the Commencement Date and, unless terminated earlier at any time in accordance with the terms of this Clause 8, shall continue for [ ] (the 'Term'). [14]

8.2 Either party may terminate this Agreement immediately by notice in writing to the other if:

8.2.1 the other commits any material breach of this Agreement which is capable of remedy and fails to remedy the same within 30 days of notice from the other party requiring the remedy; or

8.2.2 the other commits any material and irremediable breach of this Agreement or repeats any breach which has previously been the subject of a notice under Clause 9.2(a) above; or

8.2.3 if any meeting of creditors of the other party is held or any arrangement or composition with or for the benefit of its creditors (including any voluntary arrangement as defined in the Insolvency Acts 1986 and 2000 or amendments made to the same) is proposed or entered into by or in relation to the other party; if a supervisor, receiver, administrator, administrative receiver or other encumbrancer takes possession of or is appointed over or any distress, execution or other process is levied or enforced (and is not discharged within 7 days) upon the whole or any substantial part of the assets of the other party; if the other party ceases or threatens to cease to carry on business or is or becomes unable to pay its debts within the meaning of Section 123 of the Insolvency Act 1986; if a petition is presented, or a meeting is convened for the purpose of considering a resolution, for the making of an administration order, the winding-up, bankruptcy, or dissolution of the other party; or if an event which is analogous to any of the foregoing under the laws of any country in which the other party is incorporated or established shall occur in relation to such other party.

8.3 On termination of this Agreement for any reason the Distributor shall immediately cease distribution of the Information and destroy or permanently delete all copies of the Information then in its possession of control.

8.4 Termination of this Agreement for any reason shall be without prejudice to any other rights or remedies a party may be entitled to under this Agreement or at law and shall not affect any accrued rights or liabilities of either party.

14 Obviously a range of supply periods might apply—with set terms and renewal arrangements or else the ability for either side to terminate on agreed notice. The fee provisions might be adapted as a result.

9. CONFIDENTIALITY

Each party undertakes to the other that it will treat as confidential the terms of this Agreement together with all information whether of a technical nature or otherwise relating in any manner to the business or affairs of the other party as may be communicated to it hereunder or otherwise in connection with this Agreement and will not disclose such information to any person (other than to its auditors and other professional advisers under a n equivalent obligation of confidence) and will not use such information other than for the purposes of this Agreement subject always to any proper specific authorization in writing by the disclosing party to such disclosure or use. The provisions of this Clause shall not apply to any information which is in the public domain other than by default of the recipient party or is obtained by the recipient party from a bona fide third party having no apparent restraint on its free right of disposal of such information or is required to be disclosed by law (or applicable regulation) or the valid order of a court of competent jurisdiction, or the request or direction of any governmental or other regulatory authority or agency.

10. NOTICES

Any notice given under this Agreement shall be in writing and signed by or on behalf of the party giving it and shall be delivered to the other party by hand or by pre-paid post or fax transmission to the address or transmission number of that party specified above or such other address or number as may be notified by time to time for this purpose. Any notice given or made under this Agreement shall be deemed to have been received as follows: (a) if delivered by hand, at the time of actual delivery; or (b) if posted on the 2nd clear working day following the day on which it was dispatched by pre-paid post; or (c) if sent by fax transmission, with a confirmed receipt of transmission from the receiving machine, on the day on which transmitted if that day is a working day and if that day is not a working day, the next working day.

11. GENERAL

Neither party shall be liable to the other if it is unable to perform or is delayed in performing its obligations under this agreement due to circumstances over which it has no control (such as extremes of weather or nature, government action, war, terrorism, civil unrest or act of God but excluding default of its suppliers or contractors) and provided that that it takes all practical and appropriate steps to minimize the impact of and to overcome those circumstances, it gives the other party immediate written notice of those circumstances and if such circumstances prevent performance for a period of more than 14 days, the other party may terminate this Agreement by giving immediate written notice to the party unable to perform. Each party confirms that this Agreement sets out the entire understanding between the Parties regarding the matters

hereunder and neither party has relied upon any statement, representation or warranty of any person other than as expressly set out in this Agreement but nothing in this Agreement shall limit or exclude either parties' liability for fraud. Any variation to this Agreement must be in writing and signed by both Parties. No failure or delay by any party in exercising its rights under this Agreement shall operate as a waiver of that right. No term of this Agreement is enforceable pursuant to the Contracts (Rights of Third Parties) Act 1999 by any person who is not a party. Neither party may assign or transfer this agreement without the prior written consent of the other.

12. LAW

This Agreement shall be governed by English law and the Parties agree to submit to the exclusive jurisdiction of the English Courts.

SIGNED by the parties or their duly authorized representatives:

SIGNED by)
duly authorized for and)
on behalf of)
SUPPLIER:)

SIGNED by)
duly authorized for and)
on behalf of)
DISTRIBUTOR:)

SCHEDULES

B3

ONLINE ADVERTISING TERMS

Introduction

Advertising has always been a key revenue model for many digital media businesses, especially for web-based consumer content services, and this continues to be the case, although there have been some successful examples of charged-for services, and some high profile recent movements toward this model as content has moved behind the 'pay wall'.

Websites provide online real estate, the value of which will depend on the reach of their online audience and its demographic profile. Larger sites and networks of sites will be able to attract advertisers directly; smaller sites are likely to work with advertising networks that aggregate web space across multiple individual sites—larger sites may use networks to monetize their remnant inventory. Online advertising also encompasses other sources of real estate such as instant messaging, email marketing, RSS feeds, and applications and widgets.

Networks may offer advertisers the ability to target where their adverts appear, in terms of specific sites or types of site—in vertical channels such as automotive, holidays etc. Others will offer 'run of network' where advertisers have no control over where an advert will appear, although some networks will allow advertisers to opt out of certain types of site. Run of network is less costly for the advertiser than run of site, given the minimal degree of audience targeting it allows. Targeting techniques have been developed to increase the value of such networks either by context (positioning the ad in a relevant context) or by behaviour of the online user (generally by use of cookies to track the web-surfing patterns of unique users).

Where sites work with advertising networks it will generally be on the network's standard terms and conditions. The sample agreement is from the perspective of a website that is providing media in its own right. The main issue is the metrics of a campaign—how many times has an advert been served, in which time period, etc. The publisher will want to avoid commitment on these aspects, and require the advertiser to accept its metrics.

Sitting behind the commercial arrangements are the usual legal concerns with any form of content: that it does not infringe intellectual property rights or contain defamatory or other unlawful elements. As commercial marketing material there will also be specific advertising restrictions, consumer protection and product liability issues. In addition there may be compliance requirements with regulatory codes or best practice requirements applicable to advertising generally, to the promotion of particular products or with certain forms of online advertising. The latter have become increasingly focused on privacy issues as the use of the targeting methods described above has triggered concerns that users' personal information might be used in an inappropriate or unlawful manner. Actually, most targeting technology used in this form of so-called 'behaviourial advertising' is based on the use of non-personally identifiable forms of data but the need to maintain public confidence and the potential for misuse have stimulated action by the online advertising industry.

In the US the Network Advertising Initiative (<http://www.networkadvertising.org>) and in Europe the Interactive Advertising Bureau (<http://www.iabeurope.eu>) have produced specific codes of practice in this area.

Online Advertising Terms

1. GENERAL

(a) These terms and conditions, along with the PUBLISHER ratecard as set out here at [*add link*] (the **Rate Card**) and any other documents referred to below, (together, the **Agreement**) set out the sole basis upon which [ ] (**PUBLISHER**) agrees to accept any advertising material whether hosted by PUBLISHER and/or on any third party ad server (an **Advertisement**) provided by any party, whether as the advertiser or as the agent, media buyer or other party on behalf of the advertiser, (the **Advertiser**) for inclusion in the website at [www.] and any associated online, wireless and/or messaging service or campaign provided by PUBLISHER (the **Website**). [1]

(b) The Advertiser agrees to be bound by this Agreement upon submission of an Advertisement for inclusion in the Website. PUBLISHER shall not have accepted any Advertisement, regardless of whether it has been reviewed or approved by PUBLISHER, until its inclusion in the Website and PUBLISHER may at any time and at its absolute discretion reject, exclude, delay or alter the placement of, or demand changes to, any Advertisement.

(c) If the Advertiser is an agent, media buyer or other party representing another party (the **Client**), then the Advertiser and the Client shall each be deemed to be a party to this Agreement and to be jointly and severally liable to PUBLISHER. Such Advertiser must make the Client aware of the provisions of this Agreement and agrees and acknowledges that it is contracting with PUBLISHER under this Agreement as a principal. Reference to the Advertiser below shall be deemed to include any Client. [2]

(d) PUBLISHER and the Advertiser agree that this Agreement shall apply to the exclusion of all other terms, including any terms and conditions used by the Advertiser, and supersede all previous oral and written terms, representations, understandings or arrangements. No changes may be made to the Agreement without the prior written agreement of PUBLISHER. [3]

(e) The Advertiser hereby undertakes that the information it provides to PUBLISHER (whether online or otherwise) shall be accurate and up-to-date and also to notify PUBLISHER promptly of any changes.

2. ADVERTISEMENTS

(a) PUBLISHER reserves the right, but does not undertake, to review and approve every Advertisement prior to it being included in the Website. Any subsequent changes to a specific Advertisement or its placement must also be approved in writing in advance by PUBLISHER. [4]

(b) Advertisements must be provided to PUBLISHER in accordance with the technical specifications established by PUBLISHER from time to time

1 The clause avoids a 'battle of forms' by making it clear that any advertising that is placed on the site is accepted under these terms and conditions.

2 It is unlikely that the advertiser itself will submit the advertisement to the Publisher; rather this will be done on its behalf by an intermediary such as an agency or media buyer. This clause attempts to bind the underlying players to the terms to avoid any argument in the event of dispute.

3 Entire agreement clause.

4 The question of whether a publisher should pre-review the advertising hosted on its site is a finely balanced one—there is legal advantage in attempting to fall within the hosting exemption under the E-Commerce Directive, balanced against brand/reputation exposure. This clause leaves the issue open to the publisher.

(the **Specifications**). The Specifications are set out here at [*add link*] and available on request from PUBLISHER.

(c) Each Advertisement must be received by PUBLISHER no later than 5 (five) working days before the Run Date. For the purposes of this Agreement the **Run Date** is the date on which the overall campaign of which the Advertisement forms part is first intended to be included in the Website. If an Advertisement is provided after this time PUBLISHER may still agree to include the Advertisement in the Website but shall not be responsible for errors arising out of the late delivery. The Advertiser shall remain liable to pay for the requested space on the Website in full. If the Advertiser wishes to cancel, suspend or transfer an Advertisement, or its placement, it must give the Advertiser at least 15 (fifteen) working days prior written notice.

(d) PUBLISHER does not guarantee the inclusion of any Advertisement within the Website, nor the publication dates or placement of any Advertisement that is included. If the Advertiser is not in breach of this Agreement or otherwise at fault and an Advertisement for which a Run Date has been agreed by PUBLISHER is not included in the Website at all, PUBLISHER will try to offer an alternative inclusion date for that Advertisement. If the Advertiser does not accept that alternative date or if PUBLISHER is unable to offer such an alternative the Advertiser's order shall be deemed cancelled and PUBLISHER shall refund the Advertiser any pre-paid moneys on a pro-rata basis for any Advertisements not included in the Website at all. The Advertiser agrees and acknowledges that this is its sole remedy and that, without limitation, the Advertiser shall have no claim for any damages, costs or expenses.

(e) The Advertiser agrees and acknowledges that:

(i) where an Advertisement is hosted by PUBLISHER, the Advertiser shall accept the results of PUBLISHER's systems for recording and reporting on the Advertisements;

(ii) where an Advertisement is hosted on a third party ad server, targeting based on IP addresses or subsequent analysis of IP addresses will not include any breakdown other than to determine country, region and city and targeting of an Advertisement based on referring pages or subsequent analysis will not include any analysis of the page content; and

(iii) where an Advertisement is hosted on a third party ad server, all impression, click-thru, unique user, repeat user, time-on-site and conversion sales data shall be shared with PUBLISHER on a weekly basis;

(f) Where an Advertisement is inserted into a PUBLISHER messaging service the Advertiser agrees and acknowledges that:

(i) additional controls regarding format and content of the Advertisement may apply;

(ii) rates shall be charged on the number of Advertisements sent and no commitment is made regarding the number of Advertisements received; and

(iii) no information of any kind relating to recipients or intended recipients will be made available to the Advertiser or any third party and no representation is made as to the accuracy or completeness of PUBLISHER's user database of recipients or intended recipients, and PUBLISHER accepts no liability whatsoever from any inaccuracy or incompleteness of its database. [5]

(g) The Advertiser grants to PUBLISHER (at no cost to PUBLISHER) a non-exclusive worldwide licence of all such rights in the Advertisement as are necessary to allow PUBLISHER to include the Advertisement in the Website in accordance with this Agreement. For the avoidance of doubt, as between PUBLISHER and the Advertiser, the Website, the PUBLISHER user database and all data, information and analysis relating to them are owned by PUBLISHER. [6]

3. WARRANTY

(a) Each of the Advertiser and PUBLISHER warrants, represents and undertakes to the other that it has the corporate power and authority to enter into this Agreement (including, in the case of the Advertiser, on behalf of any Client) and perform its obligations under this Agreement.

(b) The Advertiser warrants, represents and undertakes that each Advertisement provided for inclusion in the Website and any website or associated material, service or campaign to which such an Advertisement links:

(i) shall not prejudice or be detrimental to PUBLISHER or otherwise bring PUBLISHER into disrepute (and no reference to PUBLISHER shall be made without PUBLISHER's prior written consent);

(ii) shall not (directly or indirectly, in whole or in part): be fraudulent, misleading, false, defamatory, obscene or offensive; infringe or prejudice the interests and/or proprietary rights (including the copyright, trade mark rights or other intellectual property or related rights) of any third party; unlawfully discriminate on grounds of age, sex, religion or belief, disability, race or ethnicity or sexual orientation; or contain a computer virus, or any other harmful, contaminating, disruptive or destructive agent or component or code; and

(iii) shall comply with the requirements from time to time of data protection and privacy legislation and regulation as well as the British Code of Advertising Practice and Sales Promotion;

and otherwise comply with all applicable laws, regulations, codes of practice or similar in countries where the Website is available. The Advertiser agrees and acknowledges that the Website and the Advertisements included in it will be made available without geographic restriction. [7]

5 Advertisements may be inserted into Publisher communications to users, such as email newsletters; these clauses make set expectations in terms of calculations being based on numbers sent with no commitment as to number received, nor as to the recipients.

6 A simple licence of rights in the advertisement to enable the agreed insertion.

4. LIABILITY

(a) The Advertiser will indemnify and hold PUBLISHER, its directors, officers, agents, employees, suppliers, vendors, and service providers harmless against any claims liability, and expenses, including reasonable lawyers' fees, whether in contract, tort, negligence, strict liability or otherwise that it or any of them may incur by reason of or arising out of any breach or alleged breach by the Advertiser of its warranties, representations and/or undertakings in Paragraph 3 above or any other terms and conditions of this Agreement or otherwise arising as a result or in connection with the Advertisements. [8]

(b) In no event shall PUBLISHER, or any of its directors, officers, employees, agents, vendors, and/or suppliers be liable to the Advertiser or any other person, for any indirect, punitive, incidental, special, or consequential damages, including, without limitation, damages for loss of use, loss of data, loss of goodwill, loss of profits, work stoppage, accuracy of results, or computer failure or malfunction, arising out of or in any way connected with this Agreement, whether based on contract, tort, negligence, strict liability or otherwise, even if PUBLISHER or any of its directors, officers, employees, agents, vendors, or suppliers have been advised of the possibility of damages. PUBLISHER's total liability under this Agreement shall be limited to direct damages actually incurred by the Advertiser and shall not exceed the fees actually paid by Advertiser and received by PUBLISHER during the 3 (three) months preceding the claim under which the damages arose. The limitations on direct and indirect, punitive, incidental, special, or consequential damages are independent of one another and any other limitations set forth in the Agreement. Nothing in the foregoing shall be construed as excluding or limiting PUBLISHER's liability for death or personal injury caused by its negligence.

(c) The Advertiser must notify PUBLISHER in writing within 5 (five) working days of becoming aware of any complaints about any of its Advertisements.

(d) The Advertiser agrees and acknowledges that PUBLISHER does not commit to nor make any representations regarding or otherwise accept any liability in respect of any impression, click-through, sales conversion or other rates or figures for any Advertisements.

5. PAYMENT

(a) The Advertiser shall pay the rates for Advertisements as set out in the Rate Card as amended from time to time. These are exclusive of any VAT or other applicable sales taxes that shall be payable by the Advertiser in addition.

(b) PUBLISHER may require the Advertiser to make advance payment as a condition of any order for the inclusion of an Advertisement in the Website, otherwise payment in cleared funds is required within 30 (thirty) days of the date of PUBLISHER's invoice.

7 Standard warranties given in respect of the advertisement, intended to ring fence the Publisher from any liability in the advertisements.

8 Standard indemnity given by the Advertiser to ring fence the Publisher from liability.

(c) Any amounts which remain outstanding after the due date shall bear interest at the rate of 5% (five percent) per annum above the base lending rate of HSBC Bank Plc from time to time from the due date until the date of actual payment whether before or after judgment.

6. GENERAL

(a) Neither PUBLISHER nor the Advertiser may assign all or any of its rights or obligations or transfer all or any of its obligations under this Agreement without the prior written approval of the other.

(b) PUBLISHER's failure to exercise or enforce any right or provision under this Agreement shall not constitute a waiver of such right or provision.

(c) Except as expressly provided in this Agreement, nothing in this Agreement shall confer on any third party any benefit or the right to enforce any term of this Agreement.

(d) PUBLISHER shall not be liable for any failure or delay in performance under this Agreement to the extent and for so long that this is caused by any circumstances beyond its reasonable control (including extreme weather, strikes, civil disturbance, acts of cyber-terrorism, hacking or system downtime).

(e) If any provision of this Agreement is determined to be invalid, it shall be deemed severed from the remainder of such terms to the extent of such invalidity, and all other provisions shall remain in full force and effect.

(f) PUBLISHER may in its absolute discretion and without notice modify, suspend, or discontinue any part of this Agreement. Changes to this Agreement shall be effective when posted. The Advertiser is responsible for reviewing this Agreement each time the Advertiser submits an Advertisement.

(g) The Advertiser and PUBLISHER each agree that the substantive laws of England and Wales will govern with respect to all matters relating to or arising out of this Agreement and that such laws will apply without regard to principles of conflict of laws. The Advertiser and PUBLISHER agree and hereby submit to the exclusive jurisdiction and venue of the appropriate courts in London, England with respect to such matters; provided, however, that nothing in this clause shall limit the rights of PUBLISHER (or its affiliates, heirs and successors) to bring proceedings in any other court of competent jurisdiction if such proceedings are required to preserve PUBLISHER's rights.

(h) The Advertiser acknowledges and agrees that any violation of this Agreement may result in irreparable injury and damage to PUBLISHER that may not be adequately compensable in money damages, and for which PUBLISHER will have no adequate remedy at law. The Advertiser, therefore, consents and agrees that PUBLISHER may obtain injunctions, orders, or decrees as may be reasonably necessary to ensure compliance with this Agreement.

The Advertiser waives any requirement of the posting of a bond that may apply for issuance of any injunctions, orders, or decrees.

(i) In this Agreement, unless otherwise stated, words in the singular shall include the plural and vice versa; the headings are for convenience only and shall not affect interpretation; and reference to **including** shall mean including without limitation.

B4

WEBSITE AFFILIATE AGREEMENT

Introduction

The act of linking from one online destination to another is a fundamental element of the online world. It is therefore unsurprising that people have tried to monetize that and asked their lawyers to control it. Some of the first Internet case law developed around disputed links.

In fact, it remains a matter of debate in many territories whether website A can take legal action against website B if A objects to B's linking. There have been many cases around the world that have featured such disputes and the courts have heard and applied a range of legal arguments including aspects of copyright, trade mark and unfair competition law, database rights (in the EU), trespass to goods and breach of contract. The outcomes of those cases vary. Much has depended on the context of the link and the particular circumstances of the parties. In most of the cases, additional content usage has been involved: such as the copying of titles and headlines within a link or the creation of an abstract or summary of the content from the linked site. In the US, most recently, the so-called 'hot news' doctrine has been successfully re-invented to protect the re-use of time-sensitive content on websites (see discussion in Part I).

An additional consideration may be whether C can take legal action against B if C objects to B's linking to unlawful material on website A—whether that is material infringing C's copyright or containing comments defamatory of C, and regardless of whether C can also take action against A. This has been a particular issue for search engines and other location tool providers. Many jurisdictions now have specific statutory defences, such as under the Digital Millennium Copyright Act in the US or the E-Commerce Directive in the EU, for intermediaries that have been applied in (even if they were not specifically designed for) such disputes. Although there are conflicting decisions in several jurisdictions on the legal status of search engines, courts have generally distinguished between truly independent service providers linking to or even hosting a third party's unlawful material, who have able to benefit from such defences, and those that have some closer commercial or operational connection with the third party, who have not.

In practice, of course, many links will be created without any contact between the two sites involved. A link can be disabled on receipt of an objection and the Internet would never have developed in the way it has if objections were common. Even where there is contact this may simply take the form of an exchange of emails or a telephone call. Where the planned linking is more involved, however, perhaps where framing and content sharing will allow the parties to present a more inter-connected experience to the user, or where there is some form of wider commercial understanding between the parties and, in particular, where there is an expected payment or other benefit flowing between them then some form of written agreement is needed.

Linking agreements first appeared with the rise of the portals, ie entry websites, often linked to dial-up internet access providers, many of which grew up out of the proprietary online services that had predated the web. The portals offered new users—and back then most of the public was new to the Internet—an easy-to-use starting point to online content and services. Other sites would agree to link to the portals, share content and perhaps agree specific promotional and commercial activity. These often short-term arrangements were set out in linking agreements that had to be easy to use and flexible to allow for a range of different deals that could be agreed and documented quickly. The need to sign up a regular stream of deals sometimes obscured the underlying dynamics—was the portal promoting the link or the link supporting the portal?

The rise of the search engine—and the gradual development of a more sophisticated Internet audience—largely brought an end to the portal concept. But the social networks, virtual worlds, user-generated content sites and major e-commerce sites that now dominate the online world still need linking arrangements in various forms. There is still a value, and potential liability, in directing users from one online destination to another. Linking of course remains at the heart of the power of any search engine and most forms of online advertising. Indeed the need to establish the legal basis of links ever more quickly and with a wider range of sites and services now means agreements may be presented in the form of standard terms to be accepted online on a click-through basis. The document set out below, however, maintains the traditional approach—a sample document that the destination site might offer to the linking site (its affiliate) a set of terms and conditions, ideally agreed on the basis of little negotiation, with only the specifics of the term sheets needing to change.

Website Affiliate Agreement

WEB OPERATOR CO

100 Website Operator Co Drive, New Town 20035

<table>
<tr><td colspan="5">WEBSITE AFFILIATE AGREEMENT—DEAL SHEET (1)</td><td>Agreement date</td></tr>
<tr><td>Web Operator Co Contact:</td><td></td><td>Contact Details:</td><td></td><td>Contract Ref No:</td><td></td></tr>
<tr><td>Website Affiliate:</td><td colspan="5">[insert details of party]</td></tr>
<tr><td>Website Affiliate Contact:
Email/Telephone/ Mobile/Fax:</td><td colspan="5"></td></tr>
<tr><td>Linking Website:</td><td colspan="5">[insert details of Website Affiliate's site]</td></tr>
<tr><td>Promotion: (2)</td><td colspan="5">[insert details of promotion on Web Operator Co site]</td></tr>
<tr><td>Affiliate Fees: (3)</td><td colspan="5">[insert details of fees payable or refer to separate Appendix]</td></tr>
<tr><td>Initial Term: (4)</td><td colspan="2">[insert period]</td><td colspan="2">Start Date:</td><td>[insert date]</td></tr>
<tr><td>Automatic Renewal:</td><td colspan="2">YES □ NO □</td><td colspan="2">Cancellation Notice Period:</td><td>[insert period]</td></tr>
<tr><td>Launch Date: (5)</td><td colspan="5">[insert date]</td></tr>
<tr><td>Timetable:</td><td colspan="5">[insert dates and milestones or refer to separate Appendix]</td></tr>
<tr><td colspan="6">Web Operator Co (Web Op Co) and the Website Affiliate agree to the provisions of this Website Affiliate Agreement (which includes this Deal Sheet, the attached Terms & Conditions and any documents referred to in the Terms & Conditions) as of the Agreement Date above</td></tr>
<tr><td colspan="3">Signed by:____________________
For and on behalf of WEB OPERATOR CO</td><td colspan="3">Signed by:____________________
For and on behalf of WEBSITE AFFILIATE</td></tr>
</table>

1 Deal Sheet—The intention is that deal specifics are included upfront in an easy-to-use tabular format that can be amended and expanded to reflect technical and commercial requirements.

2 Promotion—The focus here is some form of promotion or marketing opportunity within the Website Operator Co website to which the Linking Website will drive online traffic but the structure and format could work for any situation where two online locations link up.

3 Affiliate Fees—The commercial assumption here is that the Website Affiliate will receive some form of payment. One common form of deal would involve the Website Affiliate receiving a share in an agreed commercial benefit enjoyed by the Website Operator Co from the traffic generated through the linking arrangement. This is more likely to be an agreed percentage of specific revenue actually received, probably from e-commerce or possibly advertising, rather than payments for traffic per se or a set overall fee, but a wide range of alternative structures could be developed. Even a purely fee-free promotional arrangement might be worthwhile and still deserve some form of agreement.

4 Initial Term—Here an initial period for the arrangements to run and a specific start date are identified along with provision for automatic renewal to be agreed and, if so, a set notice period needed to override that automatic renewal—as set out in Clause 6.1.

5 Launch Date—This is identified as a specific date—subject to the Website Operator Co's ability to vary it under Clause 3.1. That right to vary might be made mutual or else a looser estimate included. By contrast if a specific date is crucial then Clause 3.1 might link to a specific termination right or at least some explicit options if the date is not met.

WEBSITE OPERATOR CO

WEBSITE AFFILIATE AGREEMENT—TERMS & CONDITIONS

1. DEFINITIONS

1.1 In this Agreement capitalized terms shall bear the meanings set out in the attached Deal Sheet or below:

Branded Materials: the text, images, audio, video, data and other content and materials including the Web Op Co Branding in any form including any related usage guides or information which Web Op Co may make available from time to time.

Intellectual Property Rights: copyright, database, trade mark and all other intellectual and industrial property rights and related or similar rights whether or not registered or capable of registration including all renewals, revivals and extensions for their full period of protection throughout the world.

Links: the hypertext links between the Linking Website and the Promotion and associated graphics and layout for the linking and landing pages.

SLA: the service level agreement set out in the attached Appendix 1. [6]

Specification: the design parameters, placement commitments and other agreed specifications for the Links set out in the attached Appendix 2.

Term: the term of this Agreement as set out in Clause 6.1.

Web Op Co API: Web Op Co's proprietary application programming interfaces and other tools from time to time available.

Web Op Co Branding: the trade and service marks, logos, names, brands, website styling and other distinctive features of Web Op Co.

1.2 In these Terms, unless otherwise stated: words in the singular shall include the plural and vice versa; the headings are for convenience only and shall not affect interpretation; references to *Clauses* and *Appendices* relate to this Agreement; references to a *person* include an individual, firm, government body or authority, unincorporated association or body corporate; reference to a *Party* is to a party to this Agreement and reference to *including* or *include* shall not be construed to limit the sense of the preceding words.

2. ESTABLISHMENT OF THE LINKS [7]

2.1 The Website Affiliate shall develop the Links incorporating the Branded Materials in accordance with the Timetable and the design parameters set out in the Specification and supply them in such form as may be requested by Web Op Co for written approval by Web Op Co.

2.2 Following written approval by Web Op Co the Website Affiliate shall implement the Links on the Linking Website in accordance with the Timetable and

6 Service Level Agreement—The Website Operator Co is expecting the Website Affiliate to comply with some form of SLA—see Chapter A6. This is in contrast to the limited obligation on the Website Operator Co at Clause 3.2. If the Affiliate Fee is linked to performance anyway then an SLA might be felt not to be needed. Or else it might be replaced by a relatively limited mutual commitment on both sides to ensure that their sites and, in particular, the links and the promotion are reasonably available.

7 Establishment of the Links—It is assumed that there will be an agreed specification and timetable for creating and implementing the Links that can be attached to the agreement in an appendix. Alternatively, the process of establishing those key documents might itself be a first stage in performing the agreement, or in very simple arrangements short descriptions of each might be dropped into the Deal Sheet and/or definitions section. For more complicated arrangements the straightforward notion of 'written approval' might need to be replaced with more detailed provisions on integration and testing.

the placement commitments set out in the Specification. The Website Affiliate shall ensure that the Links do not go live before the Launch Date (or such other date as the Web Op Co may specify in writing).

2.3 Following the Launch Date (or such other date as the Web Op Co may specify in writing) the Website Affiliate shall ensure that the Links are made available at all times in accordance with the SLA.

3. THE PROMOTION

3.1 The Web Op Co shall make available any Branded Materials for the Links to the Website Affiliate including via the Web Op Co API. The Website Affiliate agrees to enter into and comply with Web Op Co's separate terms and conditions for access to the Web Op Co API from time to time in force. [8]

3.2 Web Op Co does not commit, and has no obligation to the Website Affiliate, to operate the Promotion at all times. The content and operation of the Promotion shall be at the sole discretion of Web Op Co. Web Op Co may request an update of the Specification and the Links to reflect any changes in the Promotion.

3.3 Notwithstanding any other provision of this Agreement, if Web Op Co reasonably believes that the Links and/or the Promotion may create liability for Web Op Co (whether or not due to a breach of this Agreement by Website Affiliate) Web Op Co may remove or suspend the Links and/or the Promotion and/or require by immediate written notice that Website Affiliate remove or suspend the Links. [9]

4. AFFILIATE FEES [10]

4.1 Subject to and in consideration of the Website Affiliate complying with its obligations under this Agreement Web Op Co shall pay the Affiliate Fees to the Website Affiliate.

4.2 Web Op Co shall issue a quarterly report in an agreed format showing the Affiliate Fees payable to the Website Affiliate. Following receipt of the report the Website Affiliate shall issue a valid VAT invoice for the relevant amount which shall be payable by Web Op Co within sixty (60) days of receipt.

4.3 If the Affiliate Fees payable in any quarter are less than £xxx Web Op Co may hold over payment until the next quarter in which aggregate Affiliate Fees exceed that amount.

4.4 Web Op Co will pay VAT at the applicable rate on any of the payments due under this Agreement on receipt of a valid VAT invoice.

5. Intellectual Property Rights [11]

5.1 Web Op Co (and/or its licensors) is the owner of all Intellectual Property Rights in the Branded Materials, the Promotion, the Web Op Co API, the

8 Branded Material—The Linking Website will carry material provided by the Website Operator Co. This could be provided in physical format or more likely via email or FTP. Here the Website Operator Co provides access to their material though an API that may in some cases require a similar but separate set of standard terms. This is becoming more common with larger content operators seeking to provide material to a large distribution base.

9 Suspension/Take Down—The Website Operator Co reserves a broad suspension right: not just in the event of the Website Affiliate's breach but in any circumstance where it believes there may be liability. On top of the limited commitment at Clause 3.2 this gives the Website Operator Co a broad degree of flexibility. Again this might be made a mutual right effectively giving each side the same protection.

10 Payment Terms—Where the standard terms are produced by the paying party these provisions will usually include the bare minimum. Accordingly, the Website Affiliate will want to tighten these payment provisions with the usual additions requested by the receiving party: details of payment (eg specifying electronic settlement to a nominated bank account); an audit right; confirmation of interest on late payment; and, if these are cross-border payments, detail on currency, tax and withholdings.

11 Intellectual Property Rights—The primary focus here is the Branded Materials and the value of that content may influence the level of detail included here. The Website Affiliate might look for a similar level of detail in respect of its rights but unless content from the Website Affiliate is also being provided to the Website Operator Co or if there is any kind of link back to the Website Affiliate site there is limited usage of those rights involved.

Web Op Co Branding (and all goodwill arising from its use) and any other materials provided by or on behalf of Web Op Co to Website Affiliate under or in connection with this Agreement. Web Op Co grants to the Website Affiliate a revocable, limited, non-transferable, non-exclusive licence of such rights solely to the extent and in so far as is necessary to allow the Website Affiliate to develop and operate the Links in accordance with this Agreement during the Term. The Web Op Co Branding and any other trade marks within the Branded Materials or other materials provided must be used in accordance with any applicable branding guidelines. Copyright, trade mark and other notices must be shown as requested by Web Op Co at all times. All other rights are expressly reserved by and to Web Op Co.

5.2 Subject always to Clause 5.1, the Website Affiliate (and/or its licensors) is the owner of the Intellectual Property Rights in the Linking Website.

6. TERM AND TERMINATION

6.1 This Agreement shall commence on the Start Date and unless terminated earlier by either Party in accordance with Clause 6.2 shall continue for the Initial Term and if the Parties have agreed to Automatic Renewal in the Deal Sheet this Agreement shall automatically extend for further successive periods equal to the Initial Term unless and until either Party gives written cancellation notice to the other of not less than the Cancellation Notice Period before the commencement of any such start period.

6.2 This Agreement may be terminated by either Party on immediate written notice to the other Party if the other Party:

6.2.1 resolves to go into a voluntary liquidation (other than a members' voluntary winding up for the purposes of a reconstruction of its affairs), presents or has presented against itself a winding up petition, makes a composition with its creditors, has a receiver, manager or administrative receiver appointed over to the whole or any part of its assets or property, presents or has presented against itself a petition for the making of an administrative order or becomes unable to pay its debts within the meaning of section 123 of the Insolvency Act 1986; or

6.2.2 is in material breach of any of its obligations under this Agreement which is capable of remedy and has not remedied such breach or agreed to a satisfactory course of action within fourteen (14) days of having received written notice of the same from the terminating Party; or

6.2.3 is in material breach of any of its obligation under this Agreement which is not capable of remedy or repeats any breach as has previously been the subject of a notice under Clause 6.2.2; or

6.2.4 is precluded by a force majeure event in accordance with Clause 8 from performing its obligations for a period more than twenty-eight (28) days.

6.3 Web Op Co may terminate this Agreement on immediate written notice at any time if Web Op Co ceases or intends to cease to operate the Promotion.

6.4 On termination or expiry of this Agreement the Website Affiliate shall immediately and permanently:

6.4.1 disable and remove the Links; and

6.4.2 delete or destroy all Branded Materials in its possession or control; and

6.4.3 cease to access the Web Op Co API.

6.5 Any termination of this Agreement by either Party shall be without prejudice to any other rights or remedies it may have, and shall not affect any rights accrued or obligations arising on or before the date of termination.

7. WARRANTIES AND INDEMNITIES 12

7.1 Each Party warrants and undertakes to the other that:

7.1.1 it has the full right, power and authority to enter into and perform its obligations under this Agreement;

7.1.2 it is entitled to perform its obligations under this Agreement and to grant any licences hereunder free from any third party claims; and

7.1.3 it shall use reasonable skill and care in performing its obligations under this Agreement.

7.2 The Website Affiliate further warrants and undertakes that it shall operate the Links and the Linking Website in accordance will all applicable laws and regulations and shall not infringe the Intellectual Property Rights or any privacy, publicity or other right of any person or be defamatory or obscene or otherwise unlawful.

7.3 The Website Affiliate shall indemnify and hold harmless Web Op Co against any costs, liabilities, losses, damage or expenses arising from any breach of any of the Website Affiliate's warranties and undertakings set out in this Clause 7.

8. FORCE MAJEURE

Neither Party shall be liable to the other if it is unable to perform or is late in performing its obligations under this Agreement due to extremes of weather or event of nature, industrial action, government action, interruptions in public order, accidents, epidemics or acts of God, provided that the Party relying on this clause gives immediate written notice to the other Party and takes all

12 Warranties and Indemnities—A short and simple set of broadly mutual standard warranties regarding the performance of the Agreement. The Website Affiliate would probably want some form of equivalent additional warranty to Clause 7.2 regarding the Website Operator Co site or at least the Promotion. It would also look for an equivalent indemnity from the Website Operator Co.

reasonable steps to overcome such circumstances (and any payment obligations of the other Party are suspended during such period). If such an event continues for a period of twenty (20) days or longer, the other Party may terminate this Agreement by giving immediate written notice to the Party unable to perform.

9. CONFIDENTIALITY AND PRIVACY 13

9.1 Each Party undertakes to the other that, subject to Clause 9.2 below, it will treat as confidential the terms of this Agreement together with all information whether of a technical nature or otherwise relating in any manner to the business or affairs of the other Party as may be communicated to it hereunder or otherwise in connection with this Agreement and will not disclose such information to any person firm or company (other than to its auditors and other professional advisers) or to the media and will not use such information other than for the purposes of this Agreement subject always to any proper specific authorization in writing by the disclosing Party to such disclosure or use.

9.2 The provisions of Clause 9.1 above shall not apply to any information which:

9.2.1 is in the public domain other than by default of the recipient Party;

9.2.2 is obtained by the recipient Party from a bona fide third party having no apparent restraint on its free right of disposal of such information;

9.2.3 is required to be disclosed by law (or applicable regulation) or the valid order of a court of competent jurisdiction, or the request or direction of any governmental or other regulatory authority or agency.

9.3 Each party will comply with its obligations under the Data Protection Act 1998 (as amended or replaced) and any associated legislation or regulations regarding personal data including implementing and maintaining appropriate technical and organizational measures to prevent damage, loss or corruption of, or unauthorized access to such data.

10. NOTICES

Any notice given under this Agreement shall be in writing and may be delivered to the other Party or sent by pre-paid post or facsimile transmission to the address or transmission number of that Party specified in the Term Sheet or such other address or number as may be notified under this Agreement by that Party from time to time for that purpose.

11. NO ASSIGNMENT

The Website Affiliate shall not assign or sub-license the benefit of or subcontract any of the obligations under this Agreement (or any part thereof) without the prior written consent of Web Op Co, which may be given or withheld in its absolute discretion.

13 Confidentiality and Privacy—Since it is users of the Website Affiliate site who are linking to the Website Operator Co site the Website Affiliate might want more detailed assurances from the Website Operator Co regarding privacy and data protection law to protect those users. The Website Affiliate might even look for some form of data sharing arrangement. The Website Operator Co view may be that once the users are on the Website Operator Co site then subject to a generic obligation to comply with the law, in line with Clause 9.2, the Website Operator Co should be free to collect and use personal data as it wants (see Chapter B9).

12. GENERAL

12.1 A waiver by either Party of any of the terms or conditions of this Agreement in any instance shall not be deemed or construed to be a waiver of such term or condition for the future, or of any subsequent breach thereof. The rights and remedies of the Parties under this Agreement are cumulative and in addition to any rights and remedies provided by law.

12.2 This Agreement constitutes the entire agreement and understanding between the Website Affiliate and Web Op Co and that it supersedes all previous agreements, arrangements and understandings between them. Any variation to this Agreement must be in writing and agreed by the Parties.

12.3 Subject to the final sentence of this Clause 12.3, neither Party shall be entitled to (and both parties irrevocably and unconditionally waive any right they may have to) any remedies for any misrepresentation whether or not contained in this Agreement or breach of any warranty not contained in the Agreement. Nothing in this Agreement shall restrict or exclude liability for (or remedy in respect of) fraud or fraudulent misrepresentation.

12.4 A person who is not a Party to this Agreement has no right under the Contracts (Rights of Third Parties) Act 1999 to enforce the benefit of any term of this Agreement and to the extent permitted by law the Parties hereby exclude the application of such Act to this Agreement.

12.5 Nothing in this Agreement shall be deemed to create a partnership or joint venture between the Parties.

13. GOVERNING LAW AND JURISDICTION

This Agreement shall be governed by and construed in all respects in accordance with English law and the Parties agree to submit to the non-exclusive jurisdiction of the English Courts as regards any claim or matter arising in relation to this Agreement.

B5

WIRELESS CONTENT AGREEMENT

Introduction

The wireless/mobile content market has boomed over the last five to ten years, driven by the increasing power and sophistication of mobile devices and the advent of high bandwidth GPRS and 3G mobile networks, which make a mobile internet experience a far more user-friendly and powerful one.

The role of the networks in this market is strategically interesting—are they simply connectivity providers, mobile ISPs, or can they offer incremental value to their user base? All the networks have invested in content services and portals, in an attempt to stimulate network data usage, and to drive revenue per user. At the same time, the increasingly friction-free mobile internet experience enables third parties to use mobile as a legitimate distribution channel 'off portal', and a number of mobile businesses work outside the scope of the mobile networks.

The advent of the iPhone and the 'app', now replicated across networks and competitor smart-phone devices, has provided another mobile distribution path, under which consumers interact with content in discrete application packages, with the mobile network purely in the background, providing the distribution of the app and enabling location-based interaction. There is debate in the industry whether the app will supplant the browsing experience within the mobile domain, and certainly consumers have demonstrated a readiness to pay for apps in a way that they are reluctant to do for the 'Internet browsing' model. The introduction of new categories of wireless device such as e-book readers like the Amazon Kindle and tablet devices like the Apple iPad will serve to stimulate this debate.

One of the concepts much discussed in mobile delivery is super-distribution, which attempts to harness the viral effect of users sharing content for commercial benefit. A sale of one piece of content to one device for one dollar locked to that device will only make the supplier one dollar. If however the buyer is permitted to forward that content to ten friends and they to ten more *and* there is some form of DRM in place to ensure the friends pay then the supplier has made considerably more than one dollar. This concept is at the heart of a set of specific mobile DRM standards that allow content and the rights to use it to be delivered over the mobile network (see the Open Mobile Alliance (<http://www.openmobilealliance.org>)).

This may even allow the supplier to charge the friends less than the first buyer. Differential payments may become increasingly important in the content business with content not converging but actually diverging onto different platforms and devices at different price points. Ringtones were a great example—fans were happily downloading what was effectively part of a music track to their phone for up to \$5—when they could have downloaded the whole thing to their PC for less than \$1.

In each case the key focus is being able to create a viable content 'ecosystem', ie provide an environment where mainstream user demand can be created for content and services on a given platform that is financially rewarding for the networks, the device manufacturers and the content/service suppliers. Crucially of course key players may be fulfilling more than one role in that environment.

Content procurement for mobile is similar to that for other areas of digital media, but there are some specific issues that we highlight in the sample agreement below.

Wireless Content Agreement

Mobile Content Distribution—General provisions

1. BASIC PRINCIPLES

1. The following provisions set forth the terms and conditions ('Standard Terms') governing the supply and use of all text, data, images, graphics, audio and/or audiovisual material, games, software programs, marks, logos, brands and/or other material as relevant and more particularly specified in the Special Conditions (together, the 'Content') by Supplier to [Distributor] (hereinafter referred to as 'Distributor').

2. Capitalized expressions used in these Standard Terms shall have the meanings set out in the Special Conditions and the Standard Terms. The Standard Terms, Special Conditions and any documents referred to therein together constitute an agreement for granting of a licence in and to the Content by the Supplier to Distributor (the 'Agreement').

3. In the event of inconsistency between parts of this Agreement, the Special Conditions shall take precedence over these Standard Terms.

2. PROVISION OF CONTENT

1. The Supplier shall provide the Content to Distributor in accordance with the Special Conditions including any timetable or update schedule contained therein.

3. LICENSING

1. The Supplier grants to Distributor by way of [non] exclusive licence the right to make available and distribute the Content by means of [the Site] to users of Mobile Devices and for their personal use in one or more of the territories listed in the Special Conditions ('Territory'), including without limitation by [browsing, streaming, downloading, playback, storage and purchase].

2. The Supplier grants Distributor the right to use the brands, logos, names and trade marks relating to Supplier and the Content, together with screenshots, demos and/or excerpts of the Content, on the Site (and on all other media subject to the prior approval of Supplier) for the purpose of marketing or advertising the availability of the Content. The Distributor shall comply with the Supplier's usage guidelines in respect thereof (if any), as may be supplied to Distributor from time to time.

3. The Supplier grants to Distributor the right to make the Content available for demonstration, order and/or purchase by users via the Internet with delivery of such Content to the users' Mobile Device. [1]

1 Allows the Distributor to offer users the ability to demo and order the content via web portal or other site, with the delivery of the content being made to the user's mobile device.

4. Unless otherwise agreed or where technically unfeasible in the circumstances, Distributor shall not remove or conceal any copyright notices contained in the Content.

5. The Distributor may not modify the Content except solely as is necessary to enable delivery of the Content to a Mobile Device. [2]

6. The Distributor shall be responsible for procuring and maintaining all necessary licences in respect of any underlying musical compositions contained in the Content required for the Distributor to exercise its rights under this Agreement. [3]

7. [Supplier grants to Distributor the right to make the Content available to users as part of a bundle with other content, products or services provided by the Supplier [and/or by third parties] (with the bundle structure and pricing determined by Distributor)]. [4]

4. OBLIGATIONS ON DISTRIBUTOR

1. The Distributor shall use all reasonable technical measures to prevent unauthorized access to or use of the Content. The Distributor shall ensure that the Content is delivered to users enabled with industry-standard DRM technology in accordance with good industry practice and in any event employing 'forward-lock' protection wherever possible. [5]

2. [The Distributor may not bundle any Content with any other content without the prior written consent of the Supplier.] [6]

3. The Distributor may not use the Content, nor any part of the Content (including but without limitation cover art, artist name or likeness) for marketing and promotional purposes, without the prior written consent of the Supplier. The Distributor may not use any trade mark of the Supplier or its licensor, nor any Content (or part thereof) in such a manner that implies an endorsement of any goods or services by the Supplier, any of its licensors and/or any individual or entity featured in the Content. [7]

4. The Distributor may not allow the delivery of any Content to any Mobile Device that does not meet such minimum technical standards as have been notified by the Supplier. [8]

5. FEES

1. Within [x] working days from the end of each month, the Distributor shall provide the Supplier with a report detailing the amount of the Content sold by the Distributor in the preceding month. The Supplier shall issue Distributor with an invoice for the agreed Fees indicated on the Special Conditions within [y] days of receipt of the Distributor's report. Within [z] days of receipt of the Supplier's invoice, Distributor shall transfer the Fees to the Supplier.

2 Given the differing technical specifications and form factors of mobile devices, it may be necessary for content to be re-formatted to enable it to be correctly displayed on a specific type of device. Some Suppliers will provide this as part of their service, but it may be that the Distributor requires a limited right to make changes here.

3 Much mobile content has been derived from music—ringtones, and mobile downloads of full tracks. While the general practice is for 'all rights cleared' deals, the rights in the underlying musical compositions are generally held by Collecting Societies who prefer to license 'the last link in the chain' to the end consumer, that is the Distributor. This clause is included given that musical content has played a key role in the mobile sector, although it will not be relevant in content that does not feature music.

4 The bundling of content together into packages has become interesting to mobile networks as a pricing mechanism to drive user uptake. Bundling complicates the mechanism of payment for the Supplier—will the fee be based on a pro-rating of the actual or notional value of the bundle? How this is structured will need to be addressed in the commercial terms. If a Supplier does not want its content to be bundled this should be made an express restriction—see Clause 4.2 for this alternative.

5 Digital Rights Management is a controversial topic but is still relatively common in mobile content distribution, aiming to prevent onward, unauthorized distribution of content by end-users. There are a number of rival standards and implementations, and some detail may be gone into on this issue, perhaps referencing a DRM schedule. This clause is relatively light, obliging the Distributor to utilize industry standard technology, including forward lock where possible.

6 The negative alternative to the bundling Clause 3.7.

7 Typically a supplier will wish, and/or be obliged by its own licensors, to prohibit use of the content, or artists featuring in the content, to 'endorse' any product or service, to avoid potential legal exposure

8 Quality standards are becoming less of an issue given the increasing sophistication of mobile devices but this may remain an issue for certain high quality/high value content.

2. Unless otherwise specified, the Fees exclude VAT or other applicable sales tax, which must be levied, if necessary, on the Fees and set out on the Supplier's invoice, in addition to any withholding or other applicable tax which may be imposed by any relevant taxing authority or government.

6. WARRANTIES

The Supplier represents and warrants that: (a) it holds the unlimited right and title to grant the rights granted under this Agreement, and that no additional licences, permissions, waivers, consents or payments with regard to copyrights trademark rights, patents, rights to names/personality/likeness/image, performers rights, database rights, moral rights, design rights, rights to images or other industrial or intellectual property rights of any kind ('IPR') are necessary in order for Distributor to exercise the rights granted to it in accordance with this Agreement, and that such use will not infringe any third party rights of any kind; (b) it shall use its best efforts to prevent the Content from being infected by viruses or other harmful programs or code; (c) the Content will not be, or contain anything which is, illegal, obscene, or defamatory in any part of the Territory.

7. LIABILITY

1. Neither party limits its liability to the other for (a) fraudulent misrepresentation or (b) death or personal injury caused by the negligence of, in either case, that Party or the employees, agents or sub-contractors of that Party.

2. Subject to sub-clause (1), neither Party shall be liable under contract, tort or any other head of law, to the other Party for any indirect loss, consequential loss or loss of anticipated savings. In respect of all other loss, [each Party's] aggregate liability to the other Party under this Agreement is limited to [the higher of £[x] and the Fees paid or payable to the Supplier].

3. The Supplier hereby indemnifies and holds Distributor harmless against all loss, damage, costs, expenses and liabilities that Distributor may suffer as a result of (a) any claim or threatened claim (a 'Claim') by any third party relating to the Content (including without limitation a Claim for infringement of IPR in the Content); and (b) breach by the Supplier of its warranties set out in Clause 6 above. The limitation of liability set out in Clause 7(2) above shall not apply to this indemnity.

4. Distributor shall promptly notify the Supplier in writing of any Claim of which it has notice. Unless otherwise instructed by Distributor, the Supplier shall diligently conduct the defence of the Claim. The Supplier may not settle the Claim in any manner that binds the Distributor in any way without obtaining Distributor's prior written consent to the terms of such settlement (which consent shall not be unreasonably withheld or delayed).

5. The Supplier shall ensure that it carries at all times commercially adequate insurance to meet any claims by Distributor under this Agreement and shall provide Distributor with reasonable documentary evidence of compliance with this sub-clause at the written request of the Distributor.

8. CONFIDENTIALITY

1. Each party undertakes and shall ensure that its employees undertake to treat as confidential all technical and non-technical information as well as business and operating matters that come to their attention in connection with this Agreement whether in verbal, written, graphical or other form and to treat such information with at least the same degree of care as it treats its own confidential information.

9. DATA PROTECTION

1. Each party undertakes to comply with all applicable data protection laws, regulations and codes of practice in connection with the subject matter of this Agreement.

10. TERM AND TERMINATION

1. This Agreement shall come into force on signature and remain in effect for the period set out in the Special Conditions.
2. Unless otherwise provided in the Special Conditions, either Party shall have the right to terminate this Agreement forthwith:
   (a) if the other Party is in material breach of this Agreement and either such breach is not capable of remedy or such breach remains unremedied within 30 days from the date that the party in default is notified of such breach by the non-defaulting party;
   (b) upon the expiry of [30] days' written notice to the other Party; or
   (c) if the other Party enters into administration, becomes insolvent, or any similar insolvency-related event occurs.

11. MISCELLANEOUS PROVISIONS

1. No amendment to this Agreement shall be valid or enforceable unless in writing and signed by duly authorized representatives of both Parties.
2. No assignment or sub-licensing of rights or obligations under this Agreement is permitted without the prior written consent of the other Party (which consent shall not be unreasonably withheld or delayed).
3. All notices made under this Agreement shall be made in writing to the recipients indicated in the Special Conditions.
4. This Agreement constitutes the entire agreement between the parties relating to the subject matter hereof and supersedes all prior agreements.
5. Except as expressly provided in this Agreement, nothing in this Agreement is intended or shall be construed to give any person, other than the Parties

hereto, any legal or equitable right, remedy or claim under or in respect of this Agreement pursuant to the Contracts (Rights of Third Parties) Act 1999, or any provision contained herein.

12. JURISDICTION, APPLICABLE LAW

This Agreement shall be governed by and construed in accordance with the laws of England and Wales and the parties submit unconditionally to the exclusive jurisdiction of the courts of England and Wales.

B6

DOWNLOAD AGREEMENT

Introduction

There is no such thing as a standard download agreement—different sectors distribute content online differently just as they did in physical form. There are, however, some key elements to these arrangements that we have drawn together into the attached set of standard terms. These cover a content owner appointing a distributor to make the owner's content available for download on specific web stores.

One key aspect of developing any form of online distribution agreement is understanding the commercial and legal relationships it creates. In particular, how far the principal roles and relationships in any pre-existing distribution chain are replicated or replaced. For example a simplified traditional structure might involve:

- artist/author/creator delivering to developer/publisher;
- developer/publisher delivering to distributor/wholesaler/retailer; and
- retailer delivering to consumer.

All of those have had to adapt to a world of digital delivery. We discussed the first of those in Part I. The latter has usually been unwritten and straightforward: 'I am entitled to sell this book/disc/tape to you (don't worry about how ownership has passed to me via middlemen from the publisher/distributor/studio), I promise the book/disc/tape is yours to keep if in return you pay me the price I ask'. As business has moved online, that relationship has to be set out in written terms, even if they are user-friendly 'click-through' ones. And with content in digital form the elements of that relationship are open to question: how far is the work 'theirs to keep' or does DRM limit usage by time or device? Will different versions/formats cost different prices? Will the content be provided by the seller or a third party server? Even the act of (electronic) browsing may now need a contract. These are discussed further in Chapters B8 and B9.

It is the second relationship (or set of relationships) that is dealt with here. Traditionally, this agreement, which usually *is* in writing, was essentially concerned with: (a) physical title: the right to buy and sell; and (b) liability: no infringement of legal rights (copyright, obscenity or defamation) and an indemnity against claims.

But as the retailer moves from selling physical formats to digital files, and the access rights that go with them, that agreement has had to develop. In many ways it too has to transfer concepts from physical content distribution, eg delivery, returns, withdrawn stock etc and re-present them in an online context. This sample agreement is in the form of the retailer's standard terms and as such provides a typically pro-retailer stance on many of these issues. By contrast the content owner may want to take a more cautious line on many issues, especially where it is working with a new form of digital service or product without the certainties and comforts it is used to.

CHECKLIST

1. It is not just title to sell and a promise of no liability that is needed, but a wider relationship of co-operation and support to make an online relationship work.
2. The retailer needs the supplier to grant the necessary wider rights (which may or may not involve discussions with authors and rights owners) and DRM controls to match.
3. And that applies not just to the actual sale but for all aspects of the marketing and promotion—from thirty-second previews and 'look inside' functionality to search engine optimization.
4. Is the supplier willing to buy the equivalent of point-of-sale promotion and front window displays for its downloads? So-called online 'placement' is as hard fought over as shelf space—even more so the smaller the device screen.
5. Physical shops are limited to high streets, online stores are open to the world, but copyright is territorial so unless worldwide rights are granted geo-blocking policies are needed to match.
6. If international rights are granted the retailer may want protection, internationally, from say libel or breach of privacy claims; and perhaps better warranties and indemnities.
7. Who 'owns' the customer? What greater protection will each party need to reflect this? Whatever the arrangements, they must comply with data protection law (see Chapter B9)
8. Is the customer database as important as the sales, eg for advertising and other funding?
9. Books, discs and tapes do not need a user manual—downloads do: who supplies customer helpdesks?
10. Last but not least, what are the commercial terms: what the retailer pays the supplier and how the supplier gets paid by the user, eg distributorship or agency revenue shares or wholesale models, gross or net, advances or guarantees?

Download Agreement

DOWNLOAD STORE TERMS

THIS AGREEMENT is made on [date]

By and between

1. DOWNLOAD STORE (UK) LIMITED of 22 Download Court, London MP3 ('DSL'); and
2. [ ] of [ ]

('**Content Owner**')

DSL operates online stores which promote, sell and deliver digital content. The Content Owner owns rights in certain digital content. The Content Owner appoints DSL as its authorized distributor of that digital content on the terms set out below.

1. DEFINITIONS

1.1 In this Agreement capitalized terms shall bear the meanings set out below:

'**Back-up Copies**': replacement copies issued to Customers in respect of any previous Download of Content in line with the Online Stores' standard policies and consumer terms on damaged, lost or defective content from time to time in force. 1

'**Content**': any content issued by the Content Owner for digital distribution from time to time. 2

'**Customers**': any customers of the Online Stores.

'**Download**': any means of digital delivery whereby a permanent copy of the content is retained on the receiver's reception device. 3

'**Intellectual Property Rights**': copyright, database, trade mark and all other intellectual and industrial property rights and related or similar rights whether or not registered or capable of registration including all renewals, revivals and extensions for their full period of protection throughout the world.

'**Metadata**': content, distribution and rights information relating to or descriptive of the Content. 4

'**Online Stores**': the websites and e-tailing platforms which may be used, owned or operated by DSL from time to time. 5

'**Promotional Materials**': the extracts, artwork, biographical details, reviews and other ancillary and promotional materials issued by the Content Owner in respect of the Content from time to time. 6

1 Back-up Copies—DSL will want maximum flexibility in what it can offer consumers, eg to allow re-downloads according to the policies it sets. The content owner will need care here to ensure: (a) it understands what the different parameters of the policies are and (b) that it is comfortable with those both commercially and legally, eg even if the content owner agrees that the user should have an extended right to access content, what will happen if the content owner is forced to amend or even withdraw that content for legal reasons.

2 Content—This might specify certain content, include a commitment for exclusivity or else a commitment that DSL will get the same content that other similar services will.

3 Download—Often this might not be specified at all but it is always worth the Content Owner adding detail—indeed it could go further and look at the devices and the delivery means.

4 Metadata—The accompanying data that describes the content files on sale and allows them to be managed online is increasingly important and developing accurate metadata can take time and investment.

5 Online Stores—The Content Owner might want a more specific list of stores.

6 Promotional Materials—Again the Content Owner needs to take care and ensure that it can comply with whatever is required without breaching its agreements with its artists/authors/developers.

Term: the term of this Agreement as set out in Clause 9.1.

Territorial Restrictions: the distribution territories for the Content set out in the Metadata.

Wholesale Price: the wholesale price of the Content as set by the Content Owner and updated from time to time on no less than 30 days' prior written notice to DSL. 7

1.2 In these Terms, unless otherwise stated: words in the singular shall include the plural and vice versa; the headings are for convenience only and shall not affect interpretation; references to *Clauses* relate to this Agreement; references to a *person* include an individual, firm, government body or authority, unincorporated association or body corporate; reference to a *Party* is to a party to this Agreement and reference to *including* or *include* shall not be construed to limit the sense of the preceding words.

2. APPOINTMENT

2.1 DSL is hereby appointed by the Content Owner as the authorized distributor of the Content during the Term subject to and in accordance with the terms of this Agreement.

2.2 [This appointment is on a non-exclusive basis and neither DSL nor the Content Owner is restricted from entering into similar arrangements with other persons.] 8

3. GRANT OF RIGHTS

3.1 Content Owner hereby grants to DSL a [non-]exclusive, worldwide, sub-licensable right to: (a) promote, sell and deliver the Content as Downloads to Customers via the Online Stores; and (b) use and display the Promotional Materials. 9

3.2 Content Owner also grants to DSL a [non-]exclusive, worldwide, sub-licensable right to use the trade marks and branding of the Content Owner and its licensors set out in the Content and the Promotional Materials.

4. DELIVERY OF THE CONTENT

4.1 Content Owner shall be solely responsible at its cost for delivering the Content and the Promotional Materials to DSL in such format, via such means and in accordance with such timetable as DSL shall from time to time require.

4.2 Content Owner shall deliver the Content with its associated Metadata which shall be deemed part of the Content. DSL shall be able to rely on the contents of the Metadata. Content Owner shall correct and notify DSL as soon as possible upon becoming aware of any errors in the Metadata. 10

7 Wholesale Price—In this deal the Content Owner sets a wholesale price; other alternatives might be an agreed discount from list price or a revenue share—possibly with an advance or minimum guarantee to protect the Content Owner. The agreement might even be re-cast as an agency relationship with the Content Owner then able to control the retail price itself.

8 Exclusivity—Clearly if exclusivity is granted the Content Owner may want more guarantees on performance

9 Rights granted—A reservation right might be added for good measure—or else included in the IPR clause below.

10 Format—There could be significant costs in re-formatting so the Content Owner will usually want clarity on what is required.

4.3 Content Owner shall remedy any defective materials supplied as soon as possible on notice from DSL. DSL agrees to amend, update or replace Content as requested by Content Owner from time to time.

4.4 DSL shall host and store the Content using reasonable industry security measures. [11]

5. PROMOTION AND SALE OF THE CONTENT

5.1 Content Owner and DSL shall discuss marketing and promotion of the Content. [12]

5.2 Subject to 5.9, DSL shall sell and deliver the Content in the form provided by the Content Owner except where (a) amendments are made in accordance with Clause 6; or (b) where it is necessary to re-format or re-configure the Content to technically enable or assist delivery from the Online Stores to the Customer.

5.3 DSL agrees to comply with the release dates of the Content as notified to DSL but the Content Owner agrees that DSL may promote and take pre-orders for the Content before the relevant release date.

5.4 DSL agrees to include copyright, contractual and related notices with the Content as notified to DSL but shall not be liable for any inadvertent failure to do so.

5.5 As between the Parties DSL is responsible for all aspects of the operation of the Online Stores including hosting, delivery, billing and collection, VAT payments and customer support but Content Owner agrees to give all reasonable information and assistance when requested by DSL.

5.6 DSL shall use reasonable efforts to enforce the Territorial Restrictions but the Content Owner agrees and acknowledges that it is not possible to guarantee that the Content will only be received in certain territories. [13]

5.7 Where requested by the Content Owner DSL shall apply the DRM encryption and rights restrictions notified to DSL in respect of all or any Content but the Content Owner agrees and acknowledges that it is not possible to guarantee that any DRM system will be secure and cannot be circumvented. [14]

5.8 DSL may select Content for the Online Stores and determine whether or not to exercise its rights hereunder at its sole discretion. [15]

6. CONTENT WITHDRAWAL [16]

6.1 The Content Owner must notify DSL in writing immediately if Content Owner: (a) ceases to hold the rights to distribute any of the Content; (b) decides to cease distributing any of the Content or is required to do so by any court,

11 Hosting—the content owner may want more detail on how the material is held and what measures are in place to protect it—for more detail see the content protection provisions in Chapter A5.

12 Promotion—The Content Owner may look for at least some minimum commitment.

13 Territory—There are some steps that can be taken, eg credit card and address checks as well as technical steps and the Content Owner may want some further commitment.

14 DRM—Again although the principle is not unreasonable some further detail as to the usage of content that is being permitted on the specific devices downloaded to may be required.

15 Must Carry—With an exclusive deal the Content Owner may be keener to see there is some commitment to use the right

16 Content Withdrawal—Ideally the Content Owner would want some more detail on timing and communication.

regulator or third party; or (c) reasonably believes that any of the Content infringes any Intellectual Property Rights or other rights of any third part or is otherwise unlawful.

6.2 Following receipt of a notice under Clause 6.1, or if DSL otherwise determines for any reason to do so, DSL shall withdraw the relevant Content from sale on the Online Stores.

6.3 DSL may maintain archive copies of any amended or withdrawn Content. Withdrawal of any of the Content, including at the end of the Term, shall be without prejudice to DSL's right to provide Back-up Copies. [17]

7. **PRICE AND PAYMENT**

7.1 DSL shall set the retail price for the Content on the Online Stores.

7.2 DSL shall prior to sale to a Customer purchase each item of the Content from the Content Owner at the Wholesale Price then in force.

7.3 The Content Owner agrees and acknowledges that: (a) no sale will have taken place where the Download is not completed or the Content is otherwise defective and no moneys will be due to the Content Owner; and (b) relevant credit card charge-backs, fraud, discounts, refunds and other Customer costs may be set off against the total amount due to Content Owner. [18]

7.4 DSL and the Content Owner shall enter into self-billing arrangements in respect of invoices for the Wholesale Price.

7.5 DSL shall pay invoices within 30 days of the end of the month in which they are received. In the event of late payment DSL agrees to pay interest at the base rate then in force of HSBC plc plus two per cent (2%) per annum from the due date until payment is made.

7.6 DSL shall issue the Monthly Reports. All Customer data and information relating to the sale of the Content shall be owned by DSL and shall not be provided to the Content Owner save as set out in generic form in the Monthly Reports.

7.7 DSL shall make available at its premises during the Term and for one year afterwards its books and records solely as they relate to the sale of the Content to the Content Owner or its authorized representative in order for them to audit the amounts paid hereunder. Such audit may be conducted no more than once per calendar year on reasonable written notice and during usual business hours at Content Owner's cost. If any underpayment or overpayment is shown it shall be remedied and if an underpayment of over ten per cent

17 Archive—As discussed at n 1 above, the content owner may seek universal rights to withdraw content.

18 Sales revenue—As with physical sales there will usually be some debate over what can be set off against revenue and/or on what basis such deductions can be applied. With digital distribution there may be additional concern for the content owner, at least initially, as to what might be 'standard' or 'normal' levels of such deductions in any market.

(10%) is shown DSL shall refund the Content Owner's reasonable costs of audit.[19]

8. INTELLECTUAL PROPERTY RIGHTS[20]

8.1 DSL (and/or its licensors) is the owner of all Intellectual Property Rights in the Online Stores.

8.2 Subject always to Clause 3, the Content Owner (and/or its licensors) is the owner of the Intellectual Property Rights in the Content and the Promotional Material.

9. TERM AND TERMINATION

9.1 This Agreement shall commence on the Commencement Date and shall continue unless terminated by either Party on 90 days prior written notice or in accordance with Clause 9.2.

9.2 This Agreement may be terminated by either Party on immediate written notice to the other Party if the other Party: (a) resolves to go into a voluntary liquidation (other than a members' voluntary winding up for the purposes of a reconstruction of its affairs), presents or has presented against itself a winding up petition, makes a composition with its creditors, has a receiver, manager or administrative receiver appointed over to the whole or any part of its assets or property, presents or has presented against itself a petition for the making of an administrative order or becomes unable to pay its debts within the meaning of section 123 of the Insolvency Act 1986; or (b) is in material breach of any of its obligations under this Agreement which is capable of remedy and has not remedied such breach or agreed to a satisfactory course of action within fourteen (14) days of having received written notice of the same from the terminating Party; or (c) is in material breach of any of its obligation under this Agreement which is not capable of remedy or repeats any breach as has previously been the subject of a notice under Clause 9.2(b); or (d) is precluded by a force majeure event in accordance with Clause 11 from performing its obligations for a period in excess of twenty-eight (28) days.

9.3 On termination of this Agreement DSL cease to promote, sell and deliver the Content provided that it may continue to make available Back-up Copies.

9.4 Any termination of this Agreement by either Party shall be without prejudice to any other rights or remedies it may have, and shall not affect any rights accrued or obligations arising on or before the date of termination.

19 Reporting and audit—The DSL may well seek to automate much of the reporting and accounting process and limit its obligations to the content owner beyond its standard procedures. The content owner may, however, want more information and protection here as it tries to test new business models and gain a better understanding of the market.

20 Intellectual Property Rights—One issue that might be dealt with here is whether DSL itself will obtain any permissions of licences directly for the sale of the Content. This might be required for certain content such as music [link to collecting societies].

10. WARRANTIES AND INDEMNITIES [21]

10.1 Each Party warrants and undertakes to the other that: (a) it has the full right, power and authority to enter into and perform its obligations under this Agreement; (b) it is entitled to perform its obligations under this Agreement and to grant any licences hereunder free from any third party claims; and (c) it shall use reasonable skill and care in performing its obligations under this Agreement.

10.2 The Content Owner further warrants and undertakes that the Content shall not infringe the Intellectual Property Rights or any privacy, publicity or other right of any person or be defamatory, obscene or otherwise unlawful and free from virus or malicious code and technically fit for purpose.

10.3 Each Party (the 'Indemnifying Party') shall indemnify and hold harmless the other Party against any costs, liabilities, losses, damage or expenses arising from any breach of any of the Indemnifying warranties and undertakings set out in this Clause 10.

11. FORCE MAJEURE

Neither Party shall be liable to the other if it is unable to perform or is late in performing its obligations under this Agreement due to extremes of weather or event of nature, industrial action, government action, interruptions in public order, accidents, epidemics or acts of God, provided that the Party relying on this clause gives immediate written notice to the other Party and takes all reasonable steps to overcome such circumstances (and any payment obligations of the other Party are suspended during such period). If such an event continues for a period of twenty (20) days or longer, the other Party may terminate this Agreement by giving immediate written notice to the Party unable to perform.

12. CONFIDENTIALITY AND PRIVACY [22]

12.1 Each Party undertakes to the other that, subject to Clause 9.2 below, it will treat as confidential the terms of this Agreement together with all information whether of a technical nature or otherwise relating in any manner to the business or affairs of the other Party as may be communicated to it hereunder or otherwise in connection with this Agreement and will not disclose such information to any person, firm or company (other than to its auditors and other professional advisers) or to the media and will not use such information other than for the purposes of this Agreement subject always to any proper specific authorization in writing by the disclosing Party to such disclosure or use.

12.2 The provisions of Clause 9.1 above shall not apply to any information which: (a) is in the public domain other than by default of the recipient Party; (b) is

21 Warranties and Indemnities—DSL might well be asked to give a return warranty and indemnity regarding its stores and their compliance with applicable law.

22 Confidentiality and Privacy—Usually DSL will resist any sharing of data.

obtained by the recipient Party from a bona fide third party having no apparent restraint on its free right of disposal of such information; (c) is required to be disclosed by law (or applicable regulation) or the valid order of a court of competent jurisdiction, or the request or direction of any governmental or other regulatory authority or agency.

12.3 Each party will comply with its obligations under the Data Protection Act 1998 (as amended or replaced) and any associated legislation or regulations regarding personal data including implementing and maintaining appropriate technical and organizational measures to prevent damage, loss or corruption of, or unauthorized access to such data.

13. NOTICES

Any notice given under this Agreement shall be in writing and may be delivered to the other Party or sent by pre-paid post or facsimile transmission to the address or transmission number of that Party specified in the Term Sheet or such other address or number as may be notified under this Agreement by that Party from time to time for that purpose.

14. SUB-CONTRACTING AND ASSIGNMENT

The Content Owner agrees and acknowledges that DSL appoints other persons from time to time to assist DSL in the operation of the Online Stores and the distribution of the Content. Accordingly DSL may sub-license and sub-contract any of its rights or obligations hereunder. The Content Owner shall not assign or sub-license the benefit of or sub-contract any of the obligations under this Agreement (or any part thereof) without the prior written consent of DSL, which may be given or withheld in its absolute discretion.

15. GENERAL

15.1 A waiver by either Party of any of the terms or conditions of this Agreement in any instance shall not be deemed or construed to be a waiver of such term or condition for the future, or of any subsequent breach thereof. The rights and remedies of the Parties under this Agreement are cumulative and in addition to any rights and remedies provided by law.

15.2 This Agreement constitutes the entire agreement and understanding between the Content Owner and DSL and that it supersedes all previous agreements, arrangements and understandings between them. Any variation to this Agreement must be in writing and agreed by the Parties.

15.3 Subject to the final sentence of this Clause 12.3, neither Party shall be entitled to (and both parties irrevocably and unconditionally waive any right they may have to) any remedies for any misrepresentation whether or not contained in this Agreement or breach of any warranty not contained in the Agreement.

Nothing in this Agreement shall restrict or exclude liability for (or remedy in respect of) fraud or fraudulent misrepresentation.

15.4 A person who is not a Party to this Agreement has no right under the Contracts (Rights of Third Parties) Act 1999 to enforce the benefit of any term of this Agreement and to the extent permitted by law the Parties hereby exclude the application of such Act to this Agreement.

15.5 Nothing in this Agreement shall be deemed to create a partnership or joint venture between the Parties.

16. GOVERNING LAW AND JURISDICTION

This Agreement shall be governed by and construed in all respects in accordance with English law and the Parties agree to submit to the non-exclusive jurisdiction of the English Courts as regards any claim or matter arising in relation to this Agreement.

B7

PODCASTING AGREEMENT

Introduction

Podcast. Webcast. Netcast. A range of names have been used for this type of content with the former seeming gradually to replace the latter two as the success of Apple's iPod player has grown over the last five to ten years. Not of course that an iPod, or indeed any specific form of wireless device, has been necessary to receive and use such content.

There are technical arguments, too, as to what forms of distribution it covers and whether it is still a distinct type of file delivery within the usual downloads, streaming or 'cloud' access models. To many, the online syndication provided by RSS feeds are a key element of podcasting and indeed that is the format by which Apple's own iTunes application distributes and promotes them (Apple Inc uses the word 'podcast' in lower case too, suggesting it accepts a generic descriptive use).

In our experience, however, podcasting is less about technology than content. A podcast represents a particular form of specific online content—content that (and without wanting to get caught up in limiting and unhelpful definitions) usually involves regular episodes of audio, but increasingly audiovisual, made-for-web material—and, as such, content that would often not otherwise exist without this specific online form of distribution. Although broadcasters now often re-purpose traditional radio programming and re-present it online as a podcast, that sort of content is not the focus of this chapter—and indeed those broadcasters probably would not require the sample agreement set out below.

This form of agreement is for use with bespoke online programming, primarily where traditional broadcasting or recording industry parties are not involved. It is designed to be flexible but also user friendly, so terms can be agreed easily. Many podcasts by their very nature need to be produced quickly and cheaply. That is not to say that podcast content is not taken seriously. We have known the quality of microphone to be a point of particular argument in a contractual dispute between the parties behind a very popular series of podcasts. So the terms and conditions set out here are not as streamlined as might be the case if the commissioning party (here the publisher) wanted to use a very short-form version.

The agreement is presented as a letter agreement with attached technical production schedules and then standard terms and conditions added at the back. The agreement takes the approach of a publisher commissioning an individual (the presenter) to devise and deliver a range of content for inclusion within interview-style podcasts produced by the publisher but with a primary element of the presenter actively taking part in the recordings. As such it is more akin to a performance agreement acquiring rights over a performance; an agreement simply to acquire rights in previously published material would concentrate less on services and more on the material being acquired.

Podcasting Agreement

THE PUBLISHER LIMITED
Publishing House
Remainder Lane
New Media Town
NM9 2BB

To:

The Presenter
of ************ *********** ('the Presenter').

Dear [Presenter]

The Publisher Limited (we or the 'Publisher') intend, but do not undertake, to produce a '**Podcast**' (as defined below) using content (including but not limited to interviews conducted by you) collated and submitted by you, and as approved by us.

We engage you and you agree to render your services as a[n interviewer, presenter and contributor [1]] to us for and in connection with the production of the Podcast in accordance with the attached Terms and Conditions which are incorporated into this Agreement and made a part of it.

Your engagement is to:

1. collaborate with the Publisher to produce the agreed number of episodes of the Podcast including to
   - conduct interviews;
   - propose and supply [all] content for the Podcast including incidental music [2] and voiceovers;
   - act as presenter of each episode; and
   - promptly comply with all instructions of the Publisher relating to the above and to make such changes to the content of the Podcast as the Publisher directs.
2. make yourself available to attend prepublication discussions in accordance with the Prepublication Timetable;
3. comply with the Publication Timetable;
4. attend such studios and locations in the United Kingdom as the Publisher shall specify in connection with the production of the Podcast; and
5. observe any embargo conditions imposed by the Publisher from time to time (and notified to the Presenter) on third parties in respect of the Podcast (including in respect of any press releases relating to the Podcast).

We agree that the number of episodes will be: .... [3]

The Fee: [£X] and/or [20] per cent of the Net Profit.] [4]

1 Complete as necessary

2 Where music is included, clearance of appropriate rights will be required in the sound recording and the underlying composition (see pp12–13). For example, the UK collecting society PRS has a specific podcasting licence for the latter, see <http://www.prsformusic.com/users/broadcastandonline/onlinemobile/podcastlicence/Pages/podcastlicence.aspx>.

3 If it is thought relevant, allow here for an extension of the number of podcasts beyond the initial programme.

4 It would be sensible to provide for instalment payment dates; say, one-third on signature, one-third on start of performance and one-third at the end of the Term. Any royalties/share of net profits should be accounted for on an annual of half-yearly basis.

The Term: Unless terminated earlier in accordance with the Terms and Conditions, this Agreement shall come into force on the Commencement Date and shall continue in force until [*** **** 20..]. 5

The dates we have agreed for Pre-Publication and Publication are set out in the Schedules to this Letter.

Please sign and return the copy of this letter to indicate your acceptance of the Terms.

Yours sincerely etc

SCHEDULE 1

Part 1

Production Details

Part 2

Prepublication Timetable Note 6

6–8 weeks before the Publication Date ('papers accepted' stage)	The Presenter and the Publisher discuss potential items. The Presenter then to set up (with the Publisher's help where available) and conduct interviews, and edit for time.
2 weeks before the Publication Date ('issue scheduled' stage)	The Presenter and the Publisher discuss running length, order and individual items as proposed by the Presenter.
Wednesday pm, 7 days before the Publication Date.	The Presenter provide rough cuts for the Publisher to screen running order, fillers etc.
Monday pm, week of Publication Date.	The Presenter submits final completed file (in MP3 format).

SCHEDULE 2

Publication Timetable

Episode	**Publication Date**

5 The usual date would be on completion of the Services; but whatever, a date should be agreed between the parties.

6 This timetable is inserted by way of example only. Of course it will vary from programme to programme and will need to be designed afresh for each.

Terms and Conditions for Podcast Letter Agreement

1. DEFINITIONS AND INTERPRETATION

1.1 In these Terms and Conditions (unless the context otherwise requires), the following words and phrases shall have the following meanings:

'**Agreement**' means these Terms & Conditions, the Letter Agreement and any document referred to, completed or to be completed in accordance with its provisions;

'**Commencement Date**' means the date of the Letter Agreement;

'**Intellectual Property Rights**' means copyright, knowhow, trade secrets and other confidential information, registered designs, database rights, design rights, and rights affording equivalent protection to the foregoing, semiconductor topography rights, trade marks, service marks, logos, domain names, moral rights, patents, inventions, and all registrations or applications to register any of the aforesaid items, rights in the nature of any of the aforesaid items in any country or jurisdiction, rights in the nature of unfair competition rights and rights to sue for passing off; [7]

'**Podcast**' means the podcast produced by the Publisher as a result of the Services;

['**Net Profit**' means the sum remaining in the Publisher's hands after deducting all costs (including staff costs) incurred in the production [and promotion] of the Podcast from all revenue received by the Publisher as a result of (1) direct sales of the Podcast, (2) sponsorship fees relating to the Podcast, and (3) syndication of the Rights; [8]]

'**Publication Date**' means the publication date of each episode of the Podcast as set out in the Publication Timetable;

'**Prepublication Timetable**' means the timetable set out in schedule 1 to the Letter Agreement;

'**Publication Timetable**' means the timetable set out in schedule 2 [9] to the Letter Agreement;

'**Rights**' means collectively the Intellectual Property Rights and any other rights, consents, waivers and licences granted and assigned by the Presenter to the Publisher under clause 2 below;

'**Services**' means the services provided by the Presenter to the Publisher as set out in the Letter Agreement;

'**Term**' means the term of this Agreement as set out in Clause 9 below;

7 This is a not unusual IP rights definition. It embraces all rights of an IP nature.

8 A clause similar to this will be needed where there is agreement to share Net Profits. It would not be difficult to draft a clause three times as long; but whatever, care should be taken to ensure that the clause reflects the parties' intentions. It should also be taken into account that, much as this agreement owes a lot to the film and TV industry agreements for the provision of services, so the likelihood of the Presenter ever seeing any net is similarly remote. The best way to ensure receipt of something from such a clause is to tie the (smaller) share into gross receipts (and even that is not a guarantee)!

9 These timetables, where needed, should be negotiated with care; the dates have to be realistic. Nevertheless, there is a case for providing for slippage (and how that should be dealt with) and having at least one fallback date where time is of the essence.

'**Working Day**' means any day from Monday to Friday (inclusive) which is not Christmas Day, Good Friday or a statutory holiday.

1.2 In these Terms and Conditions (unless the context otherwise requires):

1.2.1 the words '**including**' and '**include**' and words of similar effect shall not be deemed to limit the general effect of the words which precede them;

1.2.2 reference to any agreement, contract, document or deed shall be construed as a reference to it as varied, supplemented or novated;

1.2.3 obligations undertaken by a party which comprises more than one person shall be deemed to be made by them jointly and severally;

1.2.4 words importing persons shall include firms, companies and bodies corporate and vice versa;

1.2.5 words importing the singular shall include the plural and vice versa;

1.2.6 words importing any one gender shall include either other gender;

1.2.7 construction of this Agreement shall ignore the headings, contents list and frontsheet (all of which are for reference only);

1.2.8 any reference to any legislative provision shall be deemed to include any subsequent re-enactment or amending provision.

2. RIGHTS [10]

2.1 Grant of Rights

In consideration of the Fee the Presenter with full title guarantee hereby irrevocably grants, assigns and confirms to the Publisher (including, where relevant, by way of present assignment of future copyright):

2.1.1 all Intellectual Property Rights throughout the world in his contribution to the Podcast and all the other products of the Services whether included in the Podcast or not for the entire period of such Intellectual Property Rights including any and all renewals, reversions and extensions thereof and thereafter to the extent permissible in perpetuity;

2.1.2 an unconditional waiver in favour of the Publisher of any rights in the Podcast and all other products of the Services to which he may be entitled under Part I of Chapter IV of the Copyright, Designs and Patents Act 1988 or any moral right or '**droit moral**' or similar right to which the Presenter might be entitled in any country;

2.1.3 all other necessary consents and waivers (including under any future legislation that may create rights in the Podcast and all other products of the Services) to enable the Publisher to make the fullest use of the Podcast and all other products of the Services, whether in ways referred to or contemplated by this Agreement or in ways not yet invented or contemplated hereby;

2.1.4 the right to edit, adapt, change, add to or delete from the Podcast.

10 This is another of the key clauses; this one seeks to take rights in the Services. Consider whether that is necessary; for this kind of Services agreement it probably is, as the Podcast is being developed specifically for the Publisher and with the Publisher's money. Where the Presenter is supplying Content (and that content is third party material), it is necessary to ensure that similar rights in that Content are acquired as specified here (preferably using an agreement in a form approved or supplied by the Publisher); and to negotiate limits on the cost of such third party material.

2.2 mark which incorporates or is confusingly similar to 'Podcast' at any time, whether during or after termination of this Agreement.

3. PRODUCTION AND PROMOTION OF THE PODCAST

3.1 The arrangements for the production of the Podcast are set out in part 1 of Schedule 1 to the Letter.

3.2 The Presenter acknowledges and agrees that the Publisher has final editorial control in respect of the Podcast. Nothing in this Agreement shall constitute an undertaking by the Publisher to publish the Podcast.

3.3 The Presenter acknowledges and agrees that the Publisher has the unlimited right throughout the world to authorize others to issue publicity concerning the Podcast and to use the Presenter's name and likeness in connection with the advertising, publicity and promotion of the Podcast. [11] For the avoidance of doubt it is hereby acknowledged and agreed that the Publisher may publicize, promote or support the Podcast by way of a website and/or other online/internet activity (including by the use of hyperlinks on [the Publisher.com]) and may submit the Podcast to the iTunes podcast directory and/or such other directory as may be operated by [eg Apple Computer Inc] and other third parties from time to time.

4. REMUNERATION [12]

4.1 Payment of the Fee is subject to the provision by the Presenter of the Services, and is in full and final consideration of the Presenter providing the Services and of the Rights granted and assigned by the Presenter hereunder.

4.2 Subject to the Publisher having pre-approved them, the Publisher will reimburse the Presenter all due and proper expenses incurred by the Presenter in providing the Services, provided that the Presenter shall submit relevant receipts for such expenses.

4.3 The Presenter is not an employee of the Publisher and will be responsible for his own national insurance, personal tax and Value Added Tax. No VAT will be paid unless the Presenter is registered for VAT and provides the Publisher with his VAT registration number on all invoices.

5. WARRANTIES

The Presenter hereby warrants, represents and undertakes to the Publisher that:

5.1 the Services will be original in the Presenter except in so far as it includes third party material included with the knowledge of the Publisher;

5.2 he is able to enter into this Agreement and that the Publisher will be able to fully exploit the Rights and the Podcast and all other products of the Services not included in the Podcast (including, but not limited to, in any Publisher

11 In the film and TV industries it would not be uncommon to find the Publisher having an obligation to get the Presenter's approval 'not to be unreasonably withheld' for specific use of the likeness, etc. It would not be unreasonable to insert such a provision here.

12 Clearly another of the key clauses. Fee: whether both a fee and a share of profits are payable will depend on the nature and extent of the Services and the Presenter's bargaining position. Expenses: always better for the Publisher to keep tight hold over expenses, as otherwise they can tend to run away! Both parties need to consider the nature and likely extent of the expenses, and budget and provide accordingly.

publication, online, in hard copy or otherwise) without infringing the Intellectual Property Rights of any third party;

5.3 he has not in the twenty four (24) months prior to the Commencement Date performed in, and shall not during the Term perform in, any podcasts produced by any of the Publisher's competitors on the same or similar subject matter as the Podcast and which will, or are likely to, compete with the Podcast; [13]

5.4 he shall render the Services to the best of his abilities at such times and places in accordance with the reasonable instructions of the Publisher pursuant to the terms of this Agreement;

5.5 he has never appeared and shall not appear in any audio or visual recording of a pornographic or obscene nature and shall not at any time utter, publish or cause or allow to be published any comment likely [14] to discredit or damage the reputation of the Publisher or the Podcast;

5.6 he is in such a state of health that the Publisher will be able to effect insurance under normal conditions upon the Presenter's inability to perform the Services and the Presenter will do everything in his power to enable the Publisher to obtain and maintain such insurance and avoid doing anything which might invalidate such insurance;

5.7 he will not incur any liabilities on behalf of the Publisher nor pledge the credit of the Publisher;

5.8 he shall comply with all the rules of the studios and other locations at which he provides the Services;

5.9 he shall at the request and expense of the Publisher do all such further acts, deeds and things and execute all such further deeds and documents and instruments from time to time reasonably required by the Publisher to vest in the Publisher the Rights and for the protection and enforcement of the same.

6. INDEMNITY [15]

The Presenter agrees to indemnify and to defend and hold harmless the Publisher against any and all demands, claims, damages, judgments, costs (including reasonable legal fees on an indemnity basis), penalties and liabilities of, based upon, inconsistent with, relating to or arising out of breach or failure of any of the warranties, representations and agreements herein contained. Upon notice of any such demand or claim against the Publisher upon written notice to the Presenter, the Publisher may withhold from all payments due to the Presenter hereunder such amounts as may be necessary to protect the Publisher and as are directly related to the potential liability thereunder until liability upon any such demand or claim has been finally settled, determined and paid and the Publisher has been reimbursed its reasonable out of pocket costs and expenses (including legal fees on an indemnity basis) incurred in connection therewith.

13 This will be unenforceable if too broad; so the Publisher must limit its application.

14 'Likely' is of course a difficult 'call', for obvious reasons. The Publisher is entitled to some protection; the Presenter might prefer the words to read 'which cause discredit to or damage …', a much more objective test.

15 The Presenter may prefer this clause to be limited or removed.

7. SUSPENSION/TERMINATION

7.1 Notwithstanding anything to the contrary in this Agreement the Publisher shall be entitled to suspend the Services during any period when the Presenter fails or is prevented from rendering them or the production of the Podcast or the Publisher's use of the Services or exploitation of the Rights may be delayed by causes outside the Publisher's control. During any suspension the Presenter will continue to comply with his obligations hereunder other than the actual rendering of the Services and will not take on any conflicting engagement and the Publisher will retain all Rights hereby granted to it. After the end of any suspension the Publisher and the Presenter shall discuss in good faith alternative dates for the provision of the Services and the Prepublication Timetable and Publication Timetable will be amended and extended to take full account of the period of delay. [16]

7.2 Without prejudice to any other remedies and/or to the Publisher's accrued rights hereunder the Publisher shall be entitled to terminate this Agreement with immediate effect on written notice to the Presenter in the event of the Presenter's death or bankruptcy or any breach or threatened breach of this Agreement including without limitation any breach or threatened breach of any of the warranties under clause 5 above by the Presenter or if the Presenter commits any act or becomes involved in any situation or occurrence which in the sole opinion of the Publisher is likely to bring the Publisher, the Podcast or the Presenter into disgrace. [17]

8. CONSEQUENCES OF TERMINATION/EXPIRY

Upon termination or expiry of this Agreement all rights and obligations of the parties shall cease to have effect immediately except that termination shall not affect accrued rights and obligations of the parties under this Agreement at the date of termination or any express obligations in this Agreement of a continuing nature.

9. ASSIGNMENT

The Publisher shall be entitled to transfer or assign any of the rights hereby granted, assigned or confirmed to it to any third party.

10. CONFIDENTIALITY

10.1 In this clause 10, '**Confidential Information**' means all information disclosed (whether in writing, orally or by another means and whether directly or indirectly) by the Publisher to the Presenter whether before or after the Commencement Date including, but not limited to, information relating to the Publisher's products, operations, processes, plans or intentions, product information, know-how, design rights, trade secrets, market opportunities and business affairs.

16 A clause of this nature is not unreasonable; after all, the Publisher wants to ensure that the Presenter remains available to complete the Services after the end of the delay. And what in this context are 'conflicting services'? However, in his turn, the Presenter will want protection from being effectively suspended for months on end, unable to earn his living. He might therefore negotiate the right, where the delay is the Publisher's, to serve notice on the Publisher (after, say, a month of suspension?) that unless they resume the production process within seven days, the agreement is to continue. (effectively requiring the Publisher to restart production or pay him off). See also Clause 2 above.

17 The termination triggers have been extended to cover a general 'non-embarrassment' provision that allows the Publisher to drop the Presenter if continued association could be harmful, eg as a result of bad press received by the latter. This is common in podcasts for commercial products in advertising and promotional campaigns.

10.2 During the term of this Agreement and after termination or expiry of this Agreement for any reason the Presenter:

10.2.1 shall not use Confidential Information for a purpose other than the performance of his obligations under this Agreement;

10.2.2 shall not disclose Confidential Information to any person except with the prior written consent of the Publisher;

10.2.3 shall make every effort to prevent the use or disclosure of Confidential Information.

10.3 Clause 10.2 does not apply to Confidential Information which:

10.3.1 is at the Commencement Date or becomes at any time after that date publicly known other than by the Presenter's breach of this Agreement;

10.3.2 can be shown by the Presenter to the Publisher's satisfaction to have been known by the Presenter before disclosure by the Publisher to the Presenter;

10.3.3 is or becomes available to the Presenter otherwise than pursuant to this Agreement and free of any restrictions as to its use or disclosure;

10.3.4 is required to be disclosed by law.

11. NOTICES

Any notice given by one party to the other under this Agreement must be in writing and may be delivered personally or by pre-paid first-class post and in the case of post will be deemed to have been given two Working Days after the date of posting. Notices shall be delivered or sent to the addresses of the parties on the first page of this Agreement or to any other address notified in writing by one party to the other for the purpose of receiving notices after the date of this Agreement. Each party may specify by notice to the other a particular individual or office holder to whom any notices served on it are to be addressed, in which case a notice shall not be validly given unless so addressed.

12. THIRD PARTIES

A person who is not party to this Agreement shall have no rights under the Contracts (Rights of Third Parties) Act 1999 to enforce any term of this Agreement. This clause does not affect any right or remedy of any person which exists or is available otherwise than pursuant to that Act.

13. NO PARTNERSHIP OR AGENCY

Nothing in this Agreement is intended to create a partnership or joint venture or legal relationship of any kind that would impose liability upon one party for the act or failure to act of the other party between the parties, or to authorize either party to act as agent for the other. Save where expressly stated in this

Agreement, neither party shall have authority to make representations, act in the name or on behalf of or otherwise to bind the other.

14. WAIVER AND CUMULATIVE REMEDIES

14.1 The rights and remedies provided by this Agreement may be waived only in writing and specifically, and any failure to exercise or any delay in exercising a right or remedy by either party shall not constitute a waiver of that right or remedy or of any other rights or remedies. A waiver of any breach of any of the terms of this Agreement or of a default under this Agreement shall not constitute a waiver of any other breach or default and shall not affect the other terms of this Agreement.

14.2 The rights and remedies provided by this Agreement are cumulative and (unless otherwise provided in this Agreement) are not exclusive of any rights or remedies provided at law or in equity.

15. VARIATION

No variation of this Agreement shall be valid unless it is in writing signed by or on behalf of each of the parties to this Agreement.

16. ENTIRE AGREEMENT

16.1 These Terms and Condition, together with the Letter Agreement constitute the entire agreement and understanding between the parties in respect of the matters dealt with in it and supersede, cancel and nullify any previous agreement between the parties or any of them relating to such matters notwithstanding the terms of any previous agreement or arrangement expressed to survive termination.

16.2 Each of the parties acknowledges and agrees that in entering into the Letter Agreement it does not rely on, and shall have no remedy in respect of, any statement, representation, warranty or understanding (whether negligently or innocently made) other than as expressly set out in the Letter Agreement. The only remedy available to either party in respect of any such statement, representation, warranty or understanding shall be for breach of contract under the terms of the Letter Agreement.

16.3 Nothing in this Clause 16 shall operate to exclude any liability for fraud.

17. GOVERNING LAW AND JURISDICTION

17.1 This Agreement and any matter arising from or in connection with it shall be governed by and construed in accordance with English law.

17.2 Each party irrevocably agrees to submit to the exclusive jurisdiction of the English courts over any claim or matter arising from or in connection with this Agreement.

B8

WEBSITE TERMS OF USE

Introduction

One of the more neglected contracts in digital media is website terms and conditions of use. As with any other product, websites and online services may require appropriate end-user notices and provisions controlling access and use. Yet many websites and services will add terms of use almost as an after-thought, perhaps copying terms wholesale from elsewhere, or not include anything at all. Neither of those options is advisable and some care should be taken with each website or service to think through the relevant issues.

There are, however, no hard-and-fast rules as to what must be covered. Indeed some websites might well be able to function safely and successfully with very limited legal wording. But that should be on the basis of a considered review rather than neglect. Certainly, free access websites with limited content and functionality might not present the same issues as more sophisticated online environments. Generally the more functionality and interactivity that is offered the more there is a need for legal input. It is then sensible to have the relevant legal material collected in one place, as terms and conditions, even if some text appears on specific parts of the website.

Once payment is required to access the website or purchase certain content then the terms become particularly important and there may be different provisions that apply to the free access material and other content behind a pay-wall etc. Of course, traditional forms of physical content have generally never required detailed legal terms: books and music LPs or CDs have usually been sold with just a few lines of text within the front (or back) matter, sleeve or cover. Digital products raise additional considerations, however, and we discuss these below and suggest possible wording in the example terms provided.

- **Licence Wording**—The user is being granted a licence to use the website and the content included within it. Rather than rely on implied terms it is sensible to set out expressly what the user can or cannot do, ie the scope of his or her licence.

This may be more important with some sites and content than others. It may also be necessary to comply with the terms that the website provider agreed in relation to that content when licensing-in from a third party. Along with the licence terms it is usually sensible to give notice of the ownership of the relevant intellectual property rights (whether required as a matter of local law, the third party licence or simply good practice) eg by referring to relevant trade marks ™ ® or to specific copyright material © and their owners.

- **Linking and Framing**—One very specific use that a website provider may wish to control is the act of linking, framing and/or other online re-use of the website or particular content within it. The ability to use intellectual property rights or other legal means to prevent such activities may be limited in many jurisdictions (see Chapter B4) so inclusion within the terms and conditions may provide a useful additional contractual argument—even if practical enforcement may still be difficult.
- **Liability**—An early driver for the development of website terms of use was concern that the wide availability of online content could bring legal exposure and liability for the website provider. Indeed terms of use are often referred to as 'disclaimers' on the grounds that their primary function is to disclaim or avoid responsibility for the contents of the website. Accordingly, broad exclusions of liability have commonly been included in most online terms. Actually, the extent to which (a) such broad provisions would really be effective, if ever tested, and (b) liability would actually arise is debatable (see Part I). Much will depend on the type of content and the intended users.
- **Information Requirements**—In many jurisdictions there are specific rules that require websites and online services to include certain information about the website provider and the service they are providing (see the Checklist for European Union rules below).
- **Specific Content**—There may be particular requirements that are necessary or advisable with special types of content. Clearly content that is only suitable for specific audiences or that may involve particular risks will require extra care/wording. In some cases specific legal or regulatory provisions will apply but it is still true in many countries that controls that would ordinarily apply in traditional/physical media, eg formal classification/certification of age-rated video material, have yet to be formally extended online (again, see Part I). Even so, best practice (and common sense) may still suggest compliance with at least the spirit of those provisions.

Once the terms are drafted it is necessary to bring them to the attention of the user—and obtain acceptance. There is still room for argument in many countries as to how far the website owner must go to ensure that the terms are legally enforceable. Indeed, there are surprisingly few clear decisions in many jurisdictions. Courts have applied general principles of non-contractual notices (eg warning notices used in physical premises) as well as traditional rules of incorporation for contractual terms.

Obviously, the more important the terms are to the website and the content, the more important it is that those terms are brought to the attention of the user on both legal and practical grounds.

CHECKLIST

Under European Union law the operators of 'information society services'—in essence this will include most non-personal websites and online services—are required to provide certain information about themselves and their service to the user. The rules, and the interpretation of them, vary slightly between members states (and are in addition to any other local requirements) but the key elements are listed below:

1. The full name of the service provider.
2. The geographical address at which the service provider operates (and also the formal registered address if different).
3. Contact details of the service provider to allow effective communication, including email but which in some cases will also require a telephone number.
4. The service provider's company registration number and/or details of any other relevant or equivalent register on which the service provider appears.
5. The service provider's VAT registration number.
6. If the service provider is a regulated business, its formal title, details of the regulating body and any applicable rules.
7. If the provision of the service is subject to an authorization scheme, details of the relevant supervisory authority.
8. If prices are referred to they must be clear and unambiguous indicating taxes and delivery costs (but further rules may apply—see below).
9. If the service is used to conclude online contracts by electronic means:
   - a description of the different technical steps needed to conclude the contract;
   - confirmation of whether or not any contract concluded will be filed and/or accessible;
   - a description of the technical means enabling the identification and correction of input errors before an order being placed;
   - the languages(s) offered for the conclusion of the online contract;
   - unless otherwise agreed in a non-consumer contract, any relevant code of conduct to which the service provider subscribes and how that can be consulted.

The information must be made 'easily, directly and permanently accessible' so with some short-form content or services with limited space to include full terms and conditions it may be necessary to include a suitable reference to where the information can be obtained.

Note Further provisions apply to the process of contracting, including rules requiring the acknowledgment of receipt of online orders and, where the website is also selling to consumers, additional, but overlapping, requirements apply under special EU distance selling provisions. These are complex and need careful consideration in respect of each specific service. Many of these requirements may be better dealt with on that part of the website where the sales are actually made.

Generally, the website owner will frame the terms of use as a contractual relationship with the user. In many jurisdictions, mandatory provisions in respect of consumer contracts could then in theory apply (in practice any dispute might be unlikely to be tested in court). Certainly within the EU these effectively place the onus on the website owner wishing to enforce terms of use against a user to be able demonstrate that the user had been given a fair and reasonable opportunity to review and accept those terms. Yet many websites feature links to terms, disclaimers or other legal wording solely in a link at the bottom of the page, below the fold, and rely on a reference to the effect that continued use amounts to acceptance of the provisions.

The ubiquity of that method may count for something—if asked, many users could probably find the location of a website's terms. Overall, however, it is still some way short of providing legal certainty. In many cases that may be an acceptable risk. With terms that the website owner is likely to want to enforce, and certainly with paid content, a more robust acceptance method is needed. Where specific legal formalities apply this can prove difficult; for example in the UK the interplay of execution formalities under particular legislation, indeed for documents signed as deeds generally, with electronic formats is problematic (see the box below on the key issue of copyright agreements in the UK). And different countries' laws do vary over such formalities.

In many cases, however, contracts can be concluded without limited legal formality so the form and method by which an online contract is agreed is essentially an issue of evidence and authentication. So, ideally, the 'click-wrap' or 'click-through' concept of an 'I AGREE' icon should, as a matter of fact, be able to show that a particular person entered into the agreement and that they understood that they were agreeing to be bound by those terms in the same way that a written signature would. As the click of an icon can clearly not be tracked to a human hand as a written signature might be, supporting evidence might be needed for important contracts.

Interestingly, and despite the existence of extensive legal frameworks anticipating their use, formal electronic signatures (ie using encryption technology to provide authentication) remain the exception even in business use.

Digital contracts—copyright issues

- Assignments of copyright in the UK must be in writing and 'signed' to be valid. Licences do not have to be, but a 'signature' confers a special status on an exclusive licensee in court proceedings.
- Though not tested fully in court, electronic signatures, a click-wrap/click-through, or just typing a name are likely to be capable of fulfilling the 'signature' requirement. A UK court has opined that a name in an email is capable of being a signature.
- Whether a technical solution meets a statutory signature requirement, ie because it has the necessary *authenticating intention*, is distinct from its *evidential reliability*. All forms of electronic signature are vulnerable to fraud to differing degrees—just as a wet signature is. That fact will not, in itself, mean it is less likely to be accepted as meeting a statutory signatory requirement.

These are UK law points and although similar issues will arise in other jurisdictions relevant local law should always be checked as necessary

Website Terms of Use

WEBSITE TERMS OF USE

1. TERMS OF USE

- These Terms set out the basis upon which we make this website available to you by whatever access means eg [ ] 1
- Please read these Terms carefully. By using this website you will be deemed to have agreed to these Terms. If you do not agree to comply with these Terms please do not use the website. We may change these Terms from time to time so please review these Terms regularly. 2
- This website is operated by [ ]. Our registered company number is [ ]. Our address is [ ]. Our VAT number is [ ].
- If you have any questions please email us at [ ] or write to us at [ ] [or call our helpdesk on [ ]]. 3

2. ACCESS AND REGISTRATION

- You must obtain, and pay for, all telecommunications services, computer equipment and software necessary to connect to and use this website. We do not provide such services, equipment or software and you will need to obtain these from other suppliers. We do not have any control over, or responsibility for, such suppliers. 4
- We provide most of this website on an open access basis but you may need to register and/or pay to use some areas. In some cases we may restrict access by age and/or location of user. You promise that all registration information you provide shall be accurate. You must inform us as soon as you can if it needs updating. It may be necessary for us to refuse some registration applications, eg to prevent fraudulent usage. Please read our *Privacy Policy* 5 [*add link*] which applies to the registration information we collect.
- We may issue you with a username, password and/or other access control for this website or certain parts of it (together, referred to as *passwords*). These are for your personal use only. You must not tell them to anyone else or allow anyone else to use them. You must not use anyone else's passwords. You must tell us if you think your passwords are no longer confidential. If you do, or if we believe it to be necessary, we may issue you with replacement passwords.
- Maintaining the security and integrity of the website is necessary to enable all our users to use it safely and effectively. You agree not to abuse the access/registration process. 6

3. CONTENTS OF THE WEBSITE

- This website features a wide range of text, photographs, sound recordings, videos, software, data and other content of all forms which we and/or our

1 It may be worth confirming the relevant forms of delivery, eg adding mobile or broadcast platforms, and/or clarifying where different versions apply.

2 As mentioned in the Introduction, while such an approach remains standard for free-access websites and online services, alternative means of user acceptance ought to be considered for premium content and/or where greater legal certainty is required. With paid-for content more formal order and acceptance procedures will be advisable and in many cases required by law. We have tried to take account of mandatory consumer law provisions, at least in the UK/EU, which will become more of a concern with pay material.

3 As mentioned in the Introduction, some jurisdictions have legal requirements for operators to provide certain information, which may vary according to the particular services offered. It is good practice to maintain an up-to-date set of details in one place on a website even if repeated elsewhere.

4 This sort of provision dates back to proprietary online services before the ubiquity of the Web but may still be worth including in user terms especially for premium content and other paid-for services.

5 See Chapter B9.

6 Even where content is provided without payment the operator may still want to develop some form of registration requirement and apply access controls. In some jurisdictions this may be required or advisable due to specific legal or regulatory requirements relating to the nature of the content and/or the audience likely to be accessing it. It may be due to the requirements of the operator's suppliers, eg granting a licence for certain territories only. Simply being able to link a user to a registration may have legal benefits (see Chapter B10). However, the process of registering can often deter users. Further, the misuse of registration procedures and access controls can be a practical concern so it is usually sensible to reserve sufficient flexibility to the operator to enable them to respond as required.

suppliers provide (together referred to as *website content*) which we want you to be able to enjoy in a fair and reasonable way. 7

- The website content is protected by copyright, trade mark rights, database rights and other intellectual property and related rights which are owned by us and/or our suppliers. You may access this website and view the website content on-screen and, where permitted by this website, print out a reasonable number of copies of parts of the website content, as long as this is for your own private and non-commercial purposes only. 8
- For certain website content, eg where payment is necessary or where our suppliers have required it, separate and/or additional usage terms may apply. These will be marked on the relevant area of this website where you will be given the opportunity to review and agree to them. 9
- You must not, nor try to, make mass, automated or systematic extractions of the website content, or use it to create or include it within another paper or electronic database, or try to re-sell it or re-distribute it. We reserve the right to prohibit or restrict the way in which other websites link to or frame or represent any of the website content. 10
- Decompiling, reverse engineering, disassembling or otherwise reducing the code used in any software on this Website into a readable form in order to examine the construction of such software is prohibited except to the extent permitted by law. If you need information on the relevant law contact us or your local consumer adviser. 11
- If you have any questions about what your may or may not do with the website content or use the website generally please contact us at [ ]. 12
- We reserve any other uses of, and rights in, the website content on behalf of both us and our suppliers, so you must obtain our prior written permission for these. We may not always be able to give our consent but to make such a request please contact us at [ ]. 13

4. LIABILITY 14

- Unless you and we agree otherwise, eg as part of any pay-per-view arrangement or where our suppliers have required us to do so and where separate and/or additional usage terms may apply which will be marked on the relevant part of the website, the website content is provided for free and is for your informational purposes only.
- Please note that the website will not be available at all times. It will be inaccessible during regular maintenance periods and it may from time to time be subject to emergency maintenance or be unavailable for other technical reasons. Like all software-based services the website cannot be promised to be free from errors or bugs. We will, however, use reasonable care and skill in fixing any problems once we become aware of them.
- Although we take reasonable care with our website content we cannot check every item or promise that typos or other errors will never appear on the website.

7 It is not uncommon for free-access website terms to include blanket restrictions on further use. That is of course unrealistic and this is a suggested form of content licence that might be more suitable, bearing in mind that policing of the terms may be difficult in practice. For more information on licensing generally see Part I.

8 This should have general application although specific rights and scope—including any permitted exceptions that a user may benefit from—will of course vary by relevant territory.

9 Some jurisdictions will not permit 'hidden' terms to be enforced—certainly against consumers—see Introduction above. Of course, further more detail could be added where necessary. It may for instance be relevant to specify more clearly when use is actually 'non-commercial'.

10 As mentioned in the Introduction, the extent to which intellectual property or related rights may prevent unauthorized scraping, linking or framing of a website remains an area of legal debate. Accordingly if an operator wishes to prevent such activities it is sensible to include express restrictions in terms of use to allow the operator to use contractual arguments in addition.

11 Some jurisdictions will have mandatory provisions relating to this area.

12 As above this attempts to strike a more helpful stance on the use of online content, although the service provider may not have the resources or the desire to encourage contact in this way.

13 A more helpful alternative to the standard 'All rights reserved'.

14 See Introduction above. This may well be far more detailed than many free-access sites would need or want, but this wording attempts to provide a more reliable and enforceable set of provisions, at least under the relevant UK consumer regulator's interpretation of EU consumer law, than the usual blanket exclusions of liability. Although experience suggests that this would be unlikely to be an issue with a free-access site where payment is involved, compliance with consumer law is more of a concern.

Unlike, traditional physical media, the website is a dynamic environment with regular changes and therefore inaccuracies may occur from time to time. Please double-check any specific instruction with us or a third party if you are in doubt.

- We cannot control and are not responsible for the user provided/generated content that appears on the website. We recommend that you apply particular caution when using that content.
- This website may contain third party advertising and links to external websites. External websites may link to this website. We choose our commercial partners with reasonable care but we do not necessarily recommend, endorse or sponsor, and cannot control and are not responsible for any third-party content that may be accessed through this website or from which this website may be accessed. Please use common sense and caution when using such third-party websites and content. You should read their own terms of use and privacy policies.
- PLEASE BEAR THE ABOVE IN MIND WHEN USING THE WEBSITE. IF YOU ARE UNCLEAR ABOUT ANYTHING THAT APPEARS ON THE WEBSITE, OR THINK THERE MAY BE AN ERROR, PLEASE CONTACT US AT [*add email*].
- [We shall not be liable and shall not compensate you for any loss or damage you may suffer unless we have failed to carry out our obligations under these Terms to a reasonable standard or breached any duties imposed on us by law, including if we have caused death or personal injury by our negligence, and that failure is not attributed to: (a) your own fault, for example your failure to implement recommendations previously advised by us; (b) a third party unconnected with our performance of this agreement, for instance problems due to communications network performance, congestion and connectivity or the performance of your computer equipment; or (c) any other events which neither we nor our suppliers could have foreseen or forestalled even if we or they had taken reasonable care.
- Accordingly, we will not be responsible for loss of or damage to your computer hardware or software or other personal property or any other losses which you suffer as a result of the website unless this is due to our neglect or failure to take reasonable precautions and such losses are reasonably foreseeable. We strongly recommend that you (a) take care to verify the suitability and compatibility of your computer system prior to use; and (b) take reasonable precautions to protect yourself against harmful programs or devices including through installation of anti-virus software.
- As this is a consumer website we shall not in any event be liable for losses related to any business such as lost data, lost profits or business interruption.] [15]

5. TERMINATION [16]

- If you wish to terminate your registration for any part of this website at any time [please contact us at [ ]].

15 In particular this example includes longer-form provisions that describe the overall limitation of liability in terms of what responsibility the service provider is accepting—in line with mandatory consumer law—rather than attempting a blanket (and prima facie unlawful and unenforceable) exclusion of any responsibility. Again this may not be suitable for every form of user terms.

16 Consumer law, certainly within the UK/EU, would prefer a more mutual position on termination—and in many cases there would neither be the need nor desire on the website owner's part to receive notice from every user when that user wishes to terminate its usage of the website and agreement with the owner. This is only likely to be an issue where payment is involved and where the practical concerns are likely to revolve around subscription periods, refunds and the specific requirements of credit card or other online payment methods. Automatic renewal mechanisms are a particular area requiring care.

- Unless you and we agree otherwise, eg as part of any pay-per-view arrangement, to which separate terms shall apply, we may terminate the provision of this website to you at any time. We shall try to give you prior notice if we do but this may not always be possible.
- If you are in breach of these Terms, or we have reasonable grounds to believe that you are, we may suspend and/or terminate your access to this website without prior notice.

6. GENERAL [17]

- If you are in breach of these Terms and we do not take any action against you, we may still take action against you later or if you breach the same term on another occasion or if you breach a different term.
- If any provision of these Terms is, for any reason, held to be unenforceable, illegal or invalid in some other way, the unenforceable, illegal or invalid provision will not affect the remainder of these Terms and they will continue in full force and effect.
- These Terms are governed by relevant UK law and you and we agree to only bring legal actions about these Terms in a UK court. We will try to solve any disagreements quickly and efficiently. If you are not happy with the way we deal with any disagreement you and we may agree to refer the matter to arbitration but you and we are not restricted from bringing court proceedings. [18]
- We intend to rely on the written terms set out in these Terms, as amended in accordance with paragraph 1 above, and the documents referred to in it, as the entire understanding between us relating to your use of the website. If you and we agree any changes, please make sure that you request that these are confirmed in writing. That way we can avoid any problems surrounding what we or you are expected to do in relation to your order.
- Only you or us have the right to enforce any provision under these Terms.

17 Contract 'boilerplate'—which in many B2B contacts is often uncontroversial and requires little negotiation (rightly or wrongly)—may fall foul of consumer law whether (a) because it is legalistic shorthand that most users will not understand or (b) because it is one-sided and pro-supplier—in either case unfair and unenforceable. This text tries to avoid that.

18 An example of the above is choice of law and courts. The UK is in fact three legal jurisdictions—England and Wales, Scotland and Northern Ireland—and while a business is free to adopt, say, the law and courts of England and Wales in its contract with other businesses, it is the view of the relevant UK regulator that this could be unfair with a consumer who should be allowed to take advantage of a local court, and potentially local law.

B9

PRIVACY POLICY

Introduction

'A communications medium transmits messages. It also may alter the message itself. A computer system processes data. It also may affect the data itself'—a prophetic statement from a 1974 book by one of the first lawyers, Milton Wessel, to write about the issues of privacy in computing. Certainly personal data—effectively defined under relevant EU law as information by which a living individual may be identified—is at the heart of the online world. Any website or other digital business that processes personal information—that is, collects, uses and/or discloses personal information—must do so in compliance with data protection law.

Despite this, data protection was for many years an often overlooked—even perceived to be boring—area of law. In a high profile privacy case in London, a data protection law specialist was famously introduced to the court as 'the anaesthetist'. Yet as a senior Google executive has memorably described, concern over privacy (for users, operators and regulators) now runs through online life like a live rail on a train track. Treading without care can bring a nasty wake-up for those still sleep-walking. Increased fines and regulatory sanctions have added to the risks.

Relevant rules vary from territory to territory. Indeed, there is a core difference between the US and the EU, with the latter basing its law around overarching regulation of all personal data while the former has more specific laws focused on particular circumstances. There are also important variances within the EU despite extensive attempts at harmonization. Further, in the particular context of digital media, a mix of data protection, electronic communications, consumer and advertising provisions can be relevant: some formal statutory provisions and others more informal industry regulations, codes and best practice. The resulting framework can therefore be complex and confusing.

The UK privacy regulator has, however, provided a helpful and relatively universal principle for handling personal data: 'always say what you are going to do, and always do what you say'. In essence that is the basis of the concept of a privacy notice or policy—a written statement explaining when and what personal data will be collected on a website, who will use it and how. As such, the document should be less a legal statement, although elements of it may help a website operator to comply with its legal and regulatory obligations, eg see discussion of cookies in the document below, than a user-friendly explanation giving practical guidance.

A privacy policy should be clear, transparent, and free of 'legalistic' or complicated language. Done properly, it should be attractive and beneficial to users as well as going a long way to satisfying fundamental legal requirements. In fact, regulators and law makers in several countries are increasingly supportive of a 'less-is-more' approach to privacy polices. The provision of lengthy descriptive documents is seen as counter-productive and instead the use of so-called layered notices, which link brief initial summaries through to additional detail, for those who wish to read it, is encouraged.

The shortest form of privacy policy is often in relation to marketing uses. That is because, in many countries special rules, additional to general data protection law, apply to marketing activities and, in particular, marketing to consumers by electronic means. The key issue here is permission. Therefore, when contact details are collected on a website, eg in a registration form or purchase screen, and the owner intends to use these for marketing purposes it is usually necessary to include a short permission request at the same time. Following the format of earlier print equivalents these are often in the form of tick or click boxes—allowing the user to opt in (or opt out—but see box below) to the marketing use requested.

For many online activities it will be common sense that personal data use is involved. So while a privacy policy is still good practice there is no need to take active steps to tell people the obvious. More should be done, however, when a site is collecting 'sensitive' personal information (under EU law stricter rules apply to data relating to health and sexuality, racial origins, political opinions and religious belief), when the information is to be shared or sold to other organizations or when the data is going to be used in a non-obvious or unexpected way. It may be necessary to take a similar approach to marketing permissions or even to send an email or other direct communication.

Care should also be taken over the amount of personal data that is collected. EU law prohibits the collection of excessive information so a website should not request personal details that are unnecessary for its relevant activities. Indeed privacy regulators generally advise against requiring registration for basic website browsing. Although, given the irritation that registration gateways can cause the user, commercial common sense probably suggests the same stance. In many cases, not just on websites but in digital media of all kinds, operators are happy to exclude any use of personal data to avoid the compliance requirements that brings.

Finally we should mention the headache of cross-border transfers of personal data. The EU places restrictions on the transfer of personal data to jurisdictions outside the EEA and certain 'white list' territories on the grounds that these may not give adequate legal protection. As mentioned above, because the US takes a different approach to data protection law the US is not on that white list. As a result additional steps have to be taken to ensure that the transfers to the US—or any non-white list other country—are lawful. These range from the user's consent to more detailed contractual solutions. Specialist advice is usually needed to select the best approach.

Opt in and opt out

There is often debate whether particular permission requests require an opt-in or opt-out.

Opt-out	Opt-in
From time to time we	*From time to time we*
would like to do X.	*would like to do Y.*
If you do NOT want us	*If you would like us*
to do X please tick here	*to do Y please tick here*

The former can result in more apparent permissions being granted, but the active step involved in the latter can be seen as being more legally effective. The relevant legal rules may not actually refer explicitly to either alternative (for example, the UK relevant regulator always focuses on the wider context of the collection process) but as digital media has developed, especially for marketing, the rules have been interpreted as moving toward the opt-in—which is certainly best practice.

In the UK it is still standard to use an opt-out for physical postal marketing and in the context of the so-called 'soft opt-in' exception where an operator can use an email obtained in the course of a sale or negotiation for a product or service if subsequent marketing is for the operator's similar products or services and where the user is given a simple opportunity to refuse originally and with each communication (ie a continuing opt-out—which is required in marketing communications generally).

Particular care is needed with:

- Children: The US has very specific controls on the way in which information from children under thirteen can be collected and used. This has resulted in thirteen becoming a default age limit for many websites in other countries. The US rules for obtaining parental consent are also often used as suggested best practice elsewhere. But other age limits and provisions for communicating with, and especially marketing to, children do apply in other countries.

- 'Recommend-a-friend' type mechanisms: Here the consent to contact someone is being provided by a third party. Legally that can expose the operator to risk especially where there are incentives for such referrals. It is common for the third party to be required to confirm they have that consent and informed that the contact will be told who gave their details. This can be important in the context of viral marketing and communication within social networks.

Privacy Policy

PRIVACY POLICY

This Policy explains our approach to online information collection, storage and use in connection with this site, as well as the specific choices you can make about your own information. Please read this Policy carefully. By using the site you will be deemed to have agreed to this Policy, so if you do not agree please do not use the site. [1]

We may post changes to this Policy from time to time so do review it regularly. This Policy was last updated on [ ]. If you have any questions about this Policy or the information which we hold please contact us: [*add email*] or write to us at [ ]. [2]

1. Information Collection

- We do not collect personally identifiable information about you, eg your name, address, telephone number, e-mail, etc, unless you choose to complete and submit a registration application to us or if you contact us directly.
- You should be aware that you may be making available personally identifiable information about yourself when you submit material to be posted to the site, eg for forums or other interactive elements of the site. Please take care when doing so. [3]
- We do automatically collect certain non-personally identifiable information when you visit our site—such as the type of browser you are using, the type of operating system you are using and the domain name of your Internet service.

2. How We Use Information We Collect

- We use non-personally identifiable information to review site usage, eg information on which pages are more popular than others, which allows us to improve the design and content of our site. We may also share this information with our current or potential commercial partners, eg investors, sponsors and advertisers for the site etc.
- We use the personally identifiable information you provide to us in your registration application to administer your registration and to provide you with the personalized features and the particular site service(s) for which that registration was necessary.
- We use the personally identifiable information you provide to us when you contact us directly to respond to your specific inquiry or to administer the relevant site activity to which it relates, eg to enter you into a site competition or to supply information or goods you have requested. [4]

1 It is important to be clear about whether a user has a choice in respect of information collection/processing. In many cases there is no real choice—the information is required to enable the site to be used, and the alternative is for the user not to use the site. As described in the information above, legalese and superfluous detail should be avoided. To aid review the headings should be helpful; with larger policies links from a contents list could be used.

2 A privacy notice should be regarded as a 'live' document. It needs to adapt as and when the business wishes to collect or use information differently. But a word on 'future proofing'. It is important to consider uses that the operator might wish to put the data to in the future so as to avoid changing the policy, but be careful not to come up with a long list of uses that it are unlikely, as personal information should only be processed for limited purposes, and be adequate, relevant and not excessive. It should also be responsive to any issues or input from users, for example feedback on language users find opaque or confusing.

3 Arguably this is obvious, but perhaps worth including to avoid any doubt (see Chapter B10).

4 A clear statement as to what use the information collected is put. Again, it is arguable that a user ought reasonably to be aware that a site will use the information the user gives to provide the user with a response or service but inclusion is common and still good practice.

- When you provide your registration application, and in some cases when you supply personally identifiable information directly to us from certain parts of the site, we may provide you with the opportunity to opt-in to certain uses, eg to provide you with information about the site or other services that you may find of interest. We will only share your personally identifiable information with anyone else for marketing purposes if you have specifically consented to that. Remember that you can opt-out of these again at any time—see **Your rights** below. 5
- If you reside in the EEA personal information you provide to us will not be transferred to other countries, including the United States, the data protection laws of which may differ from those of the European Union, unless you expressly agree to such transfer. 6
- Please be aware that it is possible, though unlikely, that we might be forced to disclose personally identifiable information in response to legal process or when we believe in good faith that the law requires it, eg in response to a court order or a law enforcement agency's request. 7

3. Cookies

- A cookie is a text-only string of information that a website transfers to the cookie file of the browser on a user's computer hard disk so that the website can remember who the user is. A cookie will typically contain the name of the domain from which the cookie has come, the 'lifetime' of the cookie, and a value, usually a randomly generated unique number.
- When you visit our site we send you a cookie. Cookies may be used in the following ways:
  - To enable the personalization features on our site, which give you the ability to recall recently viewed pages and see information which you have provided online.
  - To compile anonymous, aggregated statistics that allow us to understand how users use our site and to help us improve the structure of our site. We cannot identify you personally in this way.
  - Two types of cookies may be used on this site, session cookies, which are temporary cookies that remain in the cookie file of your browser until you leave the site, and persistent cookies, which remain in the cookie file of your browser for much longer, though how long will depend on the lifetime of the specific cookie.
- You have the ability to accept or decline cookies by modifying the settings in your browser. See for further information www.[ ]. You may not, however, be able to use all the interactive features of our site if cookies are disabled. 8

4. Our Commitment to Security

- We employ appropriate technical and organizational security measures to prevent unauthorized access to information that we collect online.

5 It is important to avoid a 'one size fits all' approach. Where a user has a real choice whether or not to provide information, it is important to present this to the user clearly. A 'layered' approach can be useful here, with key information provided at the point that the user has the opportunity to exercise choice, with a reference and link back to the main policy.

6 This is merely a placeholder and not necessary if transfers are not made. As flagged in the Introduction, transfer of Personal Data outside of the EEA is a regulated form of processing that may require the user's specific consent (if other options are not available and/or appropriate). In which case more active steps to bring this to the user's attention would be needed.

7 If there were other likely parties to whom data is transferred when taking payments, eg fraud prevention or credit agencies, these might be included.

8 Cookies are a tool to collect information about the user, and are specifically dealt with in EU law—as recently updated. The policy must set out clearly how cookies are used in the site, and the user must be given the opportunity to refuse the use of cookies—although if they do so, certain consequences will follow in terms of a lower quality of user experience. As we write, the law is being changed so these requirements will need further checking.

5. Your Rights

- You have the option at any time to request that we:
  - provide a copy of the personal information we hold relating to you (and we may make a small charge for this);
  - update or remove any such personal information; and
  - stop contacting you where we do this in accordance with your previous consent.
- To contact us please [*add email*] or write to us at [ ]. 9

9 These rights are enshrined in EU data protection law and it is good practice to communicate them in the policy, but in a user-friendly way—the user should not be put off from exercising them.

B10

USER-GENERATED CONTENT

Introduction

They say that the first version of the Internet was all about *pages*—web pages as content first moved online—but that the second, Web 2.0, was all about *people*. That, of course, is a simplification. The first bulletin boards and chat rooms were always about social interaction, and were usually the 'stickiest' areas that kept people online and the key revenue drivers for the early subscription services. In fact the home-built websites and DIY blogs of that time might be said to have been far more personalized online environments than the standardized formats of today's global platforms.

Yet, it is certainly true that digital media in the last five to ten years has been dominated by the rise of two connected elements: user-generated content (UGC) and social networks. Much has been said about both and key observations have been made by social, commercial and technical commentators around the world. Whether some of the more far-reaching claims made for them will stand up in the medium to long term remain to be seen. In the meantime, however, they are likely to remain key elements within many digital media products and services. A range of legal considerations follow from that.

Social networks, blogs and other UGC blur the boundaries between reader, publisher and author. UGC regularly appears alongside professionally produced material in mainstream media. Content users are now content suppliers not just content consumers. But are users fully aware of, or even concerned about, their legal liabilities when they supply that content? UGC sites may differ from conventional media channels in their style and purpose, but their content is still publicly consumed and they have the equivalent potential to cause harm and offence. Indeed, far from being immune from the law, UGC is in particular danger of falling foul of it.

We sponsored research which showed, of our poll, only a small number of all Internet users—5 per cent—were clear about their legal rights and responsibilities when commenting online. Even those users who had posted comments online were unsure about their legal liabilities with over three-quarters of bloggers uncertain or unaware of where the law stands. That might not be surprising when only a third of regular Internet users say they read the terms and conditions, disclaimers and guidelines for posting comment. It is not as though some have not already had cause to be concerned—in fact one in seven users had had their comments removed or taken down in the past, rising to more than one in four among those that blog.

This ignorance also persists in the face of some high profile disputes. In several countries there have been employment cases with workers sacked, or at least disciplined, for comments posted about their workplace. Perhaps many users should realize that criticizing their employer online might be something to avoid, but there are plenty of other issues to watch out for beyond defamation (see box below) and employment law. Bloggers in the UK have been prosecuted and fined under very specific provisions in UK telecommunications legislation for posting online messages deemed to be offensive or menacing. It is probably fair to say that most UK bloggers would never have heard of that law, let alone understood its impact on them.

Confusion over the relationship between the law and their online activity clearly puts users at risk, prompting calls for better—or bespoke—regulation of UGC. Suggestions have included bloggers' codes of conduct and special liability rules for UGC (see below). While half of the Internet users in our poll felt bloggers should be held to the same legal standards as the professionals, only 27 per cent of bloggers themselves thought that they should. Opinion was equally divided about self-regulation. Only half of our users would consider signing up to a voluntary charter or code.

There are two practical issues that flow from all of this:

- It is true of course that, ever since the earliest bulletin boards, users have got into difficulties with their posts, along with the online services that carried them. Yet the importance of the UGC legal framework looks likely to increase in importance. As many as 84 per cent of 18–24-year-olds have participated in some form of UGC and the overall volume of people commenting online is on a sharp increase. Whether law makers and the courts will develop lower or different standards for online feedback, commentary and citizen journalism remains to be seen. Some UK cases have suggested that the courts, or at the least the judges who have so far opined on it, might be prepared to judge the level of debate in certain online areas differently than if it had appeared in print, although many of the cases merely confirm how the law will apply in social networks as it does elsewhere. There is an even larger body of case law in the US where some of the benefits afforded to professional journalists have also been confirmed for the blogging community.
- In the meantime the operators of the online services and the platforms that deliver the UGC experience still need to set the rules of the road—as they always have—to try to help influence online behaviour, avoid problems arising and reduce their own risk of liability for the unlawful acts of others. That is the focus of the UGC terms provided below.

CHECKLIST

Defamation: The UK has tough libel laws and from the earliest Web 1.0 bulletin boards posters have got into difficulty with defamatory comments—as have the online services that carry them.

Offensive Messages: There are a range of laws from anti-harassment legislation to specific restrictions, eg the telecommunications law flagged above, that can be invoked.

Incitement: There have been high profile cases relating to terrorism but any encouragement of others to commit unlawful acts can result in prosecution.

Intellectual Property: If there is a copy-and-paste culture online, it is most prevalent in this environment.

Linking: Bloggers need to think about not only what is on their own site, but also keep an eye on the links they provide to other pages, eg linking to offensive or illegal or unauthorized material.

Reporting: The law of contempt and other statutory reporting restrictions carry strict penalties if breached

Corporate Blogging: The legal pitfalls of blogging are even more pronounced in the case of corporate blogging where additional commercial concerns will apply; corporate bloggers need to watch for: defamation or illegal content, leaking of confidential information and claims of harassment and/or cyber bullying.

Defamation

London has been called the libel capital of the world. Accordingly, and despite the weather, it attracts more than its fair share of libel tourists—those people in search of what they perceive to be a claimant-friendly jurisdiction to bring a defamation action against a publisher. (From time to time other cities can look attractive to those on such an excursion. For example, colleagues in Paris often warn us of the ways in which French law can be pro-claimant and one of the leading Internet libel cases was brought in Australia—see below—where perhaps food and climate might be better respectively.) Reforms in the US may limit the effectiveness of such an activity—and the UK itself is considering changes to defamation law—but this remains an area of risk for online media.

The essence of libel law here is that a person is entitled to his or her reputation and that can only be taken away on precise terms. The onus is effectively on the defendant not the claimant to prove their case. Unlike the US, there is no 'public figure' defence. A defendant in the UK has either to prove the truth of what he or she has written (and it is the ordinary reader's understanding of the meaning, not what the author intended, that counts); or demonstrate fair comment or privilege or a number of other lesser-used defences. Prior publication is no defence, though the fact that the libel has been published before may help to reduce any damages awarded.

General abuse is not defamatory but it was recently held that to describe an actor as 'hideously ugly' could be defamatory. Comments not intended to be taken seriously may not be defamatory but there is no specific defence for humour. It is what the reasonable reader thinks not what the author intended that counts. To bring an action the claimant needs to prove that the words in question are defamatory *plus* that they have been published to a third party *and* that they, the claimant, is recognizable from the statement.

Examples:

A message on a website or online forum will probably be published to third parties as soon as it is posted, but an email marked 'private and confidential' is probably not published to anyone other than the recipient (unless the sender should have known the recipient's PA or others would access the inbox).

'All coppers are crooks' is too wide to identify any officer, but 'all those investigating the Murder on the Clapham Express are crooks' may defame officers within an identifiably small team, even if not mentioned by name.

Online Issues

Online defamation issues tend to fall into two: for editorial content and for user-generated content (UGC). The obvious difference between editorial content online and in print is the wider potential distribution and the risk that local law in the country of download might be applied to the content.

Example:

A US publisher published an online subscription magazine hosted and aimed primarily at readers in the US. It did, however, take a small number of subscriptions from Australia. A claimant in Australia was able to bring a successful libel action in an Australian court under local law.

The UK does, however, have relatively strict defamation laws. So anyone who has cleared content for a UK audience may be less likely to run into difficulties with local libel laws, *but* some reputations vary by territory.

Example:

Someone who is thought to be a terrorist here may be considered a legitimate politician elsewhere.

Also beware the 'one-year rule'. An action for defamation may only be brought within one year of publication *but* it has long been clear that in the UK, unlike, say, the US, the publication referred to is the last publication. Any re-issue of the relevant content starts the period again. The UK is currently considering reform of this rule.

Example:

A recent case decided that where a website holds an online archive and a viewer clicks into it, the articles then viewed are 'published' again and the time period starts running for one year from that moment.

Clearly, by its very nature, UGC carries a higher risk of containing defamatory statements. There is some limited case law that suggests certain online forums should not be treated with the same seriousness as material appearing in a newspaper—but people can and do claim for defamatory postings about them in UGC areas. How far the operator of the online service that carries that content could be liable for it remains a confused and confusing issue.

The basic rule in defamation law is that anyone who is involved in the process of publication can be liable for the content. There is, however, a specific defence in defamation law for someone who is *not* the author, editor or publisher—that expressly includes someone who merely operates a computer system or communications network—*and* did not know nor should have known that the content was defamatory *and* took reasonable care (bearing in mind eg what level of control and responsibility they had and the previous nature of such content).

Example:

A large UK ISP was held liable for a defamatory statement within a USENET newsgroup which it hosted. While the ISP was judged to merely provide the technical infrastructure and so was not an author, editor or publisher it had received a written notice from the person who was defamed pointing out the statement (so had knowledge) and it had done nothing (the issue of reasonable care was not addressed).

There is now a further general defence (from EU-based law that goes beyond defamation) for any 'information society service' provider who is just hosting (or, less relevantly for many website operators, operating a cache of or acting as a mere conduit for) unlawful content *and* does not have actual knowledge of that content *but* acts 'expeditiously' to remove or disable access to it. There is no general requirement to monitor such content.

There are several problems with both the above defences but one of the main ones is deciding where the boundaries lie. Whilst they were designed (more than ten years ago) to provide protection for ISPs providing technical services, such as hosting websites and newsgroups, they may not necessarily stretch to today's website owners who are, say, operating an interactive area within their website or other UGC service. The nature and scope of these defences is currently being reviewed so changes in the next few years are likely.

Website owners are sometimes advised not to edit or moderate UGC so as to appear closer to an ISP, but there is no guarantee that this will be sufficient to obtain legal protection—especially where the website is encouraging and stimulating debate within its service (and an operator could then be argued as failing to taking reasonable care!). French and German cases have held that the defence is not available to operators in a non-passive role.

Practical Steps

- **Editorial Content**—It is not necessarily what is said but the way it is said that is relevant. Re-word contentious passages so they say no more than can be substantiated. Beware inference (unstated implication) and innuendo (statements that appear to be harmless may in fact carry a different meaning for someone in possession of certain facts).

  Repeating someone else's defamatory allegations can make the repeater as liable as the original source. Merely adding 'it is alleged that' or 'it is rumoured that' will not help. The fact that others have said something without a problem (any claim may not be public) only gives limited comfort: prior publication is no defence.

  Take care with claims over online archive content given the re-publication rule. If the option of removing the offending article or posted message is not available then it should at least be annotated in such a way that a viewer has to see the annotation, that the material was found to be defamatory.

  Linking to another online service that carries defamatory content could bring liability (international case law conflicts on the point). Be prepared to disable links if notice is given.
- **User-Generated Content**—Ultimately whether and how UGC is moderated is usually a commercial and creative decision depending on the size, genre and target audience of a site or service. Unmoderated discussion forums and UGC can often be unsuitable and unpleasant areas. It cannot be said that choosing not to moderate will necessarily ensure that the defences set out above will apply. Indeed UK government and parliamentary reports have suggested that operators of sites targeted at vulnerable groups, especially children, have a responsibility to control the online environment they provide regardless of those defences.

  If moderators are used (whether employed internally, outsourced or recruited from users) ensure they are selected carefully, know the limits of their role and the procedures with which they are expected to comply. Specific guidance on this is provided by the Home Office and other bodies.

Regardless of the strict letter of the law, operating an effective 'notice and take down' process usually makes good sense anyway. Develop a written policy for how defamatory content will be dealt with: it should cover reactive responses, internal and external escalation procedures, repeat offenders and previous conduct. Build on technical flexibility to the service and back-room functionality to allow the above procedure to be implemented quickly and effectively (it will show a court what 'reasonable care' is being taken).

Add supporting provisions for all of this into user terms and on-screen warnings. Most UGC services go further than the law and provide clear rules as to what content and conduct is or is not permitted in that service.

Final Thoughts

Online, material can be removed or amended quickly; but defamation remains a material financial risk. Many of the people defamed in UGC will not have the time or money to take action but there are several examples of complaints reaching court: recently a teacher won £1,250 in a small claims court for UGC posted about him on a website. The claimant defamed in the ISP case mentioned above settled for over £200,000.

Other remedies available may include orders to do or refrain from doing something. Huge damages awards have been restricted in recent years, but large damages awards, and so also out-of-court settlements, are possible.

More importantly, even greater legal expense may have been run up on both sides—and the loser pays a material part of the winner's costs. Also do not underestimate the investment of management time, worry, nerves and reputation.

Commercial publishers often buy libel insurance cover but it is usually treated, or certainly should be, as disaster cover: to cut in and save the business from collapse where the claim is large. It should not be there to save a service operator from the basic business of checking editorial copy and acting responsibly with UGC. Premiums will be too high in any event for that; and often the excess (the amount of risk carried by the insured before the insurance cover kicks in) is high too.

It is standard to ask for an indemnity, ie a promise to repay any costs, from third-party content providers in case of defamatory claims but obviously this is only as good as their financial worth and is hard to apply to UGC.

The bottom line is that successful online services avoid defamation issues by taking practical and proactive steps to avoid problems arising in the first place.

User-Generated Content

UGC TERMS

- This website is designed to provide a lively and interactive community for its users. We encourage all our users to interact with the website and to submit material of all kinds—known as 'user material' below. In order to ensure that this is done safely and lawfully we have established the rules set out below. For certain user material, eg as part of a competition, or where we are required by law to do so, separate and/or additional terms may apply in these Terms or as marked on the relevant part of the website.
- Unless you and we agree otherwise, you will continue to own all the user material you submit. However, we may post your user material on the website, and on our partner websites, and we may also include it in other media services [including our television programming, print publications or advertising]. It will, therefore, become accessible and may be linked to or copied from across the public Internet as well as in those other media. Please do not submit anything to us that you would not like to be used in this way and note that we may not be able to prevent further use by third parties without permission. (1)
- By submitting your user material you grant to us all rights in your user material necessary to enable the distribution of your user material in this way, including to amend or adapt it where this is reasonably necessary for those purposes, without any further approval or consent from or payment to you or any other person, and you also promise that:
  - *You have not copied from someone else or included other people's material*—Your user material must be original and you confirm that it has not been copied from elsewhere. Your user material must not feature copyright material taken from someone else or feature the trade mark, brand or name of someone else or which violates anyone's legal rights including of privacy and/or publicity;
  - *You have the permission of all the people making and appearing in it*—You must have explained to everyone who made or is in your user content, especially photographs or video, and if they are under 18 to their parents or lawful guardians, how it may be used. They, and their parents or guardians, must have provided you with their specific consent; (2)
  - *Your user content is lawful and suitable for this website*—You must not include anything in your user content which is inappropriate for a family audience and certainly anything which is of an adult-only nature including offensive, vulgar or obscene material and controversial or off-topic themes or content. It must not be defamatory or unlawful or include anything that would bring us into disrepute; (3) and
  - *You will not use the website in a manner that interferes with others*—You must not nor attempt to interfere with or disrupt anyone else's use or

1 Rights—One of the more contested issues in the terms and conditions for user-generated content and social networks is how far the service provider is granted permission to use the material provided. Originally some sites attempted to gain ownership of the material but public debate forced changes and many terms now step away from any broad grant of rights. Clearly much depends on the nature of the content and privacy issues will be relevant too. The rights granted here might be inappropriate for some services.

2 Privacy—If rights have been the key issue in user terms for UGC, social networks have grappled with privacy. The trade off between, on the one hand, allowing visibility and encouraging interaction and, on the other, supporting users in controlling access to their personal information and protecting their privacy has been a complicated and difficult balancing act. Those issues would be primarily dealt with in the relevant privacy policy and associated technical settings. However, whenever material is being shared it is important to make users aware of both their own privacy rights and those of anyone featured in their content.

3 Behaviour—Most sites will go into some detail defining and specifying what is or is not acceptable behaviour. A common approach is to include user-friendly FAQs and notes to support basic terms such as these. Clearly the content of these and the overall approach taken will vary from site to site.

enjoyment of the website, eg you must not threaten or harass or impersonate others, or otherwise use the website in an anti-social, inappropriate or unlawful way.

- We reserve the right to, but do not promise that we will, review your user content before it appears on the website. If we determine that your user content does not comply with these rules we reserve the right to, but do not promise that we will, stop it from being made available on the website or otherwise, and remove your user content, or links or any other means of access to your user content, from the website or otherwise at any time without notice to you. [4]
- Remember that you will remain responsible for your own user content and for what you do and say online. You should use the same care and consideration on the website as you do when communicating with others in any other public place. Please think before your submit!
- IF YOU DO NOT COMPLY WITH THESE RULES YOU MAY BECOME LEGALLY LIABLE TO US OR TO THIRD PARTIES OR YOU MAY OTHERWISE BE ACTING UNLAWFULLY. If anything is not clear to you, or if you think that any other user content is in breach of these rules, please contact us at [*add email*] or write to us at PO Box [ ].
- You and the other persons appearing in your user content, and if they are under 18 their parents or lawful guardians, may be required to provide further written confirmation of your compliance with these rules in such form as we may reasonably request. [5]

4 Moderation—Determining how a site should be moderated requires legal and technical input but ultimately it is a commercial question as to what sort of service the provider wants to offer, the content it wants to provide and the risks it is comfortable with. See the box on defamation for a discussion of some of the issues.

5 Children—The focus of much regulation, best practice guidance and 'soft law' in this area is around the protection of children (see Part I). The default position of US privacy law (see Chapter B9) has broadly been adopted in other countries to the effect that many providers will seek to prevent under-thirteens from using their service.

INDEX